Piaget's construction of the child's reality

Piaget's construction of the child's reality

Susan Sugarman
Princeton University

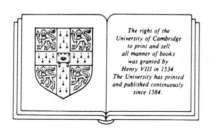

The right of the
University of Cambridge
to print and sell
all manner of books
was granted by
Henry VIII in 1534.
The University has printed
and published continuously
since 1584.

Cambridge University Press

Cambridge

New York   New Rochelle   Melbourne   Sydney

Published by the Press Syndicate of the University of Cambridge
The Pitt Building, Trumpington Street, Cambridge CB2 1RP
32 East 57th Street, New York, NY 10022, USA
10 Stamford Road, Oakleigh, Melbourne 3166, Australia

Library of Congress Cataloging-in-Publication Data

Sugarman, Susan.
Piaget's construction of the child's reality.
Bibliography: p.
Includes index.
1. Perception in children.   2. Reality – Psychological
aspects.   3. Piaget, Jean, 1896– .   I. Piaget,
Jean, 1896– .   II. Title. [DNLM: 1. Child
Psychology. ws 105 s947p]
BF723.P36S84   1987   155.4   87-10959

British Library Cataloguing in Publication Data

Sugarman, Susan
Piaget's construction of the child's reality.
1. Piaget, Jean   2. Cognition in children
I. Title
155.4'13   BF723.C5

ISBN 0 521 34164 7

Contents

Acknowledgments

I wrote this book while holding the Richard F. Stockton Bicentennial Preceptorship at Princeton University. I thank John Darley, John Harechmak, Jonas Langer, George A. Miller, Sylvia Sugarman, Cathy Urwin, and especially Raymond Geuss for comments on the manuscript. I thank Ageliki Nicolopoulou for her help in locating some of the sources cited in chapter 4 and Arlene Kronewitter for typing the manuscript. I thank Jean E. Tulis for suggesting that I write the book.

To Helen Wheeler, Edith Feinstein, and the staff at Cambridge for the care and dispatch with which they prepared the book for publication and Mary Nevader for a sensitive and penetrating copyediting job, many thanks.

I am most grateful to the Family Resource Infant Center of Princeton for allowing me to observe the children at the center as I began work on the book. I thank Annie Ballou for her suggestion that watching children might provide the impetus for writing.

Abbreviations for citation of Piaget's books

CCN	*The child's conception of number*
CCPC	*The child's conception of physical causality*
CCW	*The child's conception of the world*
CR	*The construction of reality in the child*
LT	*The language and thought of the child*
MJ	*The moral judgment of the child*
OI	*The origins of intelligence in children*
PDI	*Play, dreams, and imitation in childhood*

Introduction

Developmental psychology seeks both to understand the nature of the child's mind at the successive stages of its development and to provide an account of the process of development. We might call these aims, respectively, synchronic and diachronic analysis.[1] Swiss psychologist Jean Piaget founded the discipline in its present form, and his ideas, methods, and findings have shaped work in the field for more than half a century.

Piaget's synchronic and diachronic programs were both novel relative to the agendas of the more traditional "child psychology" (Piaget & Inhelder, 1966/1969, p. viii) of his day. Regarding synchronic analysis, Piaget, unlike traditional child psychologists, was interested not simply in providing a natural history of child behavior, but in describing the mentality behind that behavior (see, e.g., Piaget 1923/1955, especially Claparède's preface). As for diachronic analysis, Piaget's long-range aim was to explain adult thought and action. Traditional child psychology did not have this goal.

Even though much of contemporary research in developmental psychology is conceived as challenging Piaget, it shares with his work these two agendas: It has the more proximal aim of identifying the knowledge or thought process that underlies children's behavior at different ages (synchronic analysis) and the larger goal of explaining how mature "end states" come about (diachronic analysis). As with Piaget, forms of adult mentation are singled out for study, and then with the modern empirical and experimental techniques that are now available, an attempt is

---

[1] Although these terms are associated with Saussure (1966), I use them merely in their everyday sense. Synchronic analysis is the analysis of some state of affairs at a given time, and diachronic analysis, the analysis of a change in state through time.

made to identify the antecedents of these forms in children's behavior. On the basis of the antecedents that are identified, inferences are drawn about the way in which the mature, end-state forms arise.

The promise of developmental psychology and of Piaget's program in particular is, then, that it will elucidate the origins and development of mental life. No single program, not even the seminal and massive effort of Piaget, can be expected to produce a complete account or an account that will be correct in all of its details. The general conception of Piaget, held by his supporters and critics alike, is, however, that he at least charted the relevant areas to be investigated, furnished valid and fruitful directions of inquiry, and uncovered certain critical empirical findings.

This book is a critique of some of the most basic concepts underlying Piaget's theory and the empirical investigations he derived from it. It analyzes six of his classic, earlier works that have shaped thinking in the field and contain a richness of data and theory unmatched in his later works.

There are significant respects in which Piaget does not, in fact, elucidate the origins or development of mental life. My most radical claim will be that there is simply no account of mind in Piaget. In most of the works I discuss, mind is replaced by a quite striking reification of the child's thought. This avoidance of mind is deeply connected with Piaget's whole way of approaching the subject of developmental psychology.

Why devote a book to a detailed analysis of Piaget's theory? One reason is that Piaget remains the most fertile, systematic, and comprehensive thinker that the field of developmental psychology has had. Few have been as bold or as searching. Despite the overt differences between Piaget's position and that of contemporary research, his way of approaching the discipline is deeply engrained, more perhaps than is recognized. Through a close analysis of Piaget's work we can reveal its limits and hence establish a basis for the formulation of genuinely alternative lines of inquiry.

A main purpose of the book, therefore, is to begin to articulate and to pursue these alternative lines of inquiry. It is in the details of working through Piaget's often obscure and convoluted argumentation that some of these alternatives – alternative questions, methods, and substantive hypotheses – become most evident. On the whole, these alternatives are not reflected in contemporary research. They are new areas of investigation that this book is intended to open up via the discussion of Piaget.

I will not present any finished alternative theory or set of approaches. Rather, in the course of my investigation I will suggest various approaches. In some cases I will actually begin to develop an alternative account of the area under question, based on my analysis of Piaget's treatment and its shortcomings.

PLAN OF THE BOOK

The core of the book consists of a rational reconstruction and critique of the following of Piaget's works: *The child's conception of the world* (CCW), *The language and thought of the child* (LT), *The moral judgment of the child* (MJ), *The child's conception of number* (CCN), *The child's conception of reality* (CR), and *The origins of intelligence in children* (OI). These texts were written between 1920 and 1950, although Piaget continued to write prolifically and to develop his ideas until his death in 1980, at age 84.

When he wrote these relatively early works, Piaget had not yet elaborated the vast theoretical system that would dominate his later writings (although it began to be evident in *Number*). He was therefore more inclined to let the children he observed, rather than theory dictate the parameters of his descriptions. Also, the data are more diverse than they are in his later works. In this regard, each book includes, as primary or secondary data, spontaneous behaviors of everyday life and hence real phenomena that occur in the course of development. Finally, each deals with a basic psychological question, for example, the development of "objectivity," the nature of morality, or the origins of intelligence.

Piaget's later work does not ovecome the problems that I will raise in connection with these early studies and does not, in this and other respects, go beyond them. Both to document this point and to place the present investigation in the context of Piaget's later directions, I have included a final chapter dealing with his later work. The chapter also contains a brief discussion of contemporary research.

Concerning the presentation itself, I have concentrated on Piaget's conceptual framework. In doing so, I have assumed that his claims are empirically accurate, and I have attempted to put the sharpest and most consistent construction on his theoretical arguments that the texts will allow.

Each of the chapters is self-contained; no prior knowledge of Piaget is necessary. Given, however, that my aim is neither to discuss the system as such nor to provide a comprehensive review of the work, I have made no attempt to present the system or the opus as a whole. For this or other background material, readers can consult any of the numerous secondary sources on Piaget (e.g., Brainerd, 1978; Flavell, 1963; Furth, 1981; Ginsburg & Opper, 1979; Gruber & Vonèche, 1982) or Piaget and Inhelder's (1966/1969) own summary.

I begin, in turn, with Piaget's three early works: *Child's conception of the world, Language and thought,* and *Moral judgment.* I then proceed to *Number* and finally to the two infancy books (*Construction of reality* and *Origins*). The three early works allow a progressive formulation of issues of critical concern and offer a plethora of phenomena for possible reinterpretation. *Number,* which was written later and is more typical of the greater part of Piaget's work, provides a basis for examining the generality of some of the points made through the early investigations. I treat the infancy books last, because they reach back to the most foundational issues. They also, in my view, represent the best of Piaget. I conclude with the chapter on Piaget's later works.

1

"The child's conception of the world"

Piaget's stated aim in *The child's conception of the world* was to describe the conceptions of reality that children naturally form at different ages and to determine what the spontaneous thought tendencies were that might explain these conceptions. In his actual research Piaget formulated this question more narrowly as the issue of whether children distinguished, as adults do, between an internal, subjective world and external reality.

All of Piaget's early (psychological) works deal with one version of this question or another. In Piaget's customary phrasing, the question is whether children engage in "egocentric" thought. Piaget, as we shall see, came to use the term "egocentric" in many different senses. In the usual sense, the word refers to the notion that children neither adequately distinguish between self and world, nor take account of other people's points of view.

Egocentrism not only was important in its own right, but had immediate and far-reaching implications for the whole of children's cognitive life. According to Piaget, the ability to appreciate other points of view and to separate self from reality was necessary for an "objective" conception of the world as well as for logical thinking, successful communication, and the development of morality. Thus, an individual who was incapable of appreciating other points of view or of separating self from reality was thereby incapable of construing the world objectively, incapable of genuine deduction, effective communication, or truly moral judgment.

In his later works Piaget retracted the term "egocentric" in response to its alleged misconstrual by other psychologists; however, he retained the substantive theses underlying it (Piaget & Inhelder, 1966/1969, p. 61, n. 6). In the ensuing chapters I will follow Piaget's definitions as closely as possible. One of the main purposes of the discussion is to bring these and related definitions to light and examine their implications.

RECONSTRUCTION

1. The question

Piaget translated the question of whether children distinguish an inner and outer reality into three more specific questions: (a) Do children distinguish some things as mental and some as material? (b) Do they recognize a distinction between animate beings and inanimate things? (c) Do they distinguish some things as man-made and others as natural? If children draw any of these distinctions, then between what groups of things do they draw them, and how, exactly, do they define the difference?

Each of these questions corresponds to a particular type of egocentric thought that might arise. Piaget called the first type realism: roughly, the view that phenomena commonly considered to be mental (e.g., dreams, thoughts) are physical realities. The second type was animism: the attribution of consciousness and other animate properties to things that are (to civilized adults) inanimate. The third type was artificialism: the notion that all things are made in the same way that humans fabricate things.

I note in passing that Piaget is vague and somewhat inconsistent when he refers to children's "distinguishing" or not distinguishing between the internal and the external, the material and the mental, and so on. At times he seems to mean that a given distinction is or is not present in actual perception. At other times he seems to mean that a particular distinction is absent from, or is in some cases denied by, a child's conscious or implicit beliefs. On still other occasions he seems to mean only that a child's explicit explanation for a given phenomenon ignores a distinction that adults would make if they were explaining the same phenomenon with reference to the same kinds of properties. The data bear most directly on this last meaning. In the following reconstruction I will try to remain as faithful as possible to Piaget's usages and will allow such ambiguities and inconsistencies as arise to stand. I will discuss those ambiguities and inconsistencies that are pertinent to my analysis in the critique section.

2. Method

Piaget interviewed children about particular phenomena and asked them questions designed to elicit their views about whether the phenomena were "real" (material, external) or not "real," animate or inanimate, man-made or natural. Both to avoid suggesting these oppositions directly and to make the interviews comprehensible to the children, Piaget asked two kinds of questions. First, he asked the children general questions, making no mention of any alternative solutions. For example, when interviewing the children for possible artificialist explanations, he asked them simply, "How did the sun begin?" Second, he asked the children about specific properties that he regarded as representative of the category in question but not as constitutive of it. The children were not asked, for instance, whether they thought dreams were real, but whether they thought they could touch them.

For the study of realism Piaget questioned the children about three phenomena: thought, names, and dreams. He asked, for example, "Can you see thought?" "If we could open a person's head without his dying, could you touch his thought?" "Where do your dreams come from?" "Where is your dream while you are dreaming it?"

The animism interviews centered around two attributes of things: whether they were conscious and whether they were alive. Regarding consciousness, Piaget asked the children if the various items he mentioned could feel the effects of a particular action: "If I pierced the table with a pin, would the table feel anything, or nothing?" "If wood were burning, would it feel it?" "Do the clouds feel the wind?" Regarding the concept of life, the children were asked if various things were alive. These things included plants, animals, humans, inanimate objects that appeared to move spontaneously (e.g., clouds, the wind), immobile objects, and mechanical objects.

The questions concerning artificialism focused on the origins of things and on the explanation for their attributes: "How did the sun begin?" "Why is the sky blue?" "Why is it dark at night?" "Why is this stone [taken from a stream] round?"

In all three cases the questions followed a format that Piaget called the "clinical interview." The questions were tailored to the children's apparent level of understanding, the children's answers were probed by further guiding questions and countersuggestions, and, most important to Piaget, the children were asked to justify their answers.

3. Results

Piaget found evidence of realism, animism, and artificialism in the interviews and a gradual supplanting of these replies, among older children, by answers of a more objective and physical-determinist type.

In the case of realism, thought, names, and dreams were all described by the youngest children as external, material entities. Names were described as emanating from the things they represent, for example, and dreams from the light or dark. Piaget described the sequence of ensuing answers as a series of "differentiations." First the children came to distinguish between each of the three phenomena (thought, names, dreams) and their referents (the thing thought of, dreamed of, or named). Next each phenomenon was properly identified as internal rather than as external. Thought, for example, was in the head but was a physical thing. Finally, the phenomena were distinguished as immaterial and, in the case of names, arbitrary. Whereas younger children thought that fire was called "fire" because the word "fire" was hot, for instance, older children knew that the word "fire" had no physical properties and was assigned to the real entity, fire, only by convention.

A similar pattern of answers appeared in the animism interviews. Initially, the children agreed that a bench would feel something if it were burned, that a cloud knew it was moving, that a button could feel something when it was being pulled off, and so on. A series of intermediate answers could again be distinguished, each kind of answer signifying to Piaget a "differentiation" of the notions expressed by the preceding type of answer: Consciousness (whether things could "feel," etc.) was attributed first to anything that was in any way active (e.g., a burning bush, as well as a rushing brook), then only to things that could move (the sun or a bicycle but not a table or a stone), then only to things that appeared to move of their own accord (the sun, but not a bicycle), and finally only to animals. The concept of "life" followed a comparable progression.

The children's answers in the artificialism interviews exhibited a progressive detachment of physical causation from human agency, or models of it. First, all things were either fashioned by humans (or God) or arose through a process analogous to human activity. Intermediate answers contained a mixture of natural and artificialist explanations. The sun and moon were created by a condensation of clouds (collision of the stars, etc.), for instance; however, the clouds arose from the roofs of houses or the smoke of men's pipes (the stars were fires lit in the sky, etc.). Finally, the children understood that human agency has nothing to do with the origins of natural objects and either invented a physical explanation or refused to speculate.

Piaget admitted that many of the children's answers seemed forced and likely to have arisen only through the children's lack of knowledge of the topics under consideration. It was precisely his intent, however, to present the children with unfamiliar phenomena for which they would have to invent explanations and descriptions. Children's underlying tendencies of thought, he believed, were best revealed through children's attempt to comprehend the unknown or the partly known. Particularly where he could establish that particular inventions were widespread, resisted counter-suggestion, and persisted into more mature responses, Piaget believed there was evidence of these underlying tendencies.

4. Piaget's discussion

In the following account of Piaget's discussion, I will cover only his analysis of realism and animism and omit any further systematic consideration of artificialism.

In his analysis of both realism and animism Piaget tried, on the one hand, to give a theoretical account of the interview results and, on the other, to extend this account to spontaneous patterns of behavior and thought exhibited by children outside the interviews. I begin with the analysis of realism.

4.1. Realism

According to Piaget's theoretical account of realism, children are realists because they fail to distinguish between self and world. Insofar as they draw this distinction, they cease to be realists. The spontaneous phenomenon to which Piaget extended this theoretical account was children's magical practices. I treat the theoretical account first.

Self and world. If children view their mental processes, such as thinking, as existing outside themselves, then, Piaget reasoned, the boundary they draw between themselves and the external world in general must not be as clear as the boundary that adults draw. To document the generality of self–world nondifferentiation, Piaget attempted to illustrate additional confusions that children make between their inner life and the outside world.

Indicative of this confusion, Piaget believed, was what he described as children's tendency to treat their own point of view, which we know is subjective and internal, as "absolute" and as part of the external data. He cites as an example of this tendency children's notion, which he documents with spontaneous anecdotes and further interviews, that the sun, moon, and clouds follow them down the street. As we know, it is only from their point of view that the sun appears to be following them. It would not appear to be doing so from other people's perspectives. Another instance of inner–outer confusion was the claim that babies experience their own subjective sensations, such as pain, as if they existed all around them rather than solely within themselves.

Piaget takes as a major theoretical implication of this conflation of self and world the idea that consciousness of a self or of the internal or personal nature of subjective states does not result from direct intuition. It requires an intellectual construction. That intellectual construction, in turn, results from the gradual "dissociation" or "breaking up" (CCW, p. 127) of the child's primitive consciousness, in which self and world are not differentiated. Conversely, the idea of reality also "presupposes a progressive splitting-up of [this] protoplasmic consciousness into two complementary universes – the objective universe and the subjective" (CCPC, p. 242).

It is worth backing up and attempting to reconstruct exactly how Piaget arrives at this major theoretical conclusion. The argument seems to have three steps:

1. It is a property of human thought that one's concepts and prejudices intrude on the "world" one experiences. Thus, truly objec-

tive knowledge is not possible. The best we can do is recognize that indeed our vision of the world is infused with our concepts and prejudices, so that we can attempt to assess the influence of these concepts and prejudices on our perception of things.

2. This problem, of becoming aware of one's subjectivity, is an element of the larger problem of becoming aware of one's self.

3. According to Piaget's developmental argument, by a certain age, children draw explicit distinctions between various phenomena, the distinctions implying that the individual drawing them is aware of the subjectivity of his or her own point of view and the internal nature of his or her thoughts and other subjective experiences. Earlier, children fail to draw these distinctions. That failure is compatible with the idea that children do not know a "self" and are unaware of their subjectivity and the internal nature of their subjective processes. There is circumstantial evidence, beyond the results of the realism interviews, for this view. Piaget's conclusion is that the consciousness of a self is constructed; it is not a "primitive intuition" (CCW, p. 130). This construction consists specifically in the progressive "dissociation" of self and world. The path of that dissociation is shown, among other places, in the progressive "differentiations" revealed by the interviews.

Child magic. Piaget believed that children's realism, or at least the broader tendencies that explained it, could also explain children's magical practices. All magical practices, according to Piaget, presuppose the same generic relation, "participation,"[1] which involves treating two or more phenomena as materially related when there is in fact no material connection between them. It was this feature of magical practices, Piaget theorized, that was explained by children's realist tendencies. He envisioned three such connections.

The most transparent connection, Piaget claimed, was that between the form of realism involving the ascription of thought and its various "instruments" (e.g., words, images) to things and magic involving the "participation between thought and things." If thought inhered in things (the realist view), it could be used to influence things (the magical practice). To distort the name of a

---

[1] Piaget borrowed the term "participation" from Lévy-Bruhl, who used it in reference to primitive peoples. Piaget, however, disclaimed any deep connection between the thought of children and the thought of primitives (CCW, p. 132).

place in order to dissolve an event that had occurred there "follows as a natural result of regarding names as bound up in the nature of actual things and persons" (CCW, p. 155). To wish for the opposite of what one wanted in order to get what one wanted followed, similarly, from the idea that thought could "insert itself directly into the real" (CCW, p. 155).

The second kind of connection between realism and magic was that between the realist view of "signs" as dynamically laden with the realities they represent and those magical practices involving "participation between action and things." In these practices actions become signs in the same way that words and images are signs and, as signs, "participate" in the nature of the thing signified. In participating in the nature of the thing signified, these actions cum signs are seen to influence the thing, to act on it causally. Examples include the child who, in letting down the curtain at night, treats the speed with which the curtain falls as a sign of whether the house will be safe or the child who treats his or her success in touching every third stone in the wall as a sign of whether some desired state of affairs will come to pass. In both cases, Piaget alleges, the "sign" in question is taken to be both an indication and a cause of the anticipated outcome. This transmutation of a symbolic relation into a causal one would be the natural outgrowth, he thinks, of a realist mind, which tends to confuse the internal with the external or, in this case, the sign with the thing signified.

The third connection concerns magic involving the "participation between objects." Here children appear to establish a material bond between objects that we might connect only as instances of the same general law. Piaget cites as an example the case of a child who believed that by making a shadow with his hand he could bring on the night. The nonrealist mind might posit a similarity between the hand's shadow and the occurrence of night but would connect the two events only through the common principle of shadow casting. The realist mind, however, sees the shade cast by the hand as a material extension of the shade of night, because, in Piaget's account, the different elements of consciousness are just part of one undifferentiated, protoplasmic whole.

Piaget discusses a fourth group of magical practices, magic by "participation of purpose," in which he believes there is a significant element of animism as well as realism. In these instances the "will" of one object is used by the child to act on the "will" of another object. There is animism insofar as children attribute a will to objects of all kinds, not only to humans or animals. One example given by Piaget is an observation of Sully's (1914), in which a little girl thought she could make the wind subside by straightening her mother's hair, which the wind had ruffled ("Wind make Mamma's hair untidy. Babba [the child] make Mamma's hair tidy, so wind not blow again" [CCW, p. 148; Sully, p. 80]). There is animism here insofar as the wind is conceived of as a naughty child who can be disciplined to perform the appropriate behavior through a demonstration of its proper effects. There is also realism insofar as Babba believes that her own actions will influence the wind. The novelty introduced by the "magic" is the procedure of commanding something. However, Piaget thinks, the idea of commanding something will follow naturally if one is already inclined to attribute life to inanimate things and if one thinks that one's own thoughts and speech are in direct contact with them.

4.2. Animism

The spontaneous reactions to which Piaget extended his account of animism were presented mainly as further instances of the results documented by the interviews. In contrast to his treatment of magic, he did not consider them a whole new class of phenomena that might be seen as a further consequence of the theory. Therefore, I will present these supporting observations first and then turn to Piaget's theoretical analysis.

Spontaneous animism. Piaget cites evidence from several sources (mainly the early diarists) that children spontaneously ascribe animate properties to things. He notes empathic reactions beginning as early as the second year, in which a child, for example, brings a toy motor to the window to "see the snow" or, upon seeing a hollow chestnut tree, asks whether the tree cried when the hole was made (CCW, p. 212; numerous additional examples can be found in Sully, 1914). He adds the recollection of one colleague who as a child felt compelled to turn the stones in the driveway every now and then so they would have a different view.

Related to these animistic tendencies, Piaget believed, was children's belief that the sun followed them and their conception that the objects and forces of nature fulfilled their functions through a kind of moral compulsion (the sun cannot set when it wants to, because it is bound by duty to behave otherwise, to warm people, etc.).

Self, world, and the "indissociation of ideas." For Piaget, the central theoretical question regarding child animism was whether this animism arises from a nondifferentiation of self or mind and world, or whether it arises from the projection of mental properties (or other properties of the self) that are distinguished as such onto things in the world. Piaget attributed the latter view – that animism arises from the projection of mental and other properties that are distinguished as such – to various anthropologists (e.g., Frazer, Taylor) and to Freud (*Totem and taboo*).[2] According to this ascribed view, children could endow objects with a will and regard them as living only if they first recognized these properties as part of their own internal life. These properties had to be identified as internal, because it was an internal life (will, purpose, feeling, etc.) that was being ascribed to things.

Piaget denied this view. Children, in his account, did indeed recognize – that is, they experienced – will, purpose, feelings, and so forth, but not *as* properties of a mind or a self. Hence, it was not properties of a mind or a self that they were attributing to (inert) things when they offered explanations or expressed beliefs that we would call animistic. Animism arose not because children projected the psychical onto the physical but because they knew no boundary between them.

According to the same thesis, children did not in any sense "ascribe" consciousness (etc.) to things or "associate" consciousness (etc.) with things. Rather, they failed to dissociate, or alternatively they confused, subjective attributes such as consciousness and their customary physical correlates, for example, activity.

Piaget makes the further, and central, claim that the "indissociations" that result in animism are the same indissociations that explain realism. In both cases children are conflating "objective"

[2] These authors were writing primarily about primitive adults rather than about children. However, the same alternative hypotheses regarding the basis of animism can be proposed in both cases, as Piaget points out, although the answers do not have to be the same.

(or physical) and "subjective" elements of experience. The only difference between the two conceptions, in Piaget's view, is that with animism the confused terms are embodied in particular objects, whereas with realism they are situated more indeterminately "in reality."

In their replies during the animism interviews, the children exhibited an "indissociation," for example, of movement (an "objective" property) and purpose (a "subjective" property), insofar as they regarded visible movement of any sort as purposive (Piaget actually says "necessarily" [purposive] in this and the following contexts [CCW, p. 237]). Similarly, activity in general – not just movement – was seen as ("necessarily") conscious. Being and knowing were indissociated insofar as objects, by virtue of existing, were regarded ("necessarily") as knowing they existed (e.g., the wind knows it blows because it is it that blows [CCW, p. 183]). The interlocking of objective and subjective terms was equally evident in, in fact it virtually defined, the children's realist answers. The children as much as *said* that thought and its vehicles existed in things.

Paralleling the case with realism, Piaget's major conclusion regarding animism is that, if animism reflects a series of indissociations, the distinction between the inert and the living and between the physical and the psychic is not primary. It develops, Piaget thinks, as a function of children's progressive dissociation of the indissociated ideas with which they begin.

What, Piaget asks, would cause this dissociation to occur? He reflects that no positive experience – no direct experiment or acquired facts – would be sufficient to make children understand that movement is not purposive, that activity is not conscious, that things work by chance and inertia alone. This dissociation can come about, he theorizes, only through a radical change in the "habits of mind" (CCW, p. 238). This change, in turn, can be occasioned only by children's becoming aware of themselves, their thought, and their subjectivity. Then they will have the grounds on which to deny their own attributes to things.

CRITIQUE

Piaget's major theoretical conclusion in *The child's conception of the world* is a view of children's early consciousness as a kind of undifferentiated protoplasm that subsequently differentiates. He speaks alternatively of "indissociated" ideas, of the physical and psychical or the objective and subjective, that subsequently "dissociate." These views are related, in turn, to his thesis of unconscious egocentrism, according to which indissociations are attributable to a general confusion of self and world, and the subsequent dissociations are attributable to a progressive differentiation of self and world.

Three questions arise: (a) Do the facts at hand warrant the view of early consciousness as "undifferentiated protoplasm" or of (alleged) animism and realism as flip sides of the same "indissociation" of ideas? (b) Do the phenomena discussed justify the view that children are unconsciously egocentric, in any of the senses in which Piaget defines "egocentric"? (c) Do the data support the notion that more mature ways of thinking develop through the "differentiation" of children's earlier "undifferentiated" thoughts and experiences? With each of these questions we must ask not only whether the data warrant the claim being made, but whether the claim has any inherent plausibility, regardless of whether the data justify it. Finally, a fourth, separate question is whether Piaget explains or illuminates the spontaneous phenomena around which he centered his discussion, namely, children's magical practices and their spontaneous animism.

All but the third of these questions concern Piaget's "synchronic" view of children, that is, his account of the nature of children's minds at particular stages of development. The third question, concerning the manner in which more mature ways of thinking come about, concerns Piaget's "diachronic" view, his view of the way development occurs. In the following critique I will discuss first the three synchronic questions (indissociation thesis, egocentrism thesis, and magic and spontaneous animism) and then Piaget's diachronic claims. The point of reference for the first two topics (indissociation and egocentrism) will be the interview data, given that they are the original source of Piaget's arguments. The treatment of the spontaneous phenomena (magic and animism) will follow.

One of the interesting things about Piaget is his rich account of children's minds and their development. The richness consists, in part, of the fact that he gives multiple accounts of the same phenomena seen in different contexts and from different perspectives. If my discussion seems at times to backtrack, therefore, it is precisely because I am trying to grasp some of this richness.

1. The indissociation thesis

According to the indissociation thesis, both realism and animism are consequences of the same nondifferentiation of the objective and subjective elements of experience. Thus, the thesis makes a major claim about the nature of children's consciousness (that it conflates subjective and objective elements of experience) and purports, through this claim, to explain animism and realism. I will argue that the thesis fails on both counts.

I will discuss two problems in turn. The first is that Piaget uses two different and ultimately incompatible senses of "indissociation" and has insufficient grounds for either one. The second and more serious problem is that, under any of the definitions of "indissociation" that one might adopt, Piaget simply does not give a coherent account of realism and animism: Realism and animism cannot be flip sides of the same thing.

1.1. The definitional problem

Piaget's general theoretical position seems to have pulled him toward one definition of indissociation, and the data toward another. The theoretically driven definition seems to be that children do not, in their earliest thinking, distinguish between mental and physical properties at all. The mental and physical ideas that we as observers might see as inhering in a child's animistic and realist beliefs form an indissoluble whole in which neither a strictly mental nor a strictly physical term is separately identifiable from the child's point of view. The definition that emerges from Piaget's observational data seems to be that mental and physical properties are cognized by children, are even in some sense distinguished, but are seen to be necessarily connected.

That the first of these conceptions (indissoluble whole, sometimes portrayed as "protoplasmic consciousness") follows from Piaget's theoretical position can be seen if we consider the two positions that he was opposing. First, he denied that animism and realism, and their sequelae, come about through the association of atomistic ideas. To be able to say instead, as Piaget thought he could, that these ideas start out as *in*dissociated is at least to be able to say that children do not need at any stage to connect atomistic ideas. The connection is already given. The problem is how to decompose it.

Second, Piaget denied that children had pregiven notions of such qualities as movement, purpose, and the like. If we agreed that children's initial reflective state were merely one in which these ideas were present in some form but "necessarily" or rigidly connected, we would be saying that these ideas were pregiven (at the very least, we would have to ask how children acquired these ideas). This, in essence, is the empirically driven conception of in-dissociation I outlined. In view of its apriorist connotations, it would seem less congenial to Piaget's general theoretical stance than would the first conception.

I merely note that, although Piaget wishes to present his indisso-ciation theses as the natural outcome of rejecting the alternatives of atomism or innatism, we may reject these alternatives without thereby being committed in any way to Piaget's theses.

That Piaget's more empirical statements incline toward the sec-ond conception of indissociation (that children distinguish mental and physical properties in some respects but see them as necessar-ily connected) can be seen in the following example. If a child conceded that a bench would feel something if it were burning or that a wall would know if it were being knocked down, Piaget would say that the child was giving these replies because he or she regarded feeling (i.e., consciousness) and activity as necessarily connected: "All activity is regarded as necessarily conscious" (CCW, p. 237, also p. 177 and elsewhere). This account conveys the impression that children can think of "activity," can think of what it is to feel or be aware of something, and connect the two insofar as they believe that any activity ("necessarily") involves an awareness of that activity.

Some of Piaget's allegedly descriptive statements go even far-ther. Consider his summary claim that the concept of conscious-ness is first extended inappropriately to anything that is the seat of activity and is then gradually restricted to animals. The only con-cept of consciousness that could be "gradually" and "appropri-ately" restricted to animals would be a concept with connotations suitable only to animals, in other words, a concept conveying some impression of feeling and awareness as we know these terms.

Similarly, consider Piaget's comment that children "[do] not realize that there can be actions unaccompanied by consciousness" (CCW, p. 177). This statement makes sense only if we credit children with having a concept of consciousness that *should* be detached from action. That concept again, presumably, would have a distinct nonmaterial or mental component. Thus, we find Piaget describing children's supposedly indissociated concepts in a way that implies that children not only have discernible ideas, but have ideas very like our own. The ideas are "indissociated" only insofar as they are "necessarily" connected. Juxtaposed with this conception of indissociation, however, is the first conception I distinguished, the one that depicts an undifferentiated mass in which ideas of the mental and the physical cannot be distinguished at all. These two conceptions of indissociation not only differ, but conflict outright.

One might think that there are ways to resolve this apparent contradiction. One might suppose, for example, that during the period in which children are wrongly ascribing consciousness to things, the consciousness they attribute is not our full-blown sense of the term, but some weaker version that admits some kind of elementary sensibility along with some strictly physical properties. According to this view, the substantive definition of the concept (its "intension," in Piaget's [Inhelder & Piaget, 1966/1969] later terms) would develop in tandem with its progressive restriction to appropriate category members ("extension"). Piaget himself proposes such alternatives. The contradiction is never really resolved, however, because Piaget insists on seeing realism and animism as reverse sides of the same underlying tendency. This is the second and more fundamental weakness in his account.

1.2. Realism and animism as a unity

The attempt to unify diverse phenomena under the same rubric is one of the hallmarks of Piaget's approach. Indeed, some of the inferences Piaget drew on this basis are truly illuminating and have led to the serious study of whole classes of phenomena that would otherwise have passed unnoticed or remained unappreciated. Inferences based on analogies between phenomena are central to advances in any science. In developmental psychology there is an additional advantage, namely that age can be used as a determinant of what to compare and what to refrain from comparing. In Piaget's case, however, the attempted unification often goes too far. Piaget ties his phenomena into too tight a system, with the result either that the unifying concept dissolves or that the phenomena do. Piaget's attempt to construe realism and animism as reverse sides of the same "indissociations" is a case of this kind.

I begin my demonstration of this point by considering the implications of Piaget's first-order descriptions of realism and animism. Specific reference to the indissociation theses will follow.

Piaget's claim regarding realism is that children materialize mental properties. If indeed they do, and if animism is only the reverse side of realism, it is unclear whether children are really being animistic when they endow a physical object with "consciousness." According to the realism thesis, "consciousness" would not be conceived of by the children as a mental ("animate") property. The very notion of animism, however, presupposes that the properties being attributed to inert objects are seen *as* animate by the attributing agents.

It is in fact only in his discussion of the realism results that Piaget describes children as materializing mental terms to so great a degree. In his account of the original realist state, children regard mental phenomena (thought, perception, etc.) as virtually the same thing as the physical realities to which they refer. When Piaget deals with animism, however, he assumes that children understand terms that depict consciousness, such as "know" and "feel," as involving a kind of rudimentary awareness and will, enough to carry out their associated functions (e.g., the sun has to warm people, and it can do so only if it knows that it must). Piaget says that "insofar as things show an activity which is reliable in its constancy and utility to man, they must possess a psychic life" (CCW, p. 231).

Thus, it appears that Piaget is trying to have it both ways. When he discusses realism, children see mental properties as physical. When he discusses animism, they see them as mental.

Piaget's solution to this apparent contradiction is to hold that children see mental properties as *both* physical and mental; this is essentially the second, discrete-ideas, indissociation thesis (according to which children conceive distinct properties that are "necessarily connected"). Alternatively, they conceive them as *neither* strictly physical *nor* strictly mental, a view suggestive of the first, inchoate-ideas, indissociation thesis (according to which children do not distinguish mental and physical terms at all).

There is an immediate problem here insofar as Piaget's first-order descriptions simply contradict both of these views. Piaget still says (under "realism") that children construe thought as a material object and (under "animism") that they endow inert objects with thought, the ascribed thought befitting only an animate being. Piaget himself never specifies how either version of the indissociation thesis is to be understood in such a way that this contradiction can be avoided. Nonetheless, we can try to determine whether either thesis could be made coherent, independently of Piaget's account.

Consider first what I have called the inchoate-ideas indissociation thesis. Suppose, according to this thesis, that children have an idea called "thought." This is neither an idea of something strictly mental nor an idea of something strictly physical, and it is not any simple combination of the two. It is merely an impression of some sort that children know to attribute to a certain range of phenomena. According to the same view, if children also have a notion of "activity" (or "reality" or "object"), again this is neither an idea of something strictly mental nor an idea of something strictly physical, and it is not any simple combination of the two. It, too, is just a general kind of awareness.

What follows? Let us suppose that these children assert that thought is an activity or that a given activity involves thought. We would be hard-pressed to call the former assertion (about thought) "realism" and the latter (about activity) "animism," because these labels presuppose that a particular mistake concerning mental and physical properties has been made: The children have mistaken something mental for something real (physical) and have mistaken something inanimate (devoid of mental life) for something animate (in possession of "mental properties"). However, we have assumed that the children do not recognize mental and physical properties as such. Thus, this formulation of the indissociation thesis may avoid a contradiction but in return loses the phenomena it was intended to account for.

It seems, then, that insofar as children exhibit animism or realism, they must have at least some concept of mental and physical properties. This conclusion leads to the question of whether the second, "discrete ideas," indissociation thesis, which presupposes these concepts, can be made viable.

This thesis holds both that mental and physical properties are necessarily connected and that animism and realism are simply symmetrical aspects of the same necessary connection. But what could this mean, and is it true? The thesis implies that, if I think that thought inheres in its object, then I also think that that object thinks or has thought. Conversely, if I believe that a particular object thinks, I also believe that thought is a material substance. Clearly, neither of these propositions follows from the point of view of adult logic, and Piaget presents no evidence that children infer any such connections. The notions that thought inheres in its object (realism) and that objects think (animism) are not simple inverses.

Piaget's account raises another problem. In the discussion thus far I have presupposed that the data that purportedly document realism and animism are sufficiently comparable that the question of whether these two alleged tendencies are simple inverses can even be raised. The data are not, in fact, comparable in this way. Consider just the interview data, as we have been doing. The evidence for realism comes from interviews in which children were asked questions about thought (or a dream or name): what it is, where it is located, whether it can be touched or seen, and from what source it emanates. The evidence for animism, meanwhile, comes from interviews in which children were asked whether various objects that were mentioned could "feel" or were "aware of" particular things.

These two groups of questions are not commensurable. In the case of realism Piaget elicited children's reflections about terms that denote mental processes, whereas in the case of animism he observed their *use* of mental terms in their reflections about things. It is as if he assessed the children's *theories* about what a feeling (thought, etc.) is in the case of realism and examined only their intuitive *use* of "feeling" in the case of animism. Although he treats the two cases as if they were equivalent, they are not equivalent and need not coincide. If there are problems of incommensurability within the interview data, we have good reason to suspect that Piaget's extrapolations from these data to children's spontaneous practices (i.e., of magic and animism) will be at least as questionable. I defer this issue, however, until the section on spontaneous practices (section 3 under Critique). —

2. The egocentrism thesis

In Piaget's view, the indissociation of specific mental and physical ideas was a particular instance of a larger failure to differentiate self and world. Therefore, animism and realism were ultimately attributable to the same failure. This, in essence, is the egocentrism thesis as it pertains to animism and realism. Even if animism and realism are not symmetrical in the way Piaget believed (contra the indissociation thesis), either phenomenon or both might still exemplify egocentrism. For this reason, and because egocentrism is so central a notion to Piaget's theorizing, this second line of Piaget's argument merits careful consideration.

The sense of egocentrism specifically as the failure to differentiate self and world is not, however, the only egocentrism thesis that Piaget connected with animism and realism. There were others. As he did with the indissociation thesis, he treated these different versions of the thesis as equivalent, when in fact they are not the same or even conflict.

In evaluating the egocentrism thesis, then, we are again confronted with the task of sorting out the different theses Piaget was trying to assert and assessing the fit of these theses with the data and with the concepts of animism and realism. I begin with the definitional task.

2.1. The concept of egocentrism

Two main egocentrism theses can be distinguished in Piaget's account: the notion that self and world are undifferentiated and the notion of self as center of the world or of one's own point of view as absolute. We shall call these, respectively, the undifferentiation thesis and the absolutist thesis. Each of these subsumes two other theses. In the case of the undifferentiation thesis, Piaget claims both that children have no awareness, or no concept, of a self and that they draw no boundary (or at least draw an insufficient one) between self and world. In the case of the absolutist thesis, there is what I call a "negative" version of the thesis and a "positive" version. The negative thesis characterizes what children fail to do: They fail to take account of alternative points of view. The positive thesis characterizes what they do instead: They treat their own point of view as absolute, themselves as center of the world, their actions and wishes as omnipotent, and so forth.

For Piaget, all of these notions are intertranslatable. Treating one's point of view as absolute and failing to take account of other perspectives are two sides of the same thing, as are failing to draw a boundary between self and world and not having a concept of self. Further, the two main theses, failing to differentiate self and world (and its counterpart of having no concept of self) and treating one's perspective as absolute (and its counterpart of failing to take account of other perspectives), are also two sides of the same thing.

I shall argue that none of these equivalences holds. All of these concepts are much more loosely connected than Piaget assumes. Moreover, we *must* dissociate them to account for animism and realism, or at least for the spontaneous phenomena (magic and spontaneous animism) to be discussed in section 3. The end result, as I will argue in section 3, is that the very phenomena that Piaget treats as indicative of the general impoverishment of children's thinking (i.e., profoundly "egocentric" behaviors such as magic and animism) attest instead to its complexity and richness. In the present section, however, I want only to show that the equivalences Piaget sets up do not have to hold. I begin with a consideration of the absolutist thesis, analyzing first the relation between this thesis and the self–world undifferentiation thesis.

The absolutist thesis. Piaget's reasoning about the relation between the two theses seems to be as follows: Insofar as self and world or mind and thing are undifferentiated (undifferentiation thesis), children take every conception (thought, feeling, etc.) they have to be "absolute" (CCW, p. 126) or "common to all" (p. 125) (absolutist thesis). These two theses are incompatible, insofar as taking one's conceptions (etc.) to be absolute presupposes a concept of self, and Piaget's undifferentiation thesis denies a concept of self.

That the undifferentiation thesis denies a concept of self is simply an assumption on Piaget's part. Although I will ultimately dispute the assumption, I will accept it for the purposes of this discussion of the absolutist thesis.

That the absolutist thesis, however, presupposes a concept of self is less obvious and is not a consequence intended by Piaget. I am referring to the positive side of the absolutist thesis: to Piaget's positive claim that children treat their own point of view (conceptions, etc.) "as absolute," not to his negative claim that they fail to take alternative points of view. It would seem that to take one's point of view as absolute presupposes that one recognizes that one has a point of view, which presupposes, in turn, that one recognizes a self to which this point of view is attached. I would not talk about my point of view unless I had the idea that something could be "mine," and "mine" makes sense only if there is "me." Thus, we find Piaget presupposing the existence of a self through the absolutist thesis while denying it through the undifferentiation thesis.

The positive absolutist thesis makes some further problematic assumptions along similar lines. When we say of an adult that that individual is treating his or her own point of view "as absolute," we assume that that person knows what a point of view is, knows what it is for a point of view to be relative, and is denying relativity in this particular case. His or her own point of view is the *truth*. But Piaget has grounds only for a much weaker claim: Children have no notion of point of view, and no notion of relative (or absolute) points of view. Lacking these notions, they have no appreciation that there are points of view other than their own or any conception of what those points of view might be.

Under these conditions, children might hold a belief about something in the world that *we* know could arise only from their particular point of view. For example, they might believe that the sun follows them down the street. It would be odd, under these conditions, to say that *children* "feel [this] conception to be absolute" (CCW, p. 126). What one can say, and what Piaget does also say is that, if children were to consider points of view other than their own, they might see that their opinion could not be correct (e.g., if the sun follows them, how could it warm other people?). That they do not consider these other points of view is essentially the negative version of the absolutist thesis.

Even if this negative form of the thesis were true – and Piaget and others certainly provide evidence that under at least some

circumstances it is true – the positive form of the thesis does not follow as a necessary consequence. Piaget infers that, because children fail to consider other points of view (negative version), they have strange ideas about their own point of view (positive version). But under the conditions we are considering (that children have no concept of self and no notion of point of view or of relative or absolute points of view), it seems that we can conclude little more than that children have strange ideas about the *world*.
– In the light of these difficulties, there is all the more reason to question the following, equally strong claim that Piaget appears to conceive as another variant of the absolutist thesis: "Insofar as he ignores that his own point of view is subjective [the child] believes himself the centre of the world" (CCW, p. 127). It does not follow that, if *children* ignore the fact that their own point of view is subjective (i.e., relative), they believe themselves to be the center of the world. It follows virtually by Piaget's own definition that children do not believe *themselves* to be anything, because they do not know a self about whom to have beliefs. –

There might, however, be another, more compelling observation about infants and young children that lends some plausibility to this form of the absolutist thesis. Piaget points out that the early and virtually automatic receptivity of adults to children might cultivate in children the view that the world is at their disposal. The world knows, if not shares, every whim and desire children have, and it is there to fulfill (or, as the case may be, to resist) these whims and desires.

Notice, however, the presuppositions of this alleged view. There is a self for whom the world exists and a world that is there for the self. These are, again, exactly the terms Piaget wishes to deny that chldren have any concept of.

With this rejoinder I do not mean to argue that the social responsivity of which Piaget speaks does not exist or that infants do not establish certain expectations on the basis of this responsivity. It is also plausible that these expectations, or generalizations based on them, continue into childhood, at least in some form. My point thus far is that Piaget's theorizing, in particular his attempt to trace all of the phenomena under question to a lack of concept of self, rules out certain ways of talking about the phenomena. Elsewhere in his theorizing, however, in the various positive forms of the absolutist thesis, Piaget talks in exactly these ways.

At least so far, we have not considered any evidence or argument that would lead us to accept the positive absolutist thesis. Hence, we have no reason as yet to posit that children who exhibit the purportedly egocentric behavior that we have considered thus far (e.g., children's beliefs about the sun) have a concept of self. At the same time, however, we have not considered any evidence or argument that would lead us to deny that children have a concept of self or to see their lack of this concept (if indeed they lack it) as integral to their conception of the world. Piaget makes another attempt to defend exactly these claims, however, in his discussion of the undifferentiation thesis, to which I now turn.

The undifferentiation thesis. According to the undifferentiation thesis, children draw an indistinct or insufficient boundary between self and world, and this failure implies that they have no awareness of a self or of its properties (e.g., the properties of mind, personality, or subjective point of view). Children regard something that, according to Piaget, is actually internal to them, for example, their *perception* of the sun's movement, as part of external reality. Piaget saw as a deeper consequence of such inner–outer confusion the idea that children have no consciousness of self. What could a self come to if children could not distinguish the contents of their own minds from the contents of external reality?

Piaget appears to be trying here to equate self–world differentiation and the concept of self, by definition. To have a concept of self is exactly to draw the appropriate distinctions between self (or its properties) and reality.[3] But the question of whether children have a concept of self does not have to be the same as the question of whether they draw a clear boundary, or the right boundary, between self and world. One can know a self and not know its limits.

This seems, in essence, to be Freud's (1913/1952a, 1919/1952b) view of narcissism. The narcissistic stage of libidinal development is that stage in which the child takes himself or herself as love

---

[3] Piaget is not alone in this view. See, for example, Cassirer (1955).

object and in so doing "overvalues" the self and its powers. Critically, narcissism is not the original state of the child. It succeeds the stage of autoeroticism, in which the sexual instincts find satisfaction diversely in the child's own body and are distinctly not focused on a particular, single object. Freud eventually found it necessary to interpolate a developmental phase of narcissism between autoeroticism and the later stage of external object love, when he found himself otherwise unable to account for "narcissistic" disorders of adulthood. What is important for the purposes of this discussion is that Freud delineates a psychological state that both presupposes a concept of self (i.e., some unifying seat of experience) *and* has as a cardinal feature a weak boundary between this self and external reality. He can incorporate both features (i.e., some concept of self and improper self–world differentiation), because he is defining the concept of self independently of the question of the degree to which self is differentiated from the world.

I am not arguing that Freud's theory of narcissism is necessarily right or that it will account for Piaget's phenomena. I use it only to reinforce my point that in principle a separation can be made between the question of whether one has a concept of self and the question of whether and in what specific way self and world are differentiated. With this possibility in mind, I turn to Piaget's attempt to explain animism and realism through egocentrism. I treat the interview results briefly and then consider magical practices and spontaneous animism.

2.2 Realism, animism, and egocentrism

Piaget, the reader will recall, connects animism and realism with the "indissociation" or particular "subjective" and "objective" terms. Thought cannot be envisioned without a material component (realism), for example. Physical properties, such as movement, can be conceived of only in connection with a mental aspect, such as purpose (animism). The explanation of animism and realism through egocentrism is simply the further statement that each of these specific indissociations embodies a confusion of self and world, or of psychic and material reality.

The problem here is that either this alleged explanation simply restates the data or it is not true, given Piaget's data. To begin with the problem of restatement, Piaget often uses the specific indissociations themselves (e.g., children's tendency to couple activity with awareness: the branch that snaps is hurt, the burning sun feels its heat, etc.) as evidence that children confuse (properties of the) self and (properties of) reality. On these occasions it would be circular to argue that the specific indissociations occur because children confuse self and reality. At best Piaget might be construed to be labeling the specific indissociations, not explaining them.

To the extent that the argument is not circular, Piaget himself, as I discussed in the section on the indissociation thesis, denies that the mental terms that children include in these indissociations are strictly mental and that the physical terms are strictly physical. They are something in between. Thus, if children speak of activity as though the seat of activity were "aware," they are not, according to Piaget, ascribing a mental property to the object in question. Therefore, it would seem, they could not be said to be conflating a mental property with a material one. Their "error" is not an instance of some larger confusion, because, according to the theory, they have no concept of the larger categories (mental, material) between which this larger confusion would occur. The larger confusion is, rather, our creation, based on the way we interpret such terms as "awareness" (purpose, etc.) and "activity."

There is a similar problem with Piaget's example of children who think the sun follows them. Piaget construes this error alternately as an inner–outer confusion (what is really only a product of perception is taken for reality) or as a conflation of self and world (or self and others; lacking the ability to take others' perspectives, children assume that their own perspective is absolute). It is not clear, however, whether this mistake has anything to do with inner–outer, or self and world. Children are mistaking appearance for reality, but this is not necessarily the same thing as confusing inner–outer, or self and world.

Consider the illusion of the bent pencil in water. The pencil looks bent, but it is not. Given that it would look bent to any observer (other than one with correcting goggles), the illusion cannot be ascribed to a failure to take perspectives (or to its alleged converse of treating one's own perspective as absolute). In what sense is the illusion an inner–outer mistake? The illusion, that is, what I see, is a product of the optical properties of the array, the refraction of light through water, and so forth, as much as it is a product of my perception. If I think the pencil actually is bent, this probably means that I do not appreciate how the physical properties of the world make the pencil appear bent without its actually being bent (absurd though I might find the idea that it actually is bent). I have not mistaken an "inner" for an "outer" reality. I am lacking some knowledge of a further "outer" reality.

Consider, conversely, pain. I might be experiencing pain. That sensation would be internal, and it would be real; so reality need not coincide with what is external. I also might have referred pain. It would be an illusion, an "appearance," and it would be internal. Therefore, an appearance–reality confusion could occur wholly internally just as, in the bent pencil example, it can occur wholly externally, from the point of view of the perceiver.

With these few illustrations I merely want to raise the possibility that Piaget's interview data may reflect only simple mistakes that arise through a lack of specific knowledge or conceptual understandings having nothing particularly to do with the concept of self. That is, they may presuppose neither a concept of self nor its absence. Insofar as "self" theses, in any form, may be irrelevant to these examples, there is no reason as yet to attempt to distinguish among the different egocentrism theses identified in the last section.

3. Magical practices and spontaneous animism

Piaget attempts to link magic and spontaneous animism to egocentrism through the middle step of "realism," as realism is documented by the interviews. I will argue, in turn, that the connection with realism is arbitrary and that the egocentrism thesis should be replaced by a far more complex, and in a way opposite, account. I begin with the realism thesis, for which Piaget's primary point of reference is magic. Hence, I focus on magic as well.

3.1. Magic and realism

There is a simple connection between magic and realism for Piaget: If children are already disposed to think of thought or of signs (e.g., names) as inhering in things, that is, if they are "realists," it is natural for them to use thought and signs to influence those things, that is, to engage in "magic." Insofar as child magic might be attributable to these "realist" premises, then like these premises, it might be traced more generally to children's incomplete differentiation of self and world, internal and external, psychical and physical, in other words, to one version of egocentrism or another.

This connection between magic and realism is extremely tenuous. It does not follow, that is, from the point of view of adult logic, that if thought (or a name, etc.) is "in" its object (i.e., the realist position) it can be used to manipulate objects (the implicit assumption behind magic). Conversely, one might perceive one's thought to be empowered with causal significance without at the same time thinking that it is in some way part of the thing it represents or otherwise capable of coming in contact with it materially. One might envision a more indeterminate relation between the thought and the thing, if one envisions any relation at all, or one might think that the thought will somehow be heard by the thing. Especially if one is a *child,* then, precisely according to Piaget's own theory of child causality (see chapter 5), one would not see any necessary relation between causation and material contact. The concept of trying to influence things just seems to be a separate idea.

If this tight, virtually deductive connection between magic and realism is in doubt, however, Piaget also posits a weaker association: Magic and realism presuppose, separately, the same conceptual base, namely, the idea of "participation" between (what we know to be) materially unrelated phenomena. But crucial asymmetries arise here also. In the case of realism (as documented by the interviews), the children *assert,* when asked for an explanation of what thought is, that (in effect) a relationship of "participation" holds between thought and object. In the case of magic, the children engage in some practice (say, thinking the opposite of what they want), and *that practice* presupposes, to our adult way of thinking, a relation of participation between the practice and the desired outcome.

It is not clear, in this second case, whether the *children* assume that a relationship of participation holds between their actions and the event they wish to influence. Piaget does not appear to have grounds to say, as he does, "The child performs some action or mental operation (counting, etc.), and *believes that* this action or operation exercises, *through participation,* an influence on a particular event he either desires or fears" (CCW, p. 133, my emphasis). If the *child* "believes" anything on such occasions, he or she more likely believes that somehow or other he or she is influencing the probability of the outcome. More weakly still, the child may simply be doing one thing and hoping for another, with little if any sense of how his or her action might bring the outcome about.

There is the further difference that the "participation" that is evident in the children's realist answers is the product of reflection: When confronted with the intellectual puzzle of how thought could be *about* something, the children infer that the thought is somehow *in* the thing or "in" reality. It would appear to be a distinguishing characteristic of magical practices (as well as of certain spontaneous animistic reactions), however, that they are decidedly nonreflective. They are compulsive and highly emotionally driven.

Regarding this last contrast, magical practices and genuine animism (e.g., children's sympathy for or fear of inanimate objects, actions they undertake to placate or otherwise influence these objects) do not appear to be "reasoned" and may not derive (by reasoning or any other process) from any current set of beliefs children hold, either implicitly or explicitly. They might hark back to impressions children once held in a developmental period they have since passed, but that is another matter. The realist and animistic interview answers, on the contrary, are derived through a process of inference either from the children's current theories about how the world works or from more general, current trends in their thinking. Even a totally made-up answer would seem to be rationally derived, in this sense, in a way that magical practices and spontaneous reactions seem not to be.

Whether or not these speculations are correct in detail, they suggest that magic (and spontaneous animism) and realism not only are more loosely connected than Piaget thought, but differ profoundly. If, therefore, Piaget's egocentrism theses seemed largely irrelevant to the phenomena related directly to realism (i.e., the interviews), they might still be applicable to magic and spontaneous animism. I consider this possibility next.

3.2. Egocentrism as an account of magic or animism

When a child counts to 10 between rattles of the radiator to ensure the safety of the house that night or the success of the next day's outing, we could say that, regardless of what the child may think, properties of the self are in fact overflowing their bounds. Thought is immaterial and is confined to the head. It cannot affect an event in the outer world, at least not directly. Similarly, when a child feels sorry for a tree that has been hollowed out, the tree feels nothing. The *child* feels and in the tree's place would feel a great deal of pain.

In Piaget's view these phenomena (magic and animism, respectively) signify a failure to distinguish between self, or its properties, and the world. This failure is attributable, in turn, to children's lack of concept of self, or of its properties (e.g., the property "mind," or "psychic"). It is for want of a concept of mind that children fail to recognize the limits of what are in fact functions of the mind (the case of magic) and that they also endow inert objects with these same functions (animism).

I examine this view by considering, in turn, Piaget's data, the a priori plausibility of his argument, and, finally, a possible alternative.

The data. The only direct evidence Piaget cites for his view that children lack a concept of mind, and hence for the view that this deficiency mediates their magical practices and animistic reactions, is the children's comments in the realism interviews: When asked to explain what thought is, the children situated it in the external world and tended to materialize it.

For a start, Piaget is simply unjustified in generalizing from this misunderstanding of what thought is in the abstract to the claim that children do not distinguish any kind of mental life at all.[4] Even if children do conceive of thought, abstractly, as material, there is nothing to stop them from appreciating some of its mental properties at the same time. They might, for example, know that trying or wanting to do something is not the same as doing it. Piaget in fact concedes that children as young as 3 years of age

---

[4] The same general kind of point has been made by contemporary authors writing on animism (e.g., Bullock, 1985; Carey, 1985) and realism (e.g., Flavell, Flavell, & Green, 1985).

make a distinction of this sort, between thinking or wondering, on the one hand, and perceiving or knowing for a fact, on the other (CCW, p. 43; also LT, p. 232). The important datum for Piaget, however, is that children do not "deduce" (CCW, p. 43) from these distinctions that thought (wanting, wondering, etc.)is not part of the thing it represents.

But Piaget's qualification here implies nothing more than that, whatever else children may think thought is, they fail to recognize that it is also immaterial (internal, etc.). This formulation of children's understanding hardly warrants the view that they are "ignorant of the psychic" (CCW, p. 239) or that (total) "ignorance of the psychic" explains magic and animism.

Alternatively, we are left with the view that it is specifically children's failure to appreciate the nonmaterial (internal, etc.) quality of thought, in the abstract sense that Piaget documents, that explains their propensity toward magic and animism. It is difficult, however, to see how the failure to recognize in the abstract that thought is mental and immaterial could do this. Would a child who explicitly recognized the mental, nonmaterial quality of thought fail thereby to feel sympathy for the hollow tree trunk (to adjust the stones so they might have a better view, etc.) or fail to follow magical rituals at bedtime? We have no compelling reason to think so, unless the failure to recognize the mental, nonmaterial quality of thought meant exactly the failure to recognize that only animals think or the failure to abstain totally from any sort of magical preoccupation. This account, however, merely redescribes the data and also shifts Piaget's theoretical claim (which was that children do not know what thought is).

Thus far I have suggested that the data Piaget reports do not justify his argument that magic and spontaneous animism originate either in children's failure to differentiate self and world or mental and material or in their lack of a concept of any of these potential differentiae. I consider next whether these deficiencies *could* explain magic and animism in principle.

The a priori plausibility of the argument. I have already dealt with this question in part. In the discussion of the indissociation thesis (Section 1.2), I concluded that to deny that children have any concept at all of the mental would be to preclude their being animistic. There would be no sense in which *they* could be ascribing *animate* properties to things. Similarly, the idea of magic would lose its meaning if we did not assume that children conceived themselves to be at least somewhat detached from things so that they could act on them from a distance, that is, "magically." Along the same lines, to attempt to influence things with their *thought*, children must have at least some notion of what thought is and some ability to distinguish it from, say, material action or material contact with something. That is, Piaget presents no evidence – and one's subjective impression of children who engage in magical practices does not suggest – that the child who counts to 10 between rattles of the radiator actually thinks he or she is engaging in a material action. The relation of the practice to the outcome is special even to the child, however little insight the child may have into the nature of the relation, and regardless of how plainly the child might *describe* thought as a material reality.

Piaget was not unaware of these problems. He argues that the state of complete undifferentiation of self and world (mental and material, etc.) either does not exist or exists only as the original state, by which he presumably means some period during infancy. Magic, animism, and the realism evident in the interviews are all supposed to represent a later phase of development, in which this original "protoplasmic consciousness" has already begun to differentiate. Although Piaget is somewhat vague as to what has and has not differentiated at this point, he seems to think that it is the child's self as a whole that has become partly distinguished from things. Granting whatever distance may now exist between self and things, however, psychical and physical *ideas* are not yet dissociated. Subjective "aspects" still "adhere" to things (CCW, p. 250). These "adherences" explain animism, realism, and magic.

This revised view still leaves us with the difficulty, however, that if self and world are dissociated but subjective and physical ideas are not, then the "mistakes" embodied by animism, realism, and magic could not occur. Animism still requires a misattribution of *animacy* (thought, consciousness, etc.), realism a misconception of *thought,* and magic a misconstrued application of thought or other activities of the self. Piaget has simply displaced rather than solved the problems with the thesis of total undifferentiation.

All of these considerations lead to the conclusion that, even if magic and animism do involve a failure to recognize certain boundaries between the self or thought and the world, this failure cannot *explain* magic and animism. Further, if these phenomena did derive from the various failures of differentiation, we could not explain why they do not occur from earliest infancy. Indeed, some (e.g., Sully, 1914) have even speculated that superstitious practices and beliefs are more likely to occur among relatively more rather than relatively less intelligent children.

In reply to these concerns, Piaget might simply point to his concession that self and world have to have "differentiated" to some degree for magic, animism, and realism to occur. As I have just discussed, however, it is the continuum of *non*differentiation in this general conception that Piaget regards as the central explanation of these phenomena. Alternatively, it is for *want* of a concept of self or of a concept of mind that, he theorizes, children are realists and animists and practice magic. As I have also just argued, theses of this kind leave essential facets of these phenomena unexplained (e.g., the animacy within animism, the concept of thought in realism and magic, the magic in magic, and the delayed appearance of all of these reactions).

An alternative. At this point we are best off adopting the alternative tack of confronting these unexplained facets directly and attempting to identify the concepts and distinctions they seem to presuppose but that Piaget omits. I begin with the following reflection:

With magic and spontaneous animism we want to say that the ego, or the self, is not properly differentiated from the world or from things in it. We do not simply want to say that within a specific experience they might have, children do not perceive any difference between what comes from the inside and what comes from the outside. In the latter kind of experience, no mental or physical, inner or outer term can be distinguished in children's experience. There is just experience. It is only we, as external observers, who can point to the internal and external components of that experience.

When we speak of discrete magical practices, however, we are speaking of experience on another level: children's experience of their apparent influence over things. We are no longer talking just of an experience of "things," but of an experience of self in a particular relation to things. With animism as well, we could say that children have drawn an analogy to them*selves* or to their experience, based on the external signs they see (a physical condition of some kind, e.g., a hole in something). To be sure, Piaget may be correct in saying that, under certain circumstances, children have difficulty separating the physical sign from its mental correlate. But the mental correlate is nonetheless a recognizable piece of children's own experience, being observed, so children think, in some other body. Were children to say, they might tell us, "*I* can feel that way *too.*" The "I" and the "too" would be missing from the purely undifferentiated experience I described in the last paragraph.

So far I have argued that the concept of self, or at least *a* concept of self, may figure integrally in magic and animism. Compatible with this idea is the notion that this self might not know its proper boundaries. It might feel its influence where it should not (magic), and it might see its reflection where in fact none exists (animism). Once again, however, it is a *self* that has overreached its boundaries. This is not a condition simply of the indeterminate experience of (what the external observer knows to be) an inner and an outer world.

What, then, of the notions of thought and mind? I have already argued that some sense of these notions is presupposed by the mere existence of animism and also of magic, to the extent that children "manipulate" their thought (counting to 10, etc.) as part of magic and recognize some difference between doing this and materially acting on the world. Compatible with this argument is the possibility that children also materialize thought. They can still recognize some distinction between things and thoughts, even if thoughts are thinglike embodiments within those things.

Freud (1913/1952a) makes an analogous point when, following Herbert Spencer, he alludes to the primacy of the mind–body dualism in primitive, animistic belief systems. He observes that, although primitive peoples treat as animate all kinds of things that civilized adults would treat as inert, underlying these attributions is the belief that everything has a *dual nature,* a soul and a body. The soul is given a material embodiment. In effect, it is a small person. It is distinct from the body that houses it, however, insofar as it can detach itself from the body once the body dies, for example. So there is mind and body, or mind and matter, although the distinction may be closer to "matter and matter." The point is that one of these "matters" represents something that we would call thought (e.g., the ability to remember something when it is gone).

Children, of course, do not hold this set of beliefs. My purpose in bringing up Freud is, as before, to show that certain concepts and distinctions that Piaget treats as equivalent or as interdependent can be separated, and we may need to separate them to account for the phenomena in question.

The case of animism raises another set of considerations. Thus far I have been treating children's animistic reactions as though they were only simple empathic reactions to things. But at least some animistic projections may be more complicated. Following Freud's more general discussion of projection, we might conceive that on some occasions children are projecting onto external objects emotions or ideas (e.g., pain or sorrow) that they experience unconsciously but (also unconsciously) are afraid to acknowledge. The principle behind projection is that, once it is perceived to be external, the distressing feeling or thought can be escaped from, since flight is possible from external but not internal stimuli.

Piaget might describe this complex of reactions as simply another instance of the confusion of self and world that children are prone to experience. Notice, however, what this confusion presupposes. Children have a reaction that they (or part of them) acknowledge as their own. This acknowledgment is distressing. Therefore, the reaction is disowned and transferred to a distinctly external source, as a result of which it can be escaped. Embedded in this account are both a concept of self (such that a feeling can be identified as "one's own") and a distinction between inner and outer reality. According to this account children's whole reaction *depends* on this concept and this distinction.

I grant that when I speak here of children's concept of self (or "one's own") and their notion of an inner–outer distinction, I am referring to notions that are, hypothetically, unconscious. This would not, however, appear to diminish their relevance. If children could not draw the distinctions in question at some level that affects their actual experience of things, there would be no reason for projection or the conflict that motivates it to arise, either consciously or unconsciously.

In general, Piaget's egocentrism thesis seems not so much extraneous to magic and spontaneous animism as it seems wrong, or at least very seriously incomplete. The concept of self and the (or a) distinction between inner and outer reality and between mind and matter may figure in essential ways in these phenomena. At the same time, the boundaries of self may be obscure, the distinction between inner and outer reality may be easily collapsed, and the distinction between the mental and the material might not be quite the distinction that adults would make. Piaget's theory leaves no room for all of these different possibilities to exist simultaneously, yet he does not argue in such a way as to exclude them. The problem is not solved by Piaget's notion that, by the time magic and animism appear, self and world have differentiated in part and left "adherences" behind. Animism and magic do not appear to be just "further differentiations" of old categories of experience that were previously confused. They appear to be new confusions involving new categories that it would seem to be precisely the task of the theory to explain. Piaget, at best, can be seen as presupposing these categories.

The subject of Piaget's differentiation notion brings us to the question of his developmental theorizing in general.

4. The developmental thesis

Until now we have been dealing with the question of why animism and realism (and magic) occur. We have found Piaget's account wanting. The focus of Piaget's developmental theorizing, however, was the question of how more mature ways of thinking and acting come about. Through what process do children eventually draw the distinctions and develop the concepts that are denied, according to Piaget, by their animism and realism (and magic)?

Piaget offers what are in effect two complementary theses. One, an extension of the egocentrism thesis, explains the development of these distinctions and concepts through the differentiation of self and world, or the decline of egocentrism. The other, an extension of the indissociation thesis, holds that the distinctions and concepts children develop – for example, the distinction between purpose and activity or the concepts of chance and inertia – arise specifically through the differentiation of prior confusions or "indissociations" containing the poles of the distinctions and concepts in question. Thus, the decline of egocentrism permits and motivates the more specific differentiations (egocentrism thesis), and these differentiations explain how – through which specific process – children come to recognize the distinctions and concepts they do (differentiation thesis). I discuss the two theses in turn.

4.1 The differentiation of self and world

There are two ways to interpret this thesis. One way is to read it as a causal account: Insofar as children come to differentiate self and world (which for Piaget is the same as developing a concept of self), this will prompt them to distinguish, for example, between purpose and activity. The second way to interpret the thesis is to see it merely as a redescription of the data: To dissociate purpose and activity (thought and object, etc.) *is* to differentiate self and world (to have a concept of self).

Piaget seems to shift back and forth between these two versions of the thesis. They are not the same thing, however, and they are incompatible. Insofar as dissociating purpose and activity *is* to separate self and world (or separating self and world is, among other things, to dissociate purpose and activity), then separating self and world cannot be the cause of dissociating purpose and activity. Dissociating purpose and activity would simply be a particular instance of separating self and world.

There is a prior problem, however, in that neither version of the thesis is very tenable. I consider the causal thesis first.

The causal account. Piaget alludes to two ways in which the growing awareness of self and its properties comes about, such that children might then become motivated to draw the distinctions needed to eliminate animism and realism. One means is the observation of other people. As they gain experience with others, children may notice that not all behavior is intentional and hence may form "such improbable conceptions as movement without consciousness or existence without awareness" (CCW, p. 240). The second path is increasing self-knowledge, that is, introspection. The capacity to introspect comes slowly to children (according to the investigations in *Judgment and reasoning* [Piaget, 1924/1968]). Lacking this capacity, Piaget thinks, children must assume they know themselves perfectly and are fully aware of everything they do and everything that happens to them. From this illusion they must generalize to the belief that other things and other people are conscious of themselves (CCW, p. 240). Inversely, Piaget argues, once children realize that self-knowledge is never perfect, they can begin to erect an entire scale of different types of action, ranging from wholly nonconscious action to reflective and voluntary action.

The immediate problem here is that both pathways presuppose what they are trying to explain. Regarding the first pathway, Piaget thinks that children will form the idea of movement without consciousness on the basis of the observation that not all human behavior is intentional. But this thesis does not explain how children would actually *do* this, that is, how they would recognize that something is unintentional behavior. Regarding the second potential pathway, that of introspection, Piaget does not explain how children could even start to engage in introspection, given that, according to the theory, they have no notion of a self or inner world. Alternatively, they might begin to engage in a process that we would call introspection, but how, according to the theory, would *they* know that it was a *self* recalling experience particular to *it*?

Let us suppose, however, that these broader kinds of awareness (e.g., of self, thought) arise through some means. What can we make of the remainder of Piaget's causal claim, that the particular distinctions that connote the abandonment of animism and realism (e.g., the distinction between purpose and activity or intentional action and mechanical movement) would ensue? Given that we are dealing with the causal version of the thesis, we must define the broader kinds of awareness (mental–physical, self–world) in such a way that they are not automatically embodied by the more particular distinctions (e.g., purpose–activity) they are meant to explain. Let us therefore define the distinction between the mental and the physical as the recognition of thought as such, or the recognition that thought or any other mental process one could name is indeed psychic and does not inhere in the objects to which it might refer. Piaget sometimes defines the distinction in this way (e.g., CCW, p. 177).

Now, consider the assumption under which it would follow that a child who did not distinguish between the mental and the physical (in this sense) would also not distinguish between purpose and activity. The child would have to have connected purpose with thought. Otherwise it simply would not follow that, if the child failed to distinguish between thought and its objects, that child would also fail to distinguish between purpose and activity. The only alternative would be that the idea of purpose was already part of what was meant by "thought." In this alternative case, however, we would be speaking of a descriptive rather than causal claim. We are examining only causal claims here.

Or consider the assumption under which it would follow that children could come to distinguish between purpose and activity (i.e., to recognize some movements as "not purposive") only if they came to distinguish between the mental and the physical (or between thought and things). Here again, we would be requiring that these children had already regarded purpose as associated in some way with thought, so that whatever was true of the one would ipso facto be true of the other.

Either way, it seems as if Piaget is presupposing an ordered system of concepts from the start, and not just any ordered system, but our adult ordered system. If an individual failed in general to recognize the internal, nonmaterial quality of his or her mental life (or, if the assumption were warranted, of mental life in general), then it would be bizarre, specifically with respect to our adult way of thinking, if that individual distinguished purpose from the activity in which it might result. The reason we would find these views strange is that "purpose" is to us a mental term. This particular connection and the ordered system are precisely what Piaget refuses to attribute to children's thought.

In a similar vein, consider the related claims that, as children become increasingly aware of the personality and subjective activity within themselves, they will cease attributing these properties to things, and that as they come to know themselves better and hence to know how imperfectly they know themselves, they will begin to concede nonconscious actions to things. Why should these different aspects of growing self-awareness lead to a retraction of these properties from things? Indeed, why would children not transfer these new self-discoveries to things? If children can be both aware and unaware of the actions they perform, perhaps things can also be both aware and unaware of their movements. Or if children gradually discover that they have a personality in themselves or have a point of view, why would they not also attribute personalities and points of view to things?

Thus, in attempting to turn the egocentrism thesis into a causal account of animism and realism, Piaget introduces a number of extremely arbitrary assumptions. Some of these assumptions, for example, the notion that children have an articulate system of concepts from the start, run directly counter to other portions of the theory. A related difficulty is that this version of the thesis also presupposes that children are deducing one distinction from another (e.g., purpose–activity from mental–material). It is not at all clear whether conceptual development is a series of such deductions. Finally, other assumptions, for example, the idea that the increased awareness of one's own personality would lead to a retraction of personality from things, would not appear to follow from either a child's or an adult's point of view. Indeed, as I discussed in previous sections, theses that are in some sense the opposite of what Piaget proposes may hold: The explanation of animism and realism (or at least magic) may lie precisely in the discovery at some level of a psychic life, or of a self.

The descriptive account. The descriptive version of Piaget's thesis avoids all of these problems. We now assume that Piaget was attempting to do no more than redescribe the phenomena of realism and animism, but in a language that suggested their implications for egocentrism. Under this assumption, we reinterpret statements that sound as if Piaget is asserting a causal connection (e.g., insofar as children come to recognize a personality in themselves, they will refuse to attribute a personality to things; children confuse purpose and activity because they confuse the mental and the physical) to be only statements of definition, or at most of classification. The discovery of personality in oneself *is* precisely the discovery that personality is something that applies specifically to "selves" and not to other things. Or to distinguish between purpose and activity is to recognize a distinction between the mental and the physical, and other specific distinctions that children now make (e.g., between consciousness and activity) also exemplify the same basic distinction.

Even if Piaget intended nothing more than these statements of definition, the statements pose either of two significant difficulties. The first is a problem of classification. Earlier I noted numerous instances in which Piaget either grouped two different phenomena (e.g., animism and realism) inappropriately under the same unifying rubric (the indissociation of "subjective" and "objective" properties) or gave inadequate justification for linking certain reactions (e.g., children's belief that the sun follows them) to questions of self and world (mind and reality, etc.). Thus, although some of Piaget's groupings of phenomena are illuminating, many appear to be either misleading and arbitrary or irrelevant to the questions at issue (e.g., regarding self and reality).

The second difficulty is the general impoverishment of Piaget's description of his phenomena, which seems to result from his attempt to construe what he was doing as offering an explanation. Here, as I already noted, the (intentionally) descriptive account of animism and realism becomes increasingly strained the more Piaget tries to "explain" realism and animism through the indissociation thesis. The account also begs several essential questions, that is, questions that are central both to Piaget's own theory and to any understanding of the topics under investigation. Suppose, for example, Piaget were saying no more than that the discovery of a personality in oneself is the discovery that personality is something that applies only to "selves." Then, we are left to wonder what the concept of personality is that is being correctly or incorrectly applied and how children acquire this concept. The gap here is very much like the gap in the concept of egocentrism in general (in CCW). Insofar as Piaget equates the question of whether children have a concept of self with the question of whether they differentiate self and world, we are left asking what the nature of the self is that has or has not been improperly extended into the world, and how it comes about.

One last problem with Piaget's descriptive or, as we might call them, analytic hypotheses (purpose–activity "implies" mind–world) is that, as also emerged in my earlier discussion of egocentrism (and of magic and spontaneous animism), the phenomena Piaget himself was trying to account for may require that we dissociate the concepts he has interlocked. We may need, as I said then, to separate such notions as concept of self and self–world differentiation. The same might be said for the recognition of a personality (or other personal qualities) and the ascription of a personality to the right individuals.

4.2 Development as differentiation

Several problems arise from Piaget's attempt to relate the development and decline of animism and realism to the more global pattern of self–world differentiation and the trends (e.g., discovery of self, of personality) that Piaget associates with that pattern. One could, however, reject this broader theory and still find the idea of differentiation applicable to development within any one of the areas Piaget discusses, taken by itself. This more local application of the idea of differentiation appears in Piaget's earlier and later work (see chapters 4 and 6).

The standard argument (in CCW) proceeds as follows. Eventually (according to the interview data), children draw certain conceptual distinctions, for example, between purposive (intentional, or conscious) activity and purely mechanical or imparted movement. Earlier, they do not draw these distinctions, at least not explicitly, and they describe at least some events in such a way that they seem to be disregarding the distinction. For example, they speak of mechanical movement as though it were alive or conscious. Piaget infers that, when children eventually do draw the distinction in question, the distinction has arisen specifically through the dissociation of an earlier confusion; this earlier confusion is a confusion of the differentiate of the (eventual) distinction (CCW, p. 237).

This inference is arbitrary. Even if children did begin with the various confusions Piaget attributes to them, we could not assume that the distinctions that subsequently appear arise specifically by means of the "dissociation" of these earlier confusions. Here it is important to draw a distinction, analogous to the distinction I made in section 4.1, between a more descriptive and more causal version of Piaget's thesis. A descriptive version of the differentiation (dissociation) thesis would be simply the statement that, say, a 7-year-old's ideas about the movement of waterfalls and people are more highly differentiated than are those of a 4-year-old. The causal version of the thesis would say that the 7-year-old arrives at his or her more highly differentiated ideas specifically by disassembling his or her earlier confusions. I am questioning the causal thesis.

To continue, suppose (as is doubtless true) that children eventually do distinguish between purpose and activity, and in a very clear way. They know that not all activity is prompted by a purpose, and some activity is endogenously generated by a willful actor. We have no good reason to assume that children arrive at this distinction specifically by breaking apart their initially confused ideas about activity and why it occurs. They might simply be learning or inferring something new about the world that they did not know or did not think of before and that will lead them to draw a distinction that they did not previously make. Every day children learn new particulars, for instance, about how to operate mechanical objects or about how to effect certain results with other inert objects. As children learn and integrate new facts about things in the world, they might start to use this new awareness as a basis for distinguishing among things in the world where they had not previously drawn a distinction or else had made a distinction of a different sort.

Let me merely insert here, since I have already dealt with the point in previous sections (e.g., section I under Critique), that it is only Piaget's assumption that children do indeed pass through an earlier stage in which they confuse the differentiae of distinctions they will draw later. What Piaget's data usually show is only that children fail to draw a distinction (e.g., between purpose and activity), not that they confuse the poles of the undrawn distinction. Piaget, however, seems to need to attribute to children a positive view of some sort that contains the very material, in fact the actual categories, out of which the distinctions in question will later emerge. Once again, there are no empirical grounds for this attribution. Nor does it follow, as Piaget sometimes seems to suppose it does, as a logical consequence of the fact that children will eventually draw the distinctions and do not draw them earlier.

I have a more basic objection to the whole view. Piaget speaks of *ideas* dissociating into other ideas, not of *children* dissociating their ideas, as I just did (e.g., when I referred to children breaking apart their initially confused ideas about activity and why this occurs). Yet unless Piaget is making only a purely descriptive statement – that the *product* of development is such that the more differentiated ideas eventually supplant the less differentiated ones – the statement does not have a clear meaning.

Ideas do not "do" anything on their own (except perhaps in our unconscious, which is not what Piaget was discussing). Moreover, although developmental changes in ideas may be likened to differentiating germ plasm, ideas are not, in fact, material substances that endure through space and time such that *they* can in principle "differentiate." Therefore, either Piaget is presupposing an agent, namely the child, who is busy disentangling his or her earlier confusions (hence, my reference to "children" breaking apart their ideas), or he has simply reified children's thought. Alternatively, he has some other model of the developmental process that he has left obscure.

Whichever alternative is correct, Piaget has not told us what children are actually doing. Either their ideas have taken on a life of their own (the reification alternative), or Piaget has made quite arbitrary assumptions about the developmental process. Regarding the latter possibility, Piaget's differentiation image might have some intuitive appeal, insofar as it accords with our own experience in working over our own ideas. Frequently, we arrive at a cogent and differentiated view of some subject matter only after we have worked concertedly at disentangling our initially vague and confused ideas about the material. But there may be no direct or indirect sense in which *children* rework or modify their old beliefs, when, over time, they develop ideas that *we* would describe as more highly differentiated versions of their earlier ideas on the same subject. The ultimate sources of this development may be more diverse and more indeterminate, and its acquisitions more detached, than this image would suggest.

Embodied in this account is another set of assumptions, about the way in which the transition process would occur. As turned out to be implicit in the more global self–world differentiation account of development (discussed under the descriptive account in section 4.1), Piaget seems here to tie developments that might well be independent into a tight, almost deductive system. Further, as he made increasingly clear in his later work (see chapter 6), he presupposes that children explicitly falsify and reject their old views as they develop new ideas and beliefs that would seem from an adult's perspective, to contradict them. This assumption is also dangerously arbitrary. Given its prominence in Piaget's later work and the prevalence of related notions in contemporary research (see chapter 6), this early formulation is worth analyzing.

Consider an example. Piaget assumes that the development of the purely physical concepts of chance and inertia must go hand in hand with the repudiation of the "animistic" view that movement is purposive. As far as he is concerned, these are almost one and the same development (CCW, pp. 230, 238). He then searches for the common factor (i.e., the abandonment of egocentrism) that, in his view, will explain these two supposedly interdependent developments.

It is not immediately obvious, however, that in *development* these understandings (of chance and inertia, on the one hand, and of the recognition that movement is not purposive, on the other) would be interdependent or that each one would be dependent, in turn, on the same, all-encompassing additional factor. If children indeed go through a phase of repudiating their previous beliefs (e.g., in the purposiveness of movement), this repudiation might be prompted by factors or experiences having little to do with the process through which they achieve an understanding of chance and inertia. It is not even clear, however, whether children actually do go through such a phase of repudiation, or whether they undergo the same process for every belief they eventually abandon. Their earlier views might simply be superseded by new and different ideas on the same subject or by an interest in different subjects.

In a related vein, throughout the same series of theoretical statements, Piaget makes the clear presumption that children would not hold the two groups of allegedly incompatible views (i.e., the animistic or realist ones and the physical-determinist ones) at the same time. To be sure, these views are incompatible from our perspective. But that is, among other reasons, because we are explicitly juxtaposing them. It is not clear whether children do this, or to the extent that they do, it is not clear whether such episodes of focused conceptual analysis would be the primary motor of development. Children, after all, are not writing term papers or trying to solve a single sustained task over time. They are simply navigating their way about the world and trying to understand and cope with it. This would seem to leave room for a certain amount of inconsistency in the total repertory of beliefs that might be inferred from their discourse and behavior.

That these allegedly incompatible views might coexist in this way is made all the more plausible by the possibility that the views in question may not be "views" in the same sense. The sense in which Piaget's younger subjects believed that "movement is purposive" would seem to be more implicit than and different from the sense in which his older subjects believed that "movement [such as the movement of a tin can rolling down a hill] is the product of mechanical forces." The older children were aware of, and expressed, general principles from which their answers followed. There is no evidence that the younger children were aware of the general principles (that we regard as) exemplified by their answers. There would seem to be a possibility for conflict between the purportedly incompatible views held by the younger and older children only insofar as the views are stated in commensurable terms and explicitly juxtaposed.

If there is an asymmetry between the children's early and late (animist or realist and physicalist) interview answers in these respects, there would appear to be an even greater asymmetry between their spontaneous magic or animism and their late interview answers (i.e., physical-determinist beliefs). Here, as I pointed out earlier, the so-called animistic or realist premises that we might read into the children's magical and animistic reactions are not clearly held by the children, or if they are, it is not clear whether they are what motivates the magical and animistic reactions. If these beliefs would not determine whether the children will engage in magical or animistic practices, it would seem unlikely that their denial or replacement by physical-determinist views would lead to the elimination of these practices. One can envision a child who, now firmly believing that causes must be physically connected with their effects, disguises but does not abandon his or her expectation that the house will be safe if the curtain falls properly.

Here again is the argument, then, that at least certain developmental stages are unlikely to be superseded by means of a falsification of their content or by means of children's detection of contradictions between different "beliefs" that they hold implicitly or explicitly. Children might some day explicitly falsify the premises of their magical practices (or might note the inconsistency of those premises with other views they hold), and they might some day cease to indulge in magic or might come to indulge in significantly less of it. But these developments might exist in a far more complicated relationship with one another than Piaget supposed.

2

"The language and thought of the child"

Piaget's first psychological study, *The language and thought of the child,* is the original source of the egocentrism hypothesis. The book was primarily a naturalistic study of the spontaneous speech of children between 4 and 7 years of age, who were observed at play or performing small tasks in a group setting. On the basis of these observations, Piaget proposed the thesis that children engage in a unique and distinctive kind of thought, which he termed egocentric thought.

In this chapter, I undertake a cursory review of some of Piaget's findings and arguments to determine whether the egocentrism thesis, as presented in this work, comes any closer than it does in *Conception of the world* to illuminating children's thought and behavior.

RECONSTRUCTION

Much of the book concerns the sociability and adaptability of children's speech in the presence of others: How much of children's speech can be said to consist of properly directed communication as opposed to speech for oneself? What are the properties of apparently undirected speech? What are the properties of directed speech (e.g., how coherent is it, how well adjusted to the point of view of the intended listener)?

These questions were addressed through the long-term observation of all forms of speech of a small group of children, through the analysis of conversations between several pairs of children, and through a quasi-experimental arrangement in which one child had to repeat a particular story or description to another. An additional study analyzed children's understanding of proverbs, and another the spontaneous questions (especially "why" questions) of one child of 6. I will focus on the first group of studies, those concerned with children's speech in the presence of others.

Piaget's central claim in these studies is that children's speech is egocentric. At least proportionally more of it can be classified in this way than could adult speech, and this proportion can be shown to decline with age. What Piaget means when he calls children's speech egocentric is that, when children talk, they are not seeking to communicate their thought to others, and their talk does not have the effect of being communicative.

Two critical properties are absent from children's speech, according to Piaget. One is any attempt on children's part to make others understand them and, conversely, to require from others what to adults would be an appropriate response. Children are often satisfied not to be answered at all or to be answered in a way that would be inappropriate if an adult had asked the same question or made the same remark. The second missing property is logical discourse. Important connectives (e.g., "because") are lacking in children's speech, and in many instances it is not even clear what these connectives would be. There is no attempt at explanation or justification, only a concern, at best, with fact and description.

According to Piaget, children talk mainly in order to play or to accompany their own activity. On some occasions they attempt explicitly to make someone listen, and they contrive to influence that person. In such cases, Piaget believes, children are speaking from the point of view of their audience.

In between these two extremes of solitary play talk and adapted communication are various intermediate types of speech. These include numerous forms of connected discourse, which nonetheless lack crucial properties of truly listener-adapted discourse. Even though the talk of two apparently interacting speakers may converge on the same issue or the same theme (as in what Piaget calls a "collective monologue"), there is no clear give and take of ideas, but a parallel commentary on the subject matter.

These intermediate forms of exchange are egocentric because, Piaget thinks, children are not speaking from the point of view of their potential audience. They are talking only to satisfy their own needs, talking in some instances only for the functional pleasure of it. From the absence of logical analysis in children's speech and attempted comprehension, Piaget imputes egocentrism in another sense. Children adopt a subjective rather than objective attitude. They assume they understand all and that they are themselves understood by those people to whom they envision they are addressing themselves.

As usual, Piaget does not define sharply the terms in his discussion and tends to vacillate among several distinct meanings, especially of "egocentrism." In accordance with my general policy, I will present Piaget's concepts more incisively than he did in his own text. I will do this, as before, to bring out what I think is the genuine underlying structure of the argument.

Of the several meanings among which the term "egocentrism" wavers, the most deeply entrenched appears to be that children take their own point of view to be absolute (what I called the absolutist egocentrism thesis in chapter 1). To support this account, Piaget would have to point to a kind of behavior in which children attempt to communicate and fail because they think their point of view is absolute. He draws on two categories of observation, neither of which involves this kind of behavior, however. The first category is the observation of talk that is self-stimulative or in other ways directed to the self; here, by definition, there is no communicative intent. This behavior is not egocentric in the sense Piaget wants to show that it is, because children are not trying to communicate. The second class of observation consists of cases in which children are clearly attempting to communicate but fail because they lack the ability to take the listener's point of view. Cases of this kind are not clearly egocentric in the sense that Piaget wants to show that they are, because it is not clear whether these children are taking their own standpoint to be absolute. As I discussed in chapter 1, treating one's own point of view as absolute is not necessarily the reverse side of failing to take others' perspectives. Moreover, if I fail to take the listener's point of view because I am a *child* and therefore lack the resources to take the listener's point of view, that may simply show that I am aware that there is another point of view that I am trying, although failing, to take into account. I will now expand on these points.

Consider the first category of observations. On the one hand, Piaget says that, when children are exhibiting the cardinal features of egocentric speech they do not want to, or are not trying to, communicate (a conclusion also reached by Vygotsky, 1962). On the other hand, he also says that the communication embodied by such utterances is egocentric. Children are not speaking from the point of view of their audience and instead are taking their own point of view as absolute. If they are not trying to communicate, however, how can we say that their speech is egocentric, in the latter senses? If we want to say that this speech is egocentric, then we have to say either that *if* the speech were intended as communication it would be egocentric, or that the intention itself (which is not communicative) is egocentric.

The weakness of the first alternative is obvious. The speech is not intended as communication. The second alternative is also problematic, however, because it is not at all clear whether the children's actual intention is egocentric. These children are simply doing something other than communicating, and part of this activity involves talking, when talking is conventionally reserved for communicating.

Now consider the second group of observations, namely, those cases in which children are clearly attempting to communicate (e.g., when one child is trying to explain or describe something to another) and yet this attempted communication might be described as egocentric. To use Piaget's criteria, there is no real give and take of ideas, successive statements are merely juxtaposed rather than logically interconnected, or certain communications fail owing to other kinds of imprecision (e.g., inappropriate use of pronouns, use of ostensive gestures when the listener cannot see what the speaker is doing). Apparent communications exhibiting these qualities would be described by Piaget, variously, as involving a failure to take the point of view of the audience, the assumption that one is universally and immediately understood, or the assumption that one's point of view is absolute. On the basis of these attributions, the communications would be classed as egocentric.

The most apparent problem here is that these different attributions are not equivalent. Suppose that a child who is speaking does not take the point of view of his or her listener, such that that listener could not, without an undue amount of background knowledge and contextual sensitivity, understand what is being said. Imagine, for instance, a child who, in attempting to explain to another child how to operate a syringe in water, describes some of the necessary maneuvers and their consequences without making clear which maneuver is connected with which consequence. Or consider Piaget's classic "three-mountains" experiment in which a child must select a picture that depicts what a scene of three mountains, which the child is presently viewing from one angle, would look like to a doll viewing the scene from a different angle (Piaget & Inhelder, 1948/1956). In this experiment, young children typically select the picture representing their own view.

Let us assume these failures are widespread, which in Piaget's versions of these tasks they are. There are many reasons children might fail to take the listener's perspective in the senses I have described, only one of which is that they consider their own point of view to be absolute or assume they are universally and immediately understood. Children might, for example, lack the social skills or perhaps even the incentive to recognize that these are situations in which one must take the point of view of the listener. This lack of skill or incentive need not involve an assumption by the children that their own point of view is absolute or that they are immediately and universally understood. They may not be thinking about being understood. Hence, to the *children* the relativity of their point of view would not be a relevant consideration. Alternatively, and still more remote from Piaget's claim of "absolutism," children may lack the cognitive ability to take the listener's perspective in the situations I have described.

Piaget in fact argues for the second of these alternatives (that children lack the cognitive ability to adopt the listener's perspective), while arguing simultaneously that children treat their own point of view as absolute. Let us adopt Piaget's assumptions about children's cognitive ability. In the syringe experiment, children simply cannot organize the information properly and either do not know or at least do not use the appropriate connectives to express cause–effect relations. In the three-mountains experiment, children simply lack the ability to coordinate the different perspectives (e.g., they cannot make the proper front–back or left–right reversal of the items in the array). Try as they might, they simply cannot envision what the array would look like from where the doll sits.

Piaget is saying that children fail to take the listener's perspective because they *cannot* take it. If they *cannot* take the listener's perspective, they hardly need to have perceived their own perspective to be absolute in order to have failed to take the listener's perspective. They simply cannot take the listener's perspective, because they do not know how to take it.

We might say, then, with respect to Piaget's second group of observations (in which children are attempting to communicate) that the resulting *communication* is egocentric, insofar as the *communication* does not work. The listener cannot follow it. But we cannot, given Piaget's other assumptions (e.g., about the cognitive capacity of children), take the extra step that Piaget takes and argue that such children are egocentric. In fact, if, as Piaget seems prepared to say, children are genuinely trying to communicate, it might even be the case that they are trying very hard to take the listener's point of view but fail to do so because, again, they do not know how to do so.

Egocentrism would seem to be a possible state only for an agent who *could* take the perspective of the "listener," and *does not*. That individual might be egocentric in Piaget's sense, namely in the sense of making the implicit or explicit assumption that his or her own vantage point is absolute or that all of his or her utterances are automatically and immediately understood by all. Rather than a phase of development, this orientation would seem to typify what a given child or adult might *become* once the capacity to behave otherwise is in place.

3

"The moral judgment of the child"

Moral development is one of the most central, and also one of the most elusive, topics of child development. It is central insofar as moral thought is or becomes a major category of thought in which children, and adults, engage and insofar as moral judgment is or becomes a major premise for their action. It is elusive, however, insofar as there are not obvious bouts of child morality in the same way that there are obvious bouts of child magic, for example, or obvious episodes of child speech and attempted communication. Instead, our common sense tells us that after a certain point children judge some actions in moral terms, just as after a point we think that children utter some falsehoods with the express intent to deceive; that is, they lie. Not only is the phenomenon of morality elusive, however, but there is no very clear overall conception of what morality is. Widely different views are held on the question of what it is to act morally (or in defiance of morality) or to have moral opinions.

The elusiveness of the very concept of morality might seem to make the origins of morality in children all the more obscure and the study of these origins all the more intractable. But as Piaget himself would point out, particularly when we are dealing with an end state (in this case full-blown morality) that has eluded clear and unequivocal definition, study of the origins and early development of the capacity in question might provide some insight. At least it might suggest new lines of inquiry that might lead to greater clarity. Piaget's investigation of child morality was undertaken somewhat in this spirit:

In a sense, child morality throws light on adult morality. If we want to form men and women, nothing will fit us so well for the task as to study the laws that govern their formation. (MJ, p. 9)

Piaget reflects that the ideal starting point for an investigation of this kind would be the study of morality as it is actually practiced and experienced in the home and in school. However, such a project would not have been feasible as a first study, he says, because he would not have been certain what to look for in these naturalistic observations. Thus, Piaget reports a group of more structured studies that deal primarily with what he called children's "theoretical moral judgment" (e.g., MJ, p. 174): their appraisal of actions presented to them as hypothetical possibilities, for instance, in the form of stories about other children.

Nonetheless, Piaget states, this work should have implications for the questions of what morality is and how it begins. Even though his expectations in this regard are quite clear, it would still be legitimate and productive to ask whether, independently of Piaget's reflections, his general approach to moral development provides, or could potentially provide, a fruitful point of departure for a psychology of morality and moral development. Piaget reported his original findings in 1932 and essentially pursued the topic no further. Although the details of his empirical claims have been questioned and researchers now pursue somewhat different topics, Piaget's original studies, his method, and his overall definition of the area remain highly influential (see Turiel, 1983, for a review). It therefore seems worthwhile to analyze the point of departure he provides.

Because the conception of morality that informed Piaget's investigation is central to the studies he conducted, I begin the following reconstruction with an outline of that conception. My account of the empirical studies follows.

RECONSTRUCTION

1. Piaget's conception of morality

Piaget explicitly reduces the question of the nature of morality to the question of one's attitude toward rules. He reduces the question in this way because to him all morality consists of a system of rules, and the essence of morality lies in the kind of respect one acquires for these rules (MJ, p. 13).

Why did Piaget construe morality as so centrally related to the idea of rules? He appears to have reasoned as follows. A moral judgment is a judgment made according to principle. A good-hearted impulse, he says, cannot be called moral unless it involves an appeal to some norm, that is, to a rule (MJ, p. 398). Similarly, without rules to make the difference between right and wrong precise, we might speak of revenge but not of just punishment ("a feeling of punishing the guilty and defending the innocent" [MJ, p. 230]). Notions of guilt and innocence presuppose disinterested judgment, and disinterested judgment presupposes a rule.

Thus, according to Piaget, we cannot speak of morality unless we speak of the self-conscious following of rules. At the same time, however, moral conduct, in Piaget's view, involves more than mere conformity to or observance of rules. Indeed, the identification of morality with mere obedience to rules is a possible, but unfortunate and misguided view that is in fact held by children and many adults. The general thrust of development, however, is away from this conception and toward a quite different and more complex conception.

For Piaget, to speak of morality is always to speak of the attitude one holds toward the rules one follows. To begin with, the rule must be accompanied by a feeling of "obligation"; otherwise it could have the status of mere individual ritual or behavioral regularity. A sense of obligation arises once an environmental sanction is involved: The environment approves or disapproves of the action in question (MJ, p. 52). Piaget adds the further condition that the environmental sanction must emanate from, or otherwise be associated with, someone whom the individual "respects" (p. 53).

At this point Piaget introduces a crucial distinction between two attitudes an individual can adopt toward an obligatory rule; each of these attitudes, in turn, corresponds to a different kind of "respect" that one can hold for the individuals with reference to whom one follows the rule. The first possibility is that the individual regards the rule as obligatory only because it is enjoined by an external authority. In this case the background relation is one of "unilateral respect" or external "constraint," and the resulting morality is said to be "heteronomous" (i.e., coming from the outside). Under a heteronomous morality the rule will be followed merely because it is the rule. The second possibility, however, is that the rule is seen to be obligatory because it emanates from, and therefore serves, the mutual collaboration of equals. Here the background relation is that of "mutual respect," and the resulting morality is a morality of autonomy (i.e., coming from within or given to oneself). Under a morality of autonomy the obligatory rule is accepted, Piaget says, for its intrinsic value; it is regarded as one's own, is chosen. It is the outcome of a "free decision" (MJ, p. 65).

Collaboration with others contributes something to morality other than the possibility of autonomy. It provides an ideal or a "spirit of the law" toward which the content of all rules should tend. That ideal is reciprocity. This ideal emerges naturally as a requirement of any serious attempt at social interchange. Therefore, the rules arising from such collaboration ought to converge on the more abstract norm of reciprocity, which, it can be shown, all of our moral rules do.

Piaget's empirical program follows more or less directly from this total view. Most of the program concerns children's attitudes toward rules, including specific duties prescribed by the adult moral code (e.g., not to tell lies). A separate part of the program deals with the notion of justice, which Piaget considered to be the moral concept most directly related to the idea of cooperation. Indeed, he saw justice as requiring little more for its healthy development than mutual respect and solidarity among children. It will be sufficient for my purposes to restrict the present discussion to the part of the program that deals with rules.

Piaget conducted two studies concerning children's attitude toward rules. One study was an analysis of children's practice and conception of the rules of a particular social game, marbles. The other study involved an examination of children's appraisal of certain moral rules that are handed down by adults. The central question in the second study concerned the basis on which children would evaluate an act as good or bad according to the rule in question. Both studies (as well as the study of children's conception of justice) were based on individual conversations with children conducted by an adult interviewer. They were therefore similar in method to the investigations in *The child's conception of the world*. The study of marbles also included some direct observation of children as they played the game, and the study of moral rules included some anecdotal examples of a very young child's consciousness of supposed rules of conduct. I begin with the study of marbles.

2. The rules of the game

If the "essence of all morality" (MJ, p. 13) was to be sought in the "respect" an individual had acquired for (moral) rules, then, according to Piaget, the study of children's practice and conception of the rules of a children's game was a reasonable place to begin the investigation of the origins of morality. Although the rules of a game are not moral in our adult view, Piaget believed that children who played a game treated the rules as if they were moral. That is, the children's attitude toward the rules had many of the characteristics of our adult attitude toward moral rules. The rules of marbles, like moral rules, had been handed down from one generation to the next and were preserved solely by the respect the players held for them, again as in the case of moral rules.

Thus, for Piaget, the game of marbles played by children embodied properties of a miniature self-regulating society, a society that guaranteed its self-preservation by virtue of the fact that the rules according to which it operated were passed along from one generation to the next. Piaget found it advantageous to study "morality" in this context, because in play institutions, such as the game of marbles, direct adult influence was minimal. Accordingly, one could come closest to observing something like a spontaneous attitude on the part of the children. Moreover, it was in the context of a children's game that one had the greatest chance of observing an "autonomous" and rational morality, that is, a morality in which the children adopted the rules as their own and adopted them for their intrinsic value.

Piaget studied two phenomena related to the rules of the game: his subjects' actual practice of following the rules and their conception of what sort of entity these rules were. He referred to the latter issue as the children's "consciousness" of the rules. The questions about the children's consciousness of the rules were designed to address whether the children considered the rules to be external and immutable (as in a heteronomous morality) or to be subject to their own choice (as in an autonomous morality). Piaget was interested in these two types of data not only in their own right but for the relationships that might exist between them. For instance, what sort of practice of the rules (i.e., what degree of conformity to the rules) accompanied a heteronomous attitude toward the rules, and what sort of practice an autonomous attitude?

2.1. Method

For the part of the study on the practice of the rules, Piaget had the children teach him how to play the game and also observed them playing. In this way, he was able to assess the children's knowledge of the rules, the consistency of the rules stated by different children who were known to play the game together, and the consistency of each child's playing with the rules that that child, or other children in the same neighborhood, described.

In the portion of the study on the consciousness of rules, the children were asked to invent a new rule and then to indicate whether a new game could be founded on this rule (i.e., whether the rules could be changed) and, if this new rule were adopted and the old rules dropped, which rule would be the fairest. Finally, the children were asked whether people always played as they do today, and they were asked how the rules began (e.g., who invented them).

2.2. Results

Piaget distinguished four stages in what he regarded as essentially a continuum in the evolution of the children's practice of the game. The earliest observations begin with Piaget's daughter Jacqueline, when she was not quite 3 years old. Her behavior exemplifies the first stage, that of the "motor rule." At this stage children do not concern themselves with any formal rules of the game, but play with the marbles as they please and impose their own regularities on this play. For example, Jacqueline would engage in the routine of burying the marbles one by one in the ground or of lodging them in the hollow of an armchair.

The second stage, which Piaget sees as beginning between 2 and 5 years, is that of "egocentric" practice. This stage begins from the moment his subjects begin to follow the codified rules of the game. At this stage, however, they follow the rules not because they govern the game, but because they are interesting examples. Alternatively, the children follow the rules to be like the older children and therefore to be part of the group. Either way, however, the children's behavior is in fact only minimally consistent with the rules, at this point. Piaget likens practice at this stage to the "collective monologue" (LT) observed in children's speech at the parallel stage in communication. Children talk in parallel, rather than attempt to exchange ideas or influence one another.

With the third stage ("incipient cooperation"), the children try for the first time to win, and by following the rules. The interest and pleasure of the game have become social as well as motor. As with the parallel development in communication, there is an attempt to reach a "conclusion" acceptable to all, and it is the observance of common rules that makes this possible. At this stage, however, there is cooperation more in intention than in fact. The children's understanding of the rules is piecemeal and their mastery of them incomplete.

At the fourth stage there is an explicit emphasis on the codification of the rules, and the rules are followed in detail. The children are as interested in the legislation of the game as they are in winning it. They take pleasure in anticipating all possible cases and codifying them under general rules, as in formal reasoning. Piaget notes that there is decided consistency in the rules articulated by children from the same neighborhood at this stage (11 to 12 years), whereas there is considerable inconsistency among children even at the third stage.

The major dimension of development exemplified by these stages is, according to Piaget, a gradual change from crude to effective and consistent application of the rules. There is also a change in the goals of the players, from playing for the fun of it to playing to win. Finally, Piaget also observed a growing interest in the rules for their own sake.

Piaget distinguished three stages in his subjects' "consciousness" of rules. The first of these stages is largely hypothetical. Piaget extrapolates it from the general circumstances of infancy and early childhood, rather than deriving it from the children's responses to questions addressed to them about the nature of rules (very small children could not be asked these questions). At this stage "rules," so to speak, are not yet coercive or obligatory. The rules that we might distinguish in children's behavior might consist either of self-generated motor rules (as described under the first stage of practice) or of actions carried out in imitation of another person or in imitation of a rule (as in the second, "egocentric" stage of practice, where the rule might be followed because it is an interesting example). If, however, children are imitating a received rule, it is not experienced as a rule, that is to say, as an obligatory directive.

Piaget admits the possibility that even at this early stage, that is, even before children begin consciously to follow group-imposed rules, some of their behavior might be motivated by an element of "obligation." This is so because from the first, children are "bathed in an atmosphere of rules" (MJ, p. 52). There are times to sleep and times not to sleep, times to eat and times not to eat. There are certain activities that can (or must) be carried out in some places and not others. There are certain actions that one might want to engage in but that are forbidden, such as touching the stove, touching the pile of plates, or messing up the things on daddy's desk.

Some of these rites and restraints might come to be accompanied by feelings of obligation. Children might then come to attach feelings of obligation to other regularities they observe (e.g., the heating up of the stove, the setting of the sun) or in which they participate but that do not in fact involve any external sanction. In a related vein, Piaget thinks, although it is likely that the rituals very young children impose on their manipulation of marbles are completely spontaneous, these rituals could in some cases be conditioned in part by these other "obligatory" routines. Children may assume, even on first contact with marbles, that obligatory "rules" (MJ, p. 53) apply to the use of these objects.

Consciousness at the second stage, Piaget believes, is clearly influenced by these early "moral experiences" (MJ, p. 54). At this stage (the description of which is now derived from the children's answers to Piaget's interview questions) the children regard the rules of the game as sacred and immutable. They see them as emanating from adults and as having always been the way they are now. To alter them either is impossible or would be very wrong. In other words, the rules emanate from an external, virtually divine authority. The morality suggested by this view is therefore "heteronomous."

The third stage is completely different and connotes an "autonomous" morality. The rules of the game are now regarded as regulations imposed by mutual consent of the players. The rules must be followed if one is to play the game. However, they can in principle be altered, provided that one elicits the consent of the other players. The rules that now exist are assumed to have been fixed gradually over time at the players' initiative, as the need for them arose.

Finally, in conjunction with the third stage, Piaget notes some observations concerning the types of rules that the children think could exist. A fair rule is one that both enlists the support of the majority of the players and does not give any player or group of players unfair advantage over the others. In other words, the rule is consistent with the norm of reciprocity. Further, a rule is good (in the sense of appealing) if it challenges the skill of the players or has inherent aesthetic or risk-taking aspects, but not if it gives precedence to sheer luck. Piaget alleges that the children think that by discussion and mutual consent among the players they can select the fair from the unfair, and aesthetic from unaesthetic, rules (there is no direct evidence on this point in the reported protocols; the children indicate only that the rules are selected by mutual consent and that fair rules are better than unfair rules, aesthetic rules better than unaesthetic ones, etc.).

As for the relation between the two series of stages, Piaget reports that the "mystical respect" for rules (belief in their immutability, externality, etc., in other words, heteronomy) tends to coincide with the egocentric or unstable practice of rules. The concept of the rules as autonomously (and collaboratively) chosen tends to be accompanied by an effective and consistent application of the rules (some children in the third, "cooperative" stage in the practice of the rules and all children in the fourth, "codification" stage).

2.3. Piaget's discussion

Piaget considered this correspondence between the two series of stages to be the central finding of the study. He believed it confirmed the existence of the two types of morality he distinguished (heteronomous and autonomous) and also his account of the general psychological correlates of each type. His views about the correspondence can be outlined roughly as follows.

Mystical respect for rules tended to be exhibited by children who engaged in a crude and "egocentric" practice of the rules, because both mystical respect and egocentric practice signified that the rules, as such, were "external" to the children's consciousness. If children did not consider the rules to be their own and did not really understand their intent (i.e., if the rules were "external"), reasoned Piaget, it would make sense that their application of these rules would be unreliable and self-serving rather than oriented toward the conduct of the game. Similarly, the children's express view that the rules were untouchable and imposed by a supreme authority was a virtual statement that the rules were external. They were not chosen by the individuals who followed them, and they had no discernible intrinsic purpose.

Piaget also theorized that the absence of cooperation (one of the cardinal features of egocentrism) fostered both of these reactions. His reasoning seems to have been that, if children could cooperate, essentially by definition they would be following the rules (or such rules as were consensually agreed upon), and any such cooperation would tend to dispel mystical respect for the rules. Mystical respect would be dispelled because, in Piaget's view, to cooperate is to take the rules on as one's own. For Piaget's youngest subjects, however, that is, those children just learning to play marbles, cooperation simply was not possible. Therefore, the context for the "practical attitude" (MJ, p. 62) fostered by cooperation was lacking, as was the context that would mitigate against a mystical feeling toward authority or the rules perceived as coming from it. As a result, both the egocentric practice of the rules and the mystical respect for rules would flourish, together.

According to Piaget, it was at least as natural that the autonomous conception of rules should coincide with the effective practice of them as it was that mystical respect should correspond to crude practice. A rule that is thought of as depending on the "free collective will" (MJ, p. 71) thereby becomes incorporated in the mind of each participating member of the group. Individual obedience to the rule will follow naturally and spontaneously from there. Obedience (or effective practice) will also follow from the fact that the rule is agreed upon through a rational process of deliberation. If the rule is selected rationally in this way, it is selected for intrinsic reasons, and if these reasons are understood, "true respect" (p. 71) for the rule (and hence effective application of it) should increase. Finally, apart from any direct connection that might exist between the autonomous conception of the rules and their effective practice, both the conception and the practice would be fostered by the growth of cooperation and the corresponding waning of egocentrism.

From the point of view of his overall conception of morality, Piaget believed these findings supported his delineation of two different tendencies in children's attitudes toward rules. These two tendencies could be distinguished, in turn, from a third and more primitive tendency in which what we might describe as rule-following behavior was no more than a behavioral regularity. Children might execute this pattern with a sense of compulsion, but not a sense of obligation. The two other tendencies, with which Piaget was mainly concerned, presupposed a sense of obligation. It was the nature of this obligation that could vary in the two directions Piaget delineated. Either a rule was conceived as an external, immutable reality to be followed because it was the rule, or it was conceived as a freely chosen measure, alterable in principle as majority opinion might dictate and designed specifically for the furtherance of the game.

The first, heteronomous attitude was theorized by Piaget to be caused by, and to follow logically from, the relationship of inequality between child and adult and from the early and repeated "constraints" imposed on the child by the adult. The second, autonomous attitude was thought to be the logical and material consequence of children's participation in relationships of equality. These relationships were more likely to occur among children than between children and adults; however, they could in principle occur also between children and adults, if the adults cultivated an atmosphere of cooperation and equality.

Piaget emphasizes throughout his discussion that he identified two types of reactions, or two tendencies, rather than two strictly sequential stages of development. He did not think, on a priori grounds, that heteronomous morality was a necessary stepping stone to autonomous morality, and his data did not suggest a clear stagelike progression. Individual children exhibited mixtures of both attitudes, and one would expect even greater inconsistency if in place of their views of the rules of a single game, their reactions to a whole range of rules were investigated. Nonetheless, heteronomous answers peaked at an earlier age (around 7 years) than did autonomous answers (9 to 11 years), which increased in frequency over the age range (approximately 5 to 13 years) that Piaget tested.

Piaget stressed the fact that he had identified types of reactions rather than stages in part because he was convinced that the two tendencies he identified in childhood persisted into adulthood. They achieved realization not only in individual adult minds, but also in adult social and political institutions. Both conformist and mystical attitudes (each signifying heteronomy) could be found among many individual adults, and one could also identify whole sects and whole societies with these orientations (e.g., gerontocracies, theocracies, not to mention other instances of coercive rule). Autonomous rule, which was associated in Piaget's view with cooperation, was represented by sovereign and democratic government. In general, Piaget thought, the main difference between children and adults was only that the same heteronomous and autonomous tendencies were mixed in different proportions (MJ, p. 85).

3. Adult constraint and moral realism

The study of the game of marbles, in Piaget's view, was pertinent to the question of morality insofar as it dealt with the nature of children's attitudes toward rules as rules. Piaget used the rules of marbles as a case in point because for the children-he observed these rules were living rules, which the children spontaneously aspired to observe. Nonetheless, the rules of marbles are not properly moral rules; they are the rules of a game. Piaget's second study concerned specifically moral rules.

The two studies did not differ only with respect to the kind of rules investigated, however. Rather than analyze children's conception of moral rules as rules in the second study, Piaget investigated their conception of the specific duties prescribed by these rules. He did not ask, for example, whether the rule that one must not lie could be changed, but what it meant to lie or what kind of false statement constituted a particularly bad lie from a moral point of view.

The studies were connected insofar as Piaget attempted to relate these moral conceptions, in other words, the *content* of the children's specific moral opinions, to the two attitudes he discovered in the study of the rules of the game: heteronomy versus autonomy, or constraint versus cooperation.

The focal phenomenon of the second study was the literal and (as Piaget theorized, thereby) "external" way in which children interpreted received rules. Piaget called this phenomenon "moral realism," thus emphasizing its similarity to linguistic and intellectual realism, instances of which he had discussed in other works (e.g., nominal realism and the materialization of dreams, thoughts, and other mental phenomena, discussed in CWW; children's literalist interpretations of adult language, alluded to in other works).

Moral realism was, more specifically, children's tendency to regard various duties and the values they embodied as "self-subsistent" and "independent of the mind" and surrounding circumstances (MJ, p. 111). It was distinguished by three features in particular. First, it involved a concept of duty as heteronomous. Rules were received from elsewhere (the adult), one was bound to obey them, and one accepted them as they were. They were not open to judgment or interpretation. To be morally good, in this view, was to conform or obey. Second, one was supposed to obey the letter, as opposed to the spirit, of the law. Third, moral realism involved an "objective" conception of responsibility (not to be confused with an objective conception of the world, discussed in CCW and in chapter 1 of this book). According to an objective conception of responsibility, one evaluated acts in terms of their material consequences (e.g., the extent of the damage in the case of a physical act, the magnitude of departure from the truth in the case of a lie) rather than with respect to the motive or intention behind them.

Piaget contrasted moral realism with a nonrealist morality, characterized by an autonomous sense of duty, a regard for the spirit rather than merely the letter of the law, and a "subjective" as opposed to "objective" conception of responsibility under the law. To have a subjective conception of responsibility is to evaluate an act with respect to its motive rather than with respect to its consequences. (Hence, in the present context, "subjective" means inward looking or psychological, not to be equated with "egocentric," as in CCW.)

The purpose of Piaget's study was to determine which of these two lines of evaluation children's judgments of particular acts conformed to and then to explore the deeper tendencies underlying these judgments.

3.1. Method

The primary data for the study consisted of the reactions of children between 6 and 12 years of age to actions that were described to them in the form of stories. The children were asked to judge the relative gravity of different actions that were presented in pairs. In each pair, a well-intentioned act with relatively more serious material consequences was pitted against an ill-intentioned act with relatively minor material consequences. For example, in one story a boy who was called to dinner knocked over a tray of 15 cups and broke them, because they were on a tray that was concealed behind the door he was opening. This story was paired with another in which a boy, during his mother's absence, knocked over a single cup while he was trying to reach some jam on the top shelf of a cupboard.

A parallel series of stories was presented about lying. In three of the pairs, genuine lies (involving a manifest intent to deceive) with credible content were pitted against false statements lacking evil intent but involving marked departures from the truth. Thus, the story in one pair was about a boy who, after being frightened by a big dog, went home and told his mother he had seen a dog as big as a cow. The comparison story described a child who came home from school and reported that he had received good marks that day when no marks had been given at all. A separate series of lying stories involved material consequences and were patterned after the stories just referred to involving clumsiness. In one case, for example, the children were told about a very well intentioned child who tried to give a stranger directions when the child was not quite sure of the way and gave misinformation. The stranger got completely lost as a result. The comparison story told of a child who knew the way but decided to play a trick and name the wrong street. The stranger, however, found his way.

In all cases the children were asked to repeat the stories for accuracy. They were also questioned directly about the characters' intentions: "Why did he do [or say] that?" Then they were asked which child was naughtier (*plus vilain*) or whether the children were equally naughty, and were asked to explain their answers. Sometimes they were also asked who would be punished more severely and were invited to give their opinions about whether such punishment would be fair (i.e., Who *should* be punished more severely?). In the case of lying, the children were also asked to say what a lie is. In a follow-up series of questions they were asked whether it is naughtier for children to tell lies to other children (who are presumably more easily deceived than adults) or to adults. They were also asked to explain why it is naughty to lie (e.g., because lies are punishable, because they are bad, or because they are bad specifically because they violate conditions of reciprocity?).

3.2. Results

The childrens' answers to the target questions (who was naughtier and why?) fell into one of two patterns. Either the children judged the act on the basis of the gravity of its consequences (e.g., more cups broke; the lie could not possibly be true; the stranger got completely lost) or they judged it on the basis of its motive (the boy who broke the single cup was naughtier because he ought not to have taken the jam; the "lie" that the dog was as big as a cow was not so bad because the child was frightened and was only exaggerating rather than trying to fool anybody; the child who made the man get lost was not bad because he had not meant to do it). Some children revealingly pointed out that the punishment for the act with more severe material consequences would be greater than that for the ill-intentioned act with minor consequences but that this punishment would be wrong.

It should be stressed that the children giving either type of answer were able to distinguish whether the acts in question were intentional or involuntary, whether or not they were done on purpose, or whether or not the lie was meant as a trick. The children differed over whether this information counted in their evaluations.

The supplementary questions on lying produced a similar pattern of results. Some children defined a lie simply as a statement that was not true. Others defined it as what one does when one says something false on purpose. Piaget noted a graded series of answers to the question of why one should not lie. The most primitive answer was that lying is bad because one is punished for it (when pressed further these children said that it would not be bad if one did not get punished). An intermediate answer was that lying was bad whether or not one was punished; however, what made it bad was that it was not plausible. Finally, lies were bad the more (rather than the less) plausible they were, and they were bad because one "couldn't trust people any more," because "no one would know where they were" (MJ, p. 171).

The children's answers to the question of whether lies between children should be allowed corresponded to these intermediate and final answers. Corresponding to the intermediate answer was the reply that it was naughtier to tell lies to grown-ups than to children because grown-ups could tell that the lies were not true. Corresponding to the final answer was the rejoinder that it was worse to lie to another child because the child might believe the lie.

Thus, the children's answers across all the queries generally cluster into two types, one invoking "objective responsibility" (an act is wrong or bad in proportion to its material consequences or, in the case of lying, its literal departure from the truth), the other invoking "subjective responsibility" (an act is wrong if its motives are bad or if the surrounding circumstances do not excuse it). Related to objective responsibility is the further view that a lie is all the worse if it does not succeed (it is transparent, i.e., not plausible). Related to subjective responsibility is the view that a lie is all the worse if it does succeed. Finally, consistent with the idea of subjective responsibility is the notion expressed by some of the children that lying is bad specifically because it violates others' rights and makes communication and mutual trust impossible.

As with the results of the marbles study, these types do not fall into clearly demarcated stages, although, again as in the marbles study, responses of the "objective" or external type tended to peak earlier than did responses of the "subjective" or psychological type. Objective answers declined noticeably with age; subjective answers increased. Once again, however, Piaget was more concerned to have identified the types than their strict sequentiality.

I conclude this account of Piaget's results with his anecdotal observations of his daughter Jacqueline. Piaget believed he saw evidence in Jacqueline's behavior of very early objective responsibility and hence for the presence of this attitude in children's "effective," as well as "theoretical," moral thought. The observations were made on occasions when Jacqueline, as a very young child, had either intentionally or involuntarily engaged in some action that was contrary to the behavior that would normally be expected of her. After engaging in these contrary actions Jacqueline exhibited signs of shame, remorse, or guilt. Piaget believed these reactions were based on an "objective" conception of responsibility.

Piaget begins by noting (as in his account of the origins of the feeling of "obligation") that, even when caretakers have the best intentions, it is impossible for them to avoid giving children at least some commands that will be completely incomprehensible to them. Children's acceptance of such commands is virtually guaranteed to produce moral realism (conceptions of objective responsibility, etc.), that is, a tendency to associate the imperative specifically with the behavior at which it is aimed rather than with the intentions of the perpetrator. Commands of this kind are often connected to the routines of going to bed and having meals; they also include directives not to soil things and prohibitions against touching or playing with certain things. These injunctions prompt feelings of obligation, on the one hand, and feelings of remorse in the case of apparent violation, on the other.

For example, at just 2 years of age, Jacqueline is given some medicine that she is warned will make her soil her bed, which she ends up doing. Despite her mother's assurances, Jacqueline becomes extremely distressed and experiences the same feelings, Piaget thinks, that she would experience "if the thing had happened . . . through her own negligence" (MJ, p. 179). Between $2\frac{1}{2}$ and 3 years of age Jacqueline appears to show sorrow or remorse when she cannot finish her food or her medicine, even on occasions when she has been given too much or an amount that she could not be expected to finish because she has just been ill. At around 2 years of age she accidentally breaks a fragile shell that Piaget has lent her, and Piaget has the "greatest difficulty in persuading her that it is not her fault" (p. 182).

On another occasion Jacqueline, at $2\frac{1}{2}$, continues to pull the threads out of a towel, despite the fact that both parents tell her it is a pity to do that, it makes holes, "Mummy will be sad," etc. When she wakes up the next morning (having soiled her bed), she asks her mother if she isn't sad. That evening Jacqueline begins pulling apart the towel again and is told it is a pity. After her parents leave her, she cries to get them back, to make sure, Piaget believes, they bear her no grudge (MJ, p. 179).

Especially with respect to the first group of examples, Piaget is convinced that Jacqueline has regarded not having done the things she is supposed to do as a kind of moral lapse, that she feels "humiliated" at having been excused from these obligations, and that a "sense of pride" is involved even when her parents attenuate the rule (MJ, pp. 181–2). What particularly impresses Piaget is that in all of these cases right and wrong are defined strictly by overt conformity or nonconformity to the rule, without regard for the child's intentions or for other extenuating circumstances. There is only a sense of "duty violated" and no consciousness, Piaget thinks, of having done something on purpose or not having done it on purpose.[1] Thus, in the case of the bath towel, for example, Jacqueline has not intended to do anyone any harm. Nonetheless, she eventually becomes aware that she has violated her duty and done something wrong. Her conception of what is wrong, however, is purely "objective."

3.3. Piaget's discussion

Piaget's theoretical commentary centers on the conditions that foster children's "subjective" versus "objective" conceptions of their so-called moral duties. As with the children's attitudes toward the rules of the game, Piaget saw the children's conceptions of these duties as the joint product of the social relations in which the children found themselves, on the one hand, and their spontaneous mental tendencies, on the other. According to this view, moral realism (or objective responsibility, as an example of moral realism) was the result of the combination of adult constraint (and the corresponding relation of "unilateral respect") and the children's naive egocentrism. The idea of subjective responsibility

---

[1] Not until 3 years of age, Piaget notes, do children attempt to exculpate themselves in situations of this kind by appealing to the fact that they have not done something "on purpose," that it is not their "fault," and so on.

came about through the attempt to cooperate (and hence through relations of "mutual respect"), which served both to promote an understanding and interiorization of duty and to discourage any egocentric tendencies the children might have.

The account of moral realism focuses on the case of lying: As a result of their "unconscious egocentrism" (MJ, p. 163) children tend spontaneously to alter the truth in accordance with their desires in their statements to others. They do not value the truth, says Piaget. Insofar as they do not value the truth, he infers, telling the truth does not correspond to any "felt inner need" (p. 163) on children's part. If under these circumstances adults impose a rule not to lie, that rule can only remain external to children, to the point where only an "objective" interpretation of the rule is possible.

Next I consider, in turn, the way in which Piaget saw children as spontaneously "altering the truth" and the way in which unconscious egocentrism was supposed to account for this phenomenon. As for altering the truth, the phenomenon in question is what Piaget, after Stern, calls "pseudo-lying." According to Piaget, it was widely documented that, before the age of 7 or 8, children routinely distorted reality without actually attempting to deceive anyone. They fabricated the truth more as if to express a wish than to assert a statement of fact that could be called true or false. Just as young children might elude a difficult intellectual question with an impromptu myth, so in a socially or morally embarrassing situation they might invent a story that was in fact false. In doing this they would not be intending to harm or deceive anyone, but only attempting to extricate themselves from an awkward situation. Other forms of pseudolying come closer to simple romancing, that is, to unprovoked expressions of wishes to others (e.g., "I keep a 10-foot lizard in the bathtub").

Piaget believed that pseudolying could be traced to children's egocentrism, both in the sense that children had a general tendency to bend reality to their wishes, to the general (although unintentional) disregard of others, and in the sense that they had no need to speak or to seek the truth. Children would see harm in bending the facts and would be interested in the truth, he reasoned, if they were in the habit of exchanging thoughts with others and had a real desire to do so. But being egocentric they lacked precisely this habit and desire. Lacking this habit and desire, they would "see no harm in transposing facts" (in accordance with their desires) and would fail to be interested in the truth (MJ, p. 165).

It is from this vantage point that Piaget finds children's objective, or as he eventually argues, heteronomous, conception of the duty not to lie to be so natural. When parents first inform a child that what he or she has just said is a lie and is very wrong, the child will at once feel an obligation of conscience not to lie and yet will have no inner need and no set of intentions (i.e., pseudolies are not made with the intention of lying) with which to connect this obligation. That such an obligation would immediately be felt follows, Piaget thinks, from the fact that the situation is likely to be affectively charged, and the persons issuing the command are those for whom the child feels "respect" (MJ, p. 166). The total result will be the apparently paradoxical outcome that the child will go on both spontaneously altering the truth and at the same time considering it a duty not to lie. The child will say that a lie is naughty. Moreover, not understanding the real motive for not lying, he or she will evaluate this duty in purely objective terms.

Piaget hints at another, slightly different sense in which moral rules, such as the rule not to lie, remain external to children's conscience. In being felt merely as "decrees" (MJ, p. 191) from the outside, these rules are not felt as part of an inner impulse of sympathy or pity for the real or imagined others on whom one's acts might impinge. This remains the case even though, Piaget seems to think, children experience sympathy, pity, remorse, and so on from a very early age.

How, finally, are children to be "liberated" (MJ, p. 167) from their disembodied respect for external rules, and how will they come to practice those rules in a consistent fashion? Piaget's answer is, as I have noted, that cooperation alone will convince children of the necessity of rules, and this necessity will give children both a reason and an impetus to observe rules. Piaget justifies this view partly on logical grounds: "Apart from our relations to other people, there can be no moral necessity" (p. 196). He adduces additional support from the data, in particular from the statements offered by children to the effect that lying is antisocial (you couldn't trust people, you wouldn't know where you stood, etc.; p. 170).

If the values represented by prescribed duties will become

"interiorized" under the influence of cooperation, it is also under the influence of cooperation (or, alternatively, in service of reciprocity) that these duties will become autonomous. The duties will now be seen to be right for a reason, and that reason will be something other than external pressure. Further, the actual execution of the duties will be motivated by this reason rather than by external constraint.

It remains to clarify the way in which Piaget connected objective and subjective responsibility with the heteronomous and autonomous conceptions of duty he distinguished in the study of marbles. He associates objective responsibility (i.e., judging an act in terms of its consequences) with heteronomy, it seems, for two reasons. The first has to do with the content of the judgment itself. To focus on consequences is to focus on something that is external to the agent performing the act, or rather it is to detach the act from the mind that prompted it; heteronomy for Piaget seems to mean outside the mind. The second reason Piaget associates judging in terms of consequences with heteronomy is related to his ideas about the way one would come to judge an act in these terms. The argument seems to be that one would judge the gravity of an act in terms of its consequences if one did not understand the rational basis for this judgment. According to this view, one would judge that a lie was bad solely on the basis of its being untrue, because one would fail to understand *why* it is bad to say untrue things. If one understood why lying is bad, one would see that it is deceit that is serious, and one would judge the act accordingly in terms of whether it involved an attempt to deceive.

Correspondingly, to judge the gravity of an act in terms of its intent is both to conceive of good and bad acts as relative to the minds that prompt them and to understand the rational basis of the rule according to which one is making this judgment. Thus, to judge an act in terms of its intentions (subjective responsibility) is to assume an attitude that shares important features with an autonomous morality.

CRITIQUE

What we should be looking for in a theory of moral development in children is not only a series of true statements about characteristics that children develop, but an account of how specifically *moral* judgment and *moral* behavior come about. Piaget provides such an account on two levels. The first is his first-order description of emerging properties in children's thought and behavior that he thinks, when taken together, characterize the genuinely moral agent or at least a set of truly essential properties of such an agent. Second, he attempts to relate these first-order descriptions to broader aspects of children's cognitive development, his intention being, presumably, to delineate the kind of intelligence that is presupposed by the moral agent. I refer in this case to Piaget's theory of egocentrism and his associated theory of child realism.

My criticism of the account will focus on these two points. Regarding the first, I will argue that Piaget fails in significant ways to describe essential properties of moral agency or their potential antecedents. Regarding the second point, I will argue that speaking of children as moral egocentrics (or realists) makes no more sense than speaking of them as intellectual or communicative egocentrics and that the notion of egocentrism (or realism) fails to bring out the central intellectual advances that would seem to be involved in becoming moral. In both parts of the critique I will attempt progressively to formulate some of the features that Piaget omits but that seem to me to be critical to understanding morality and its development. As was my policy in the preceding chapters, I will attempt no finished account of these features, given, among other things, that such an account would require further empirical and conceptual inquiry. I will attempt only a tentative and partial outline of certain topics that would seem to merit serious consideration in further research on moral development.

1. The moral agent

1.1. Morality as rule-guided action

For Piaget, morality most centrally involves behavior in accordance with rules. The reason Piaget gives for this emphasis is that we cannot speak of good-hearted impulses as moral unless they involve an appeal to some norm. It seems to follow, for Piaget, that the way to study the development of morality is, therefore, to study children's conceptions of, and attitudes toward, "norms," that is, rules.

We may ask, to begin with, whether it is true that no benevolent impulse is moral by itself. Why does the impulse become any better because reference is made to a rule? For the most part, Piaget seems merely to assert that it is better (MJ, p. 398) and gives no explanation. He alludes to the desideratum that (moral) judgments be regulated (i.e., consistent, or principled) and also disinterested (p. 230). Here, however, he would seem only to be expressing his own view about what constitutes good or pure morality, not what makes an act or an impulse moral in the first place, from the actor's point of view. He is not saying what the subjective experience is of an individual who is appraising something morally. He is only telling us what one of the components of the appraisal *ought* to be.

Even if we were to grant, however, that full-blown morality is correctly construed as rule-guided behavior of the kind Piaget describes, it does not follow that the key to all morality lies in our attitude toward rules. Nor does it follow that the study of the development of this attitude in childhood will provide a full account of how we come to be moral agents, that is, persons who judge acts from a moral point of view and who themselves act, or refrain from acting, for moral reasons.

The problem here is that if we conceive of morality in terms of rule-guided action, we make no distinction between morality and other rule-governed actions, for example, the mere social convention of calling one's teacher by his or her proper title or observing the rules of a game (along these lines see Turiel, 1983). Correspondingly, if we focus the study of the development of morality on the development of children's attitudes toward rules, we completely disregard the question of how one comes to make specifically *moral* appraisals of action and what one is doing when one makes such appraisals. Alternatively, we assume that it is simply given that there will be moral rules and other kinds of rules, and becoming a moral agent (a person who acts for moral reasons and who appraises actions morally) consists in no more than developing the appropriate attitude toward rules and learning those particular rules that happen to be moral rules. This assumption is arbitrary, and it still does not tell us what a specifically moral appraisal of something consists of.

The different foci of Piaget's discussion might be seen to address these questions, in different ways. I next consider each of the major foci in turn. My order of treatment generally reflects a progression toward those properties that might be considered increasingly basic to moral agency from a psychological point of view.

1.2. Reciprocity

Moral rules, in Piaget's view, do not invoke just any norm, but specifically the norm of reciprocity. Morality, then, is more than rule-following behavior and more than the holding of a particular attitude toward the rules one follows. It involves following a particular kind of rule, namely, one having to do with reciprocity. Moreover, this ideal of reciprocity is not just an accidental feature of some of the rules that children acquire. It arises out of the very conditions of children's existence. These conditions are relations of "mutual respect," or cooperation. Insofar as children participate in relations of this kind, they will develop the ideal of reciprocity. Reciprocity will therefore prove immanent in their thinking; it will not be an arbitrary feature imposed from the outside.

All we gain here, however, is a notion of the kind of content we might expect a moral rule to have, not an account of what it is to be an agent who seeks recourse to that rule: who forms distinctly "moral" opinions of things, who is moved to do things (or to refrain from doing them) for "moral" reasons. When we hold a particular act to be morally reprehensible, we are doing something more than observing that the norm of reciprocity (or some derivative rule) has been violated, that norm (or the derivative rule) being traceable to the foundations of human social existence. When we believe an act to be morally reprehensible we feel that the act is *wrong,* that it *ought* to have been different, and that, indeed, it *could* have been different. The reason we hold these sentiments may be that the norm of reciprocity or some derivative rule has been violated. However, our reason for having a particular reaction is not the same as the reaction itself. It is the reaction that Piaget fails to describe and yet presupposes, insofar as he talks about the reasons for it.

In raising this objection I have assumed that Piaget is correct in assuming that all morality is based on norms of reciprocity. This assumption may be questioned, however. One could, for example, have an ethics that gives priority instead to human rights and welfare. But even if all known moral rules could be traced ultimately to some norm of reciprocity, this would not necessarily mean that the psychological basis of all morality is reciprocity.

One may feel that some action is morally right or wrong for reasons other than that the action either upholds the norm of reciprocity or violates it. One may think it is wrong to steal simply because it is bad to take other people's things, it is bad to do something that will harm others, it is bad to do something dishonest. One might even think it is wrong to steal because it is bad to do things that other people universally disapprove of, not because of any direct injury this disapproval might bring to oneself, but because acts that people disapprove of are simply bad, and that is sufficient injury in itself. The point is that none of these reasons has to extend, from the agent's point of view, all the way to the concept of reciprocity, even though as moral theoreticians *we* might trace them there.

1.3. Heteronomy and autonomy

Piaget's discussion of heteronomy and autonomy does not provide an account of the moral agent any more than does the appeal to reciprocity, although Piaget regarded this discussion either as central to a moral psychology or as a means of getting to the central questions.

In Piaget's treatment, the truly moral agent is an individual who not only follows (moral) rules, but has an autonomous conception of these rules. Piaget uses "autonomy" primarily to refer to the question of who sets the rules. Under an autonomous morality, one's duties are concieved of as given to oneself. Under heteronomous morality, one's duties are conceived of as imposed from the outside. Piaget argues, or at least he leaves us with the strong suggestion, that moral motivation and moral sentiment are possible only under an autonomous conception of our (moral) duty. It is only under an autonomous conception of our (moral) duties that we do what we do because we think it is right. Under a heteronomous conception, we do what we do because it is the rule or, in the worst cases, because we want to avoid punishment.

But these associations are false. One may do one's duty because one thinks that the act prescribed by that duty is the right thing to do, although one also thinks that that duty is prescribed externally, that is, is heteronomous. Conversely, one might perform one's duty simply because it is the rule, although one believes that the nature of that duty is self-given (determined by a consensus of peers, etc.), that is, even when one has an autonomous conception of the rules.

The game of marbles is a case in point. When questioned, some of the children (generally the younger ones) said that the rules of the game were divinely given and sacred. Piaget would say they had a heteronomous view of the rules. Other (generally older) children said that the rules were developed over time by players of the game and could in principle be altered by contemporary players under conditions of mutual consent. These children had an autonomous conception of the rules.

Now, children who think that the rules of the game are autonomous might engage in the acts prescribed by the rules only because those are the rules, not because they think those acts are intrinsically and individually "right." Conversely, a child who conceives of the rules of the game heteronomously (e.g., as arising by divine right) could think that he or she was engaging in an inherently worthy act in following a particular rule. This child could be wrong, insofar as the rule might happen to be a strictly accidental feature of the game. Nonetheless, the *child's* reasons for engaging in the prescribed act might still issue from a sincere and genuine sense that there was something inherently virtuous in acting in that way.

Piaget might reply that the children who had an autonomous conception of the rules of the game (i.e., had notions that they made or chose the rules themselves, or could do so in principle) also tended to recognize the basis of particular rules in reciprocity. If they had this recognition, the argument would run, then in following the rules because they were the rules they would still be engaging in acts the ultimate virtue of which they understood. Under these conditions, we might say they were not just following the rules, but were doing something they thought was right.

That the children might, upon reflection, understand the ultimate virtue of a particular rule, however, does not mean that this understanding would figure in their immediate reasons for following the rule on any particular occasion. They might follow the rule only because that is how one plays.

As for the children with the heteronomous conception who nonetheless thought there was something virtuous in the act prescribed by the rule, Piaget might say that these children were simply under an illusion. These children, he would say, did not yet have an understanding of reciprocity. Thus, they could not see the acts prescribed by the rules as inherently virtuous for reasons having to do with reciprocity. Therefore, either they could not, by definition, construe the prescribed act to be "right," or if they did construe it to be "right" either they would have no reason for doing so (they might, e.g., be imitating the feeling of something being "right") or they would be expressing their awe for rules.

The trouble with this potential reply is that it conflates the idea of having a sensibility of right and wrong with being able to justify that sensibility. An individual might have the sensibility, however, without having clear or appropriate grounds for it, from our point of view. It is the sensibility of (moral) right and wrong that is the more fundamental property of moral agency. Insofar as that sensibility does not depend on Piaget's notions of autonomy and reciprocity, Piaget's discussion of these notions does not provide an account of this fundamental property.

Further, insofar as Piaget's arguments regarding heteronomy and autonomy depend on his views concerning reciprocity, these arguments are subject to the objections I just raised in connection with his emphasis on reciprocity (section 1.2). To reiterate briefly, that moral judgments *ought* properly to be based on a conception of reciprocity, as seems to be Piaget's view, does not mean that those self-consciously "moral" judgments that people make *are* based on reciprocity or that their developmental origins will be best illuminated through attention to the question of whether they are.

In a similar vein, there is no clear connection between reciprocity and autonomous versus heteronomous conceptions of duty, as Piaget seems to imply there is. One could have a heteronomous conception of duty (i.e., one could think that such rules as exist are externally imposed, given by divine right, etc.) and yet place a high premium on reciprocity and indeed value highly those acts that further reciprocity. Alternatively, one might hold a distinctly autonomous view of duty (i.e., one might believe that such duties as are followed are self-imposed and could in principle be changed – e.g., by means of consensual agreement) and yet have no awareness of the reciprocity embodied by some of the rules one follows or of the need for reciprocity in general.

Many of the problems I have been describing seem to come to this: Piaget associates morality with several different ideas. We can distinguish at least four: (a) Morality consists in having an autonomous conception of duty (rules, etc.); (b) morality is the valuing of reciprocity; (c) morality involves having moral sentiments, that is, the feeling or belief that something is the morally right or wrong thing to do; and (d) morality involves having moral motivation – doing something because it is the right thing to do or refraining from doing something because it is the wrong thing to do. The central problem thus far is that these four ideas stand in far more complex relation to one another than Piaget admits. It is for this reason that moral sentiments (in which I would include what I just referred to as sensibilities of right and wrong) and moral motivation, which at best are treated only in passing, remain inadequately accounted for within Piaget's prevailing themes of rule following, reciprocity, and autonomy versus heteronomy.[2] As I have already argued, moral sentiment and moral motivation are the more basic issues. A discussion of rule following, reciprocity, and autonomy versus heteronomy would have no bearing at all on the question of morality unless we were dealing with an agent who knew what it was to appraise something morally and to act (or refrain from acting) for moral reasons (i.e., unless we were dealing with an agent who was capable of moral sentiment and moral motivation).

Piaget might protest that he intended to study only (theoretical) moral judgment, not moral motivation and moral sentiment: "It is the moral judgment that we propose to investigate, not moral behavior or sentiments" (MJ, p. 7). And Piaget, like most observers, was aware that theoretical moral judgments and the sentiments and motivations that operated in real life (i.e., in one's own moral behavior) did not always jibe. In addition to the fact that

---

[2] Throughout at least some portions of his discussion Piaget sees these four ideas as somewhat more loosely interconnected than I have made them out to be here. Notions of autonomy, according to this looser view, would only tend to go along with notions of reciprocity, and these ideas, in turn, would only tend to appear with moral evaluations (as opposed to evaluations based on the likelihood of punishment, for example) because, in Piaget's view, they all require the overcoming of egocentrism and realism in individual development. In this view, for example, a heteronomous conception of duty would tend to coincide with evaluations based on the punishability of actions because both entail the same mistake of regarding as external that which is properly internal or psychological (this is the realism thesis). I will consider this account later, when I take up Piaget's egocentrism and realism theses directly. For the present, this idea of a looser connection does not get around the fact that Piaget has drawn an unwarranted connection between heteronomy–autonomy and moral sentiment and motivation and that he has simply ignored the latter, central phenomena.

Piaget nonetheless saw his investigation as addressing "effective moral thought" (p. 174), his disclaimer raises a more insidious problem. Piaget has arbitrarily decided that one can talk about theoretical moral judgment, on the one hand, and moral action and sentiment, on the other. Although we might follow Piaget in distinguishing between abstract moral judgment and moral action, if he insists on a two-way distinction, it would seem that moral sentiment and motivation belong on the side of moral judgment. They are, as I have implied, presupposed by the capacity for moral judgment and basic to any discussion of that capacity – especially to any discussion of the development of that capacity.

Types of autonomy. Piaget's discussion of autonomy and heteronomy conflates another distinction that would seem central to the question of what it is to be a moral agent and how children come to be one. In his empirical discussions, as I have said, Piaget usually uses the term "autonomous" to refer to the idea that a rule is self-chosen. The people make the rules, and, Piaget adds, the rules can be changed at will. A related sense to which Piaget sometimes refers is the notion that the reasons that justify a particular rule are understood. Hence, we might infer, the rule is seen to exist for a reason, not merely because it is the rule. Piaget occasionally hints at another and quite different sense of autonomy. This is the notion that the autonomous agent chooses to obey a particular rule or, more essentially still, chooses his or her behavior. The first sense, by contrast, is the notion that the agent freely chooses the rule to obey (or disobey).

These two senses of autonomy are not the same thing. Under completely authoritarian rule I may choose to disobey a rule that is imposed on me and hence may also "choose" to obey it. Under completely sovereign rule I may simply follow the rule without any conscious or deliberate sense of choosing to do so. I just follow it mechanically.

Insofar as these two senses of autonomy are different and also independent, Piaget's documentation of children's views regarding the first sense (rules as self-given) tells us little about the origins and development of the second sense (choice of action). The second is the more basic sense. It is pointless to speak of moral action of any sort unless we are dealing with an agent who can be said to be choosing that way of acting over an imagined alternative that he or she regards as the wrong or immoral way to behave.

In effect, Piaget is presupposing the second sense. His view really comes to the position that the true, or autonomous, moral agent is an individual who chooses the morally right course of action (second sense of autonomy) under self-given rules (first sense). This view presupposes, but neither describes nor explains, what it is to reflect on alternative courses of action and their moral consequences and to choose the right course.

This sense of conscious reflective choice is trivial in the case of adults. Except under the most dire conditions, adults are capable of choosing a course of action in the sense I have outlined. The case of children is less straightforward. When, in the course of development, can we say that children have begun to choose a type of conduct, or to choose one type of conduct over another? Exactly what powers of reflection and what quality of action are we attributing to them when we are prepared to say that they are doing this?

To pursue these questions briefly, consider babies at those moments when an observer would say that their behavior is spontaneous, that is, not the result of immediate adult constraint. When would we say that these babies are *choosing* to behave as they do, or choosing one way over a consciously rejected alternative, rather than merely behaving? A little reflection will show that the question is complicated and becomes all the more so when compounded by the question of when this choice may be said to be motivated by moral concerns.[3] As with the question of moral sentiment and motivation more generally, Piaget has either overlooked the question or has taken an answer for granted.

---

[3] When we speak of "conscious reflective choice" motivated by specifically moral concerns in this context, we might wish to draw a further distinction among different kinds of conscious reflective choice. The child who withdraws his or her hand from the stove before touching it has made a conscious reflective choice insofar as choosing one course of action over an imagined and specifically rejected alternative. The child who decides not to take the toy another child is playing with and who does this because he or she thinks that taking the toy would be *wrong* (not just punishable) is doing something else. Although the exact nature of the difference requires further clarification, not only would the "morally" motivated choice (the toy example) seem to involve a different class of motivating reasons (from the observance of don'ts, as in the stove example), but the reasons, in a case that is actually experienced as a moral decision, would seem to figure more integrally in the moral choice.

We see again, then, that in yet a different way the primary foci of Piaget's analysis do not produce an account of basic properties of moral agency. The arguments we have considered so far, however, are limited in a particular way. They have been restricted not only to issues concerning rules and children's attitudes toward rules, but to an analysis of children's very explicit, reflective conceptions of the aspects of rules under question. To be sure, Piaget seems to think that these analyses are tantamount to, or else translate directly into, a theory of what it is to be a moral agent and how children come to be one. Nonetheless, there are occasions on which Piaget addresses these questions more directly. These occasions are his more speculative discussions regarding early development. I consider two of these discussions next.

1.4. Obligation

One of these discussions contains an account of the feeling of obligation, which Piaget believes accompanies anything we might consider to be moral conduct. A feeling of obligation arises, Piaget says, as soon as the environment sanctions a particular action, that is, provided that children have respect for the person from whom the sanction issues (MJ, p. 53). Most normal caretaking relationships are sufficient to engender this respect, and since all caretakers will impose at least some constraints, the feeling of obligation to perform particular actions will arise very early, perhaps even in infancy.

This discussion of obligation, however, presents essentially the same difficulties as Piaget's emphasis on rules. The sense of obligation (plus respect) that Piaget describes would not particularly distinguish what we feel when our action or judgment is guided by a moral principle and what we feel when we observe the rules of a game. In both cases we experience a sense of obligation insofar as we feel that engaging in the action prescribed by the rule is something we must do, and in either case, our initial receptivity to the rule could be motivated in part by our respect for the person who taught us the rule.

Piaget was aware of this problem. He emphasizes that the initial sense of obligation that children feel is not a properly moral sense. It is only a compulsion to comply with a rule because of one's feelings about the party from whom the rule emanates. It is a purely heteronomous sense of obligation, having little to do with intrinsic moral values as such.

But if obligation is initially only heteronomous obligation, Piaget is still left with the problem of explaining how nonheteronomous (i.e., autonomous) forms of morality or any other aspect of morality not covered by heteronomy, or the sense of "rule," could arise. Included among these other aspects would be the notions of moral sentiment and moral motivation discussed in the preceding sections. Piaget does make passing reference to the notion that a morality of the "good" may develop alongside a morality of duty (where duty is connected with "constraint"). This morality of the good emanates from mutual affection (MJ, p. 195) and is initially manifested in children's "sympathetic tendencies and affective reactions," which constitute the "raw material" of "all . . . moral behavior" (p. 398). These tendencies and reactions become properly moral when they are subordinated to rules. Initially, however, they are not subordinated to rules (and hence are not properly moral). Rules are wholly on the outside (they are heteronomous) and do not engage with any internal sentiments children might have.

The main difficulty here is that Piaget does not explain what these feelings of, say, sympathy really are or how they come together with rule conformity (and obligation). Moreover, if these early sentiments have nothing to do with children's reaction to rules and yet constitute the "raw material" of "all . . . moral behavior," the study of children's attitudes toward rules would seem to be an odd starting place for the study of moral development. Given Piaget's views outlined here, children's (pre)moral sentiments would be a more logical point of departure, and the study of the gradual transformation of these sentiments into properly moral judgments a more natural course for the study of moral development.

Elsewhere, however, Piaget presents an initially plausible rationale for dwelling at least in significant part on children's understanding of the idea of a rule. This brings me to the second of Piaget's two speculative discussions on early development.

1.5. The idea of a rule

Piaget notes as one potential point of origin for children's later moral reactions their responses to early, externally imposed rules (e.g., pertaining to eating, sleeping, permissible and impermissible activities). What matters here, we may infer from the account, is not so much the rules themselves or children's understanding of them, but the *idea* of a rule. If children begin to observe rules, even without understanding them, this observance will create a new and vital distinction. The distinction is the designation of a right and a wrong, or, as Piaget might prefer to say, a correct and an incorrect or valid and invalid, way of proceeding (MJ, pp. 52, 401). Any kind of moral sentiment presupposes this distinction. There is a right way and a wrong way to proceed (e.g., Winch, 1958).

It is astute of Piaget to have identified the possible relevance of these interactions to children's formation of ideas about right and wrong and hence to their eventual development of specifically moral opinions. It is not clear, however, whether he is correct in emphasizing the idea of a *rule* in reference to these interactions. From children's vantage point the interactions would seem to convey most directly the ideas of right and wrong. *We* see these ideas (as well as the specific instances they subsume) as associated with rules. However, unless we make "right" and "wrong" completely redundant with the idea of a rule, it is not evident that children see this. It is not apparent whether children initially understand much beyond the notion that some action is a bad (wrong) thing to do, and another a good (right) thing to do.

The idea of a rule is more abstract. A rule is what determines that there is a right and a wrong way to proceed and specifies what the right and wrong ways are. Merely to know that some act is wrong or bad need not involve this awareness.

In morality as well, the idea of right and wrong would seem more basic than the idea of a rule, or the fact that there is a rule, that distinguishes right from wrong. The appeal to a rule might, as Piaget would have us believe, make the morality better or purer. It is not clear, however, whether it makes the act or sentiment in question any more unequivocally "moral," in the sense of involving any specifically moral reflections on the actor's part.

At the same time, however, a moral sentiment or motivation is like the idea of a rule insofar as it involves a particular juxtaposition of judgments of right and wrong. To judge that lying is morally wrong is in part to say that one ought under the same circumstances to behave in another, specific way that is the morally right thing to do. Conversely, to think that telling the truth is morally right, or actually to tell the truth *because* it is morally right, depends on knowing what it would be to be untruthful (i.e., to lie). In other words, action undertaken for "moral" reasons presupposes the explicit rejection of alternative courses of action deemed to be immoral (Winch, 1958). Similarly, when we are aware that events follow a "rule" in a given situation, we are aware that they proceed in one way *and not in another* (or not in any other). There is again an implicit, if not an explicit, contrast of right and wrong.

But moral sentiment and motivation do not *depend* on the idea of a rule. They depend on judgments of right and wrong and on a particular juxtaposition of these judgments. The idea of a rule can be shown to have the same dependencies, but it is not the same thing. Most important, Piaget seems to have the developmental story backward. He implies that children develop the idea of a rule and derive notions of right and wrong (correct, incorrect, etc.) from this idea. If, however, we assume that in general children develop less complex notions before they develop more complex notions of the same thing, it seems likely that they would develop notions of right and wrong first. Then, in certain circumstances, they might come to think of what is right in relation to what is wrong and to think of what is wrong in relation to what is right. Insofar as both the idea of a rule and the moral appraisal of action entail this coordination, they also may develop later – even though caretakers' imposition of (*what we know to be*) rules may be one of the things that initially provokes this development.

Thus, even in this less abstract context, that is, in the realm of children's "effective moral thought," Piaget's emphasis on rules as the cornerstone of moral development appears to be either beside the point or derivative. Moral sentiments and motivations can be traced, by Piaget's own account, to origins (e.g., early sympathetic reactions) that predate or otherwise remain outside any cognizance of rules. Alternatively, at one of the potentially critical turning points for moral development (when right is seen in terms of wrong, etc.), although the idea of a rule is compatible with the conceptual organization we may infer to be present, it is neither a necessary nor a central aspect of that organization.

In the light of the problems in Piaget's account of both obligation and children's conceptualization of early, externally imposed rules, it appears that those of Piaget's discussions that were most explicitly aimed at providing descriptions of basic properties of moral agency do not advance the account very much. Piaget's concept of obligation lacks an account of any specifically moral imperative, that is, an account of what it is to do something because we think we ought to do it on moral grounds, because we think it is the morally right thing to do or even simply the right thing. Piaget separates the idea of obligation not only from any kind of moral imperative, however, but from action undertaken for any reason at all. The discussion of primitive affective reactions (e.g., sympathy) is too limited to supply the missing detail. The discussion of children's reactions to early adult constraints usefully introduces the ideas of right and wrong but traces them inappropriately to the concept of a rule. The concept of a rule is more likely to arise from than to instigate ideas about right and wrong.

The implication of all of the shortcomings of Piaget's account that I have discussed so far is that the proper subject matter for a psychology of moral development is perhaps not the question of how children acquire the abstract idea of obligation or of a rule, of an autonomous rule, of reciprocity, and so on. Far more central and pressing would seem to be the question of how children come to act for a reason, how they come to act for a reason that we would call a moral reason, and how they come to acquire the values and sentiments that become those reasons. Piaget's investigations and speculations do not address these issues, even indirectly, as he seems to have supposed they did. Although he does not construe them in this light, Piaget does, however, present data that bear on these issues. I conclude this discussion of Piaget's account of the moral agent with a brief consideration of these data.

1.6. Early moral sentiments

Piaget quite un-self-consciously describes his daugher Jacqueline's shame and remorse (or, more diffusely, regret) over various acts she committed. He also alludes to similar reports by others (e.g., Sully, 1914), from whose accounts it seems reasonable to infer that long before children have an autonomous conception of morality in Piaget's sense, they have what might be called moral, or premoral, sentiments. They have reactions of disapproval or outrage to perceived wrongdoings performed either against themselves or others, they feel shame or guilt for things they have done, they regret the harm or displeasure they have brought to someone else, and they may act on someone else's behalf not for any personal end but because they think it is the right thing to do.

Piaget was interested in these observations for what they indicated about the substantive basis of the reactions. He concluded, for instance, that Jacqueline's feelings of shame and remorse took account only of the results of her actions, not their intentions. It may be more noteworthy for the origins of morality, however, that Jacqueline felt shame or remorse – or anything like them – at all. These feelings, which carry at least a sense of wrongdoing, involve something above and beyond such feelings as fear of punishment, disappointment or astonishment over a violated expectation, or even personal regret over a lost object or a missed opportunity. *What* are the feelings children express (as near as we can tell), and what set of cognitions do they presuppose? Similarly, in the examples he describes, Piaget evidently thinks that Jacqueline perceives certain outcomes to be her own "fault" or to have come about through her own "negligence." Of course, he may be mistaken either in these attributions or in the ascriptions of shame, remorse, and so on. But let us suppose that, by some age, these attributions are correct. If Jacqueline perceived something to be her fault, for instance, does this mean that she (rightly or wrongly) envisioned that she had a choice in the matter? At whatever juncture we are willing to ascribe something like a perception of choice, or an assumption of responsibility for having made one choice as opposed to another, we are pointing to an important moment in moral development.

Although the outline of an empirical research program based on these observations is beyond this book, I would at least venture to suggest that even a fairly gross and approximate analysis of these early moral (or premoral) reactions might make it possible to begin to describe how moral agency begins and how it develops.

2. Moral egocentrism

I turn now to the series of arguments through which Piaget connected the topic of morality to his general psychological theory. The thesis is that children's egocentrism keeps them from being moral in the proper (autonomous, etc.) sense. The development of morality proper, therefore, is to be explained at least in significant part by the decline in egocentrism. One component of the egocentrism thesis is the realism thesis: The reason children hold certain views of morality is that they are not as capable as adults of distinguishing between what comes from the outside and what is an inner, psychological reality. I begin with a brief reconstruction of the two theses.

2.1. Reconstruction

In what ways did Piaget consider children to be morally egocentric? Primarily, their actual practice of following rules was inconsistent and was driven by their own needs and desires rather than by the ends for which the rules were designed (regulation of social relations, regulation of a game, etc.). For example, in the game of marbles, some of the younger children used the rules they were aware of as interesting examples rather than as conditions for acting. They improvised around these examples, and although they played in the company of other children, they played largely for themselves. Piaget projects further that as part of their egocentrism the children had the "illusion" of participating in the game.

The case with lying was similar. Here Piaget noted the well-documented observation of pseudolying, whereby children invent the truth to suit their needs of the moment. According to Piaget, this behavior represents an egocentric application of the rule about lying insofar as children are applying the rule inconsistently and acting so as to suit their own interests rather than the interests of others. There is egocentrism also, in Piaget's view, insofar as children do not envision that they are bringing any potential harm or inconvenience to others. They are not thinking about others, only about themselves. Finally, as with the egocentric practice of following the rules of marbles, children are exhibiting a generic tendency, characteristic of egocentric thought and action, merely to "utilize" reality and "distort" its objects (MJ, p. 164) for play and for the exercise of faculties. In short, thought and action are directed at satisfaction, not at "truth." Children "neglect the value of veracity" (MJ, p. 163).

Speaking in a more general way, Piaget says that "from a moral point of view, egocentrism involves a sort of anomie such that tenderness and disinterestedness can go hand in hand with a naive selfishness, and yet the child does not feel spontaneously himself to be better in one case than the other" (MJ, p. 400). The source of this pattern of reactions is, again, children's failure to distinguish their own perspective from that of other people. This distinction would arise if children compared themselves with other people. That, however, is precisely, in Piaget's view, what children do not yet do.

The arguments in support of realism follow similar lines. First, however, let us recall the general phenomenon of realism, as Piaget understood it. A realist conception of reality, according to Piaget, is a conception that places what are in fact contents or properties of the mind outside the mind, that is, in reality. Realism arises, in Piaget's account, through children's failure to draw the appropriate boundaries between themselves and the external world, a failure that is in turn associated with children's lack of consciousness of self.

Piaget found in several notions that his subjects expressed a specifically *moral* realism. First was the notion of heteronomous duty itself. The rules that we follow are necessarily external to us. The extreme version of this notion is that they are sacred and immutable. This view is realistic insofar as it regards as wholly external to the acting subject that which ought to be conceived of as at least partially internal. To conceive of rules as subject in principle to the decision of the agents who follow them (i.e., to have an autonomous view of duty) is, on the other hand, to grant this internal aspect. Realism was also exhibited insofar as children did not recognize (intrinsic, given by the mind) reasons that the rules should be followed and appealed instead to a purely external criterion, for example, avoidance of punishment. Finally, there was the concept of objective responsibility, which involved realism in two senses. First, the concept itself ignores anything internal to the actors involved, for example, their intentions. To assign objective responsibility is to judge acts solely on the basis of their external consequences. Second, insofar as one judges acts on this basis, then, as made explicit by the immediately preceding point, one has not looked for a reason as to why actions that normally lead to such consequences are bad. In having failed to look for a reason, one has, again, made morality a purely external matter, that is, a matter that is independent of the mind and hence "real."

Piaget carries this realism thesis one step farther, to resolve what he thinks might seem a paradoxical result. He finds that it is at just the point when children express a decidedly heteronomous view of rules that the practice of these rules is most "egocentric" and hence inconsistent. The heteronomous view in question is the notion that rules are imposed by the authorities and are virtually sacred. They are obligatory in the strongest sense. This view might appear to conflict with the fact that the practice of rules is so uneven. The realism thesis can resolve this conflict through the notion that at the source of both reactions – the heteronomous attitude and uneven practice – is the idea that the rule is external to the child; it corresponds to no "felt inner need" (MJ, p. 163). Because the rule remains external in this sense, that is, external to children's "conscience," it cannot really transform their conduct. Hence, inconsistent practice would ensue. It is also congruent with this externality that children regard the rule as emanating from a source totally outside themselves and thus as being beyond their reach in the sense that they cannot change it.

In Piaget's larger framework, each of these attitudes coming under the heading of moral realism would be seen as part of a broader tendency of children to project mental contents onto the outside, or to "reify" them. Insofar as this broader tendency can be explained within the theory by children's failure to distinguish a self and its properties, it must be possible to explain the different attitudes associated with moral realism in the same way.

I next present a critique of arguments supporting moral egocentrism and realism in the order in which I have just presented them.

2.2 Critique of egocentrism

I begin with the arguments bearing directly on the claim that children are moral egocentrics and conclude with some brief comments on the associated claims of apparent "anomie," "naive selfishness," and so forth.

Egocentrism per se. Piaget discusses the two specific cases of children's egocentric practice of the rules of marbles and their egocentric practice of the rule against lying. The argument, in brief, is that children are egocentric in these two cases because they do not follow the rules. By itself, this is a weak basis for the attribution of egocentrism, because it ignores the reasons children fail to follow the rules.

In the case of marbles, Piaget's subjects, according to his account, were not trying to play the game. They were using what we know to be the rules of the game as prototypes for a game of their own, played, however, in the company of others. It could even be that, under the constraints of the goals of which they were capable, they were participating in the collective effort as well as they knew how. Piaget depicts them, for instance, as aspiring to enter into the spirit of the game. Under these circumstances, it seems that the most we can say is that the children were egocentric in the specific sense that they lacked a particular social skill (i.e., were not capable of it) and perhaps lacked (again, were not capable of) certain kinds of social motivations or social goals. That they "failed" to employ these skills or to adopt these motivations and goals seems beside the point if they were not *capable* of employing or adopting them.

An adult exhibiting the same behavior might reasonably be said to be failing to do these things. To that degree, the adult might be said to be behaving egocentrically, that is, just like a child. But I think that what we really mean here is that the adult, in behaving like a child, is behaving egocentrically. The adult is disregarding the rules of the game and the needs and concerns of others, when he or she should not be. The child does not have the option to regard or disregard the rules of the game and the needs and concerns of others. He or she *cannot* pay attention to these things. So whereas the adult who behaves like a child might be behaving egocentrically, the child in behaving like a child would simply be behaving like a child.

In view of the fact that I have already raised the same general objection several times (see, e.g., chapter 2), I want now to state what I take to be Piaget's basic, underlying difficulty. I will then discuss the specific case of lying, which will bring out the difficulties more clearly and in detail.

The problem is endemic to Piaget's entire approach to his investigations. It concerns what I call his capacity argument. The vast majority of Piaget's interpretive claims assume this form, not only his egocentrism theses, which are at issue here. The capacity argument depends on drawing a very strong analogy between given modes of adult behavior that presuppose the full development of certain underlying capacities and the behavior of children who, by hypothesis, have not yet developed those underlying capacities fully. For the purposes of this discussion I will accept Piaget's empirical claim that children lack certain capacities.[4] There are, in principle, weaknesses in the analogies through which Piaget interprets children's resulting behavior.

More specifically, some adult behaviors that are correctly characterized in certain evaluative ways, for instance, as egocentric, are appropriately characterized in those ways precisely because they can generally be seen as the result of a failure to exercise a fully developed capacity. Alternatively, they can be seen as the result of an intentional decision to use that capacity in one way rather than in another. The apparently analogous behavior of children is not properly or correctly characterized with the same (negative) evaluative vocabulary, precisely because it is behavior produced by an agent who has not yet developed the capacity to behave differently.

An equally problematic outcome of Piaget's approach is that the retreat to this kind of language, which as we now see is largely metaphoric, prevents Piaget from carrying out his central task. That task is the substantive description of the missing capacity,

---

[4] Even contemporary critics of Piaget who challenge Piaget's sweeping claims that children lack such-and-such capacity would nonetheless say that in contexts in which children fail to demonstrate the capacity in question they fail because (for performance or other reasons) they *cannot* demonstrate the capacity in those situations. This is still different from what we would say about adults, namely that they *do not* demonstrate the capacity on certain occasions when we would expect them to.

and the description of what children are doing when they still lack that capacity. It is this paucity of description, along with the inappropriate use of the capacity argument, that emerges in Piaget's treatment of lying, to which I now turn.

Consider the adult. A normal adult is said to have lied in what I call the full-blown sense if that individual has intentionally told an untruth for the purpose of deceiving another. So telling a full-blown lie presupposes certain capacities. These include (a) the capacity to distinguish truth from falsity, (b) the capacity to recognize those situations in which human utterance will be construed by others to be an assertion of truth, and (c) the capacity to form the intention to deceive. Only individuals who have these capacities are able to lie.

The difficulty, then, in speaking of children's lies consists, first, in the fact that in many cases children may not have a clear grasp of the distinction between true and false. Second, in some cases children may lack the social skills to perceive that in certain situations their actions will be construed as the assertion of propositions and therefore that there is an expectation that what is asserted will be true. Third, in many cases children may easily lack the quite complex capacity to form an intention to deceive.

Piaget's discussion of children's lies actually takes place in the context of a set of distinctions that are slightly different from those I have just described and whose relationship to the preceding distinctions is not immediately or completely evident. Piaget is clear that children (who tell only pseudolies) do not "lie" intentionally. In many of the instances Piaget cites it is difficult to say they lie at all. They exaggerate, or they invent something. They do not mean to deceive or harm anyone and presumably (by definition of pseudolie) do not know at the time that they are doing anything wrong or anything that might conceivably be construed as wrong.

The ambiguity comes with Piaget's further claim that children tell pseudolies because they do not "value" (MJ, p. 163) the truth. This claim seems to mean that children are able to distinguish between true and false, and then any one of several further conditions applies. I will distinguish three: First, children may be able under most circumstances to distinguish between truth and falsity (they know a true statement from a false one or a real bottle from a fake) but are not interested in the distinction or do not see its relevance. Second, they may recognize the distinction and even in some way think it is important, but for one reason or another fail to draw the distinction in the socially expected situations. For instance, they might not be skilled in recognizing when true statements are expected or appropriate, or they might recognize such situations but not think it important to comply with expectations. Third, they might know what the truth is, and know generally when they should produce it, but fail to appreciate the general reasons for its overriding importance in these contexts.

To elaborate the third possibility, children might know that they are supposed to tell the truth but might recognize that doing so will have immediate bad consequences for them, and they might not see that these consequences are outweighed by the social consequences of saying false things. Here we may envision a little child who knows what the truth is, and knows that he or she is expected to tell it in a certain situation, but does not know clearly why it is important for everyone to tell the truth in those circumstances. This child may come quite understandably to give exceptional weight to the consequences of telling or not telling the truth for itself in those circumstances.

In none of these three cases, however, are children correctly described as egocentric in the sense in which adults might be called egocentric in comparable situations. Adults who lie, either intentionally or, for example, through intense self-preoccupation, may be said to be egocentric in the sense that they are *breaking* a rule that is vital to social solidarity (trust, reciprocity, etc.) or in the sense that they are not taking account of others' points of view. We can say this, however, because we presuppose that adults know in principle how to maintain social solidarity (and therefore can be said to be "breaking" it) or in principle how to take others' points of view (and therefore can be correctly described as failing to do so).

All we can say of children is that, for the reasons given in the preceding paragraphs, they do not know how to do these things. They *cannot* do them. The result is that they engage in behavior that performed by an adult would be egocentric in the senses just given. But for the very same reasons, it is inappropriate and misleading to say that children are "breaking" the bonds of social solidarity or that they are "failing" to take others' points of view. It is inappropriate to say that they are "breaking" the bonds of social solidarity, because they do not know how their behavior could in principle maintain or break these bounds. It is inappropriate to say that they are "failing" to take others' points of view, because they do not know that their behavior has, or could in principle have, consequences that would make these points of view relevant to consider.

In brief, Piaget's capacity argument and the evaluative language into which it translates are inappropriate once again, in this case with respect to lying. I will merely add in passing that in the course of following Piaget's argument, *I* had to supply the missing analysis of lying (e.g., the tentative three-way distinction among the different capacities involved in lying) that might clarify the sort of act in which children might be engaged. Piaget either deals with this level of analysis haphazardly or else ignores it altogether.

I have been criticizing Piaget's application of the concept of egocentrism in general to his data on morality. Piaget speaks more specifically, however, of a *moral* egocentrism. If the concept of egocentrism in general poses difficulties because it reduces only to a claim about capacity, the attribution of moral egocentrism would seem all the more problematic. In what sense are children being *morally* egocentric when they play marbles without really playing, or utter falsehoods without really lying, because they simply lack the skill (and lack the skill because they lack the capacity) to behave otherwise?

Egocentrism and anomie. I conclude this section with some comments on Piaget's summary statement regarding moral egocentrism. This statement begins with the claim that the "egocentric" children of whom we have been speaking exhibit a kind of "anomie" (Durkheim's term). By this Piaget presumably means that children do not follow consistent norms. They have no norms.

The most it would seem we could say here, however, is that children do not follow our norms, or do not follow them consistently. We have no grounds to conclude from the behavior Piaget describes that children do not follow any norms or that they are inconsistent with respect to the norms they follow. For instance, if children do not lie intentionally, the case could be made that they are not inconsistent with respect to the norm of (not) lying. That norm is simply not a relevant dimension for evaluating their behavior.

The term "anomie" ordinarily has additional connotations that are even more inappropriate. The individual who has a sense of anomie has *given up* following norms and feels disoriented. The child who shares his or her toys willingly one day and snatches someone else's toys the next can hardly be said to have given up a norm or to be disoriented for want of a norm.

On a similar note, consider Piaget's further remark that children can exhibit a "naive selfishness." We might judge them to be callous as well, for example, for the physical pain they can inflict on animals and the hardships they can cause people precisely through the so-called rules that they "break."

I cannot resist citing Sully's (1914) very apt remarks on this point. In calling children "callous" under these circumstances, Sully says, we are projecting the way we would feel if we were doing the same thing they are doing. With the full knowledge of suffering that we have, to torment a pet cat the way a child does would indeed require an immense feeling of indifference (i.e., callousness) on our part. The child, however, probably has no intention of inflicting pain, but only the impulse to "hold, possess, and completely dominate" (Sully, 1914, p. 240) the animal. The child's problem here (if it can justly be called a problem) is not that he or she is without norms, but that certain acts have consequences that may not have been intended and that, if understood and attended to at the time, would provide a reason for checking a particular impulse.

I do not mean here to portray children as slighted moral heros and heroines. Rather, I wish to claim that Piaget makes the mistake of attributing to children's behavior a moral dimension in instances where there does not appear to be one. It is only on the basis of that attribution that children could be called morally egocentric or, as Piaget says, egocentric "from a moral point of view" (MJ, p. 400). Moral egocentrism might exist, but normal child behavior, when exhibited by children, does not appear to be an instance of it.

2.3. Critique of moral realism

I turn now to the thesis of moral realism. I first discuss the moral realism thesis itself and then Piaget's attempt to relate moral realism to intellectual realism.

Moral realism. Piaget's discussion of moral realism poses an immediate problem insofar as the reactions he groups under moral realism seem only very tenuously interrelated. The connection is especially remote, for example, between the notion of whether children take intentions into account in judging the gravity of an act, that is, the notion of subjective versus objective responsibility, and the notion of whether the rules that prescribe acts are conceived as emanating from an internal or external source (as having reasons, etc.), that is, the notion of heteronomy or autonomy.

These two senses in which phenomena are supposed to be in the mind (or the connections of the two phenomena to the mind) are very different. The first case (intentions) concerns whether children see the relevance of what went on in someone's mind to what the person did (specifically, to the question of whether what that person did was good or bad). The second (reflections on the origins of rules) concerns whether children can conceive of the phenomenon in question (a rule) as being explicable with reference to a process (e.g., mutual decision of peers, the reason of the individual) that we would describe as taking place in part in their minds.

Similar problems arise with Piaget's attempt to solve the "paradox" of the coincidence of the egocentric practice of rules and children's heteronomous attitude (specifically "mystical respect") toward them. At least three problems are evident.

First, it is surprising that Piaget labored so hard to connect these two phenomena through the same motivating belief (i.e., children's alleged conception of rules as external). It would seem simpler to assume that in the actual play situation (in which children play for themselves, use a rule only as an interesting example, etc.), the rule is only a prototype and not an imperative. However, in talking about rules, that is, in their abstract reflections on what rules are, children construe the rule as a given and as an imperative. It is plausible enough that children's practice of the rule is "egocentric" because they do not really understand the rule, because the underlying motivation for the rule does not correspond to any "felt inner need," and so on. But this in itself would not explain why children think the rule is divine and immutable. They could, for example, both fail to understand the real purpose of the rule and think that rules are changed every day.

What ought to be explained is, rather, why children think the rule is divine and immutable *despite* their failure to understand it. That explanation would seem likely to have something to do with children's relations to authority.

Children who are repeatedly told to share things but who do not yet understand fully what it is to share provide a useful comparison here. On some occasions these children remember what they are supposed to do and refrain from taking another child's toy. On others, they snatch the toy because it is attractive and forget that they are not supposed to take it or may not really understand why they are not supposed to take it. At the same time, they will give every indication that they think sharing is important when the issue of sharing arises in the abstract. But the reason for this attitude is not that the rationale for sharing remains beyond the children's comprehension, but that Mommy (Daddy, teacher, etc.) tells them to share.

Here we might say, with Piaget, that children might be less prone to adopt the "Mommy says" position if they understood the real point of a rule. Seeing its inherent virtues, they might not need an external rationale either to motivate the consistent practice of the rule or to explain its apparent importance. But then we are talking about a further development that might have the potential of eradicating the two earlier reactions (egocentric practice and heteronomous attitude). We would not, thereby, have an explanation of why the two reactions occur in the first place.

Second, Piaget appears to believe that there is not only a plausible, but a necessary connection between the externality of a rule to children's conscience and their egocentric or inconsistent practice of it. Here I will only point out that Freud, like Piaget after him, had the notion that some of the values we hold were internalized irrationally, that is, without proper comprehension and because of our particular relation to authority figures when we were young. Freud does not seem to think, however, that unstable application of these values would follow as a result of this irrational internalization. If anything, fanatical and unyielding adherence might occur.

Third, even if a rule that remained external to children's "conscience" could not, or at least did not, transform their conduct, it would not follow necessarily that children would regard the rule as emanating from the outside. Rather, in parallel with Piaget's theorizing about numerous other allegedly egocentric phenomena, children could harbor the "illusion" that the rule came from within themselves.

Thus, in his attempt to link children's "consciousness" of rules with their practice of rules, as with his attempt to interrelate different aspects of their consciousness of rules (e.g., heteronomy and objective responsibility), we find again that Piaget is oversimplifying his classification of the phenomena. The attitudes and behaviors he wishes to draw together exist in either much looser or much more complex relation to one another than he describes. The individual relation of each of the phenomena to the idea of externality (or realism or mind) is equally obscure.

Moral realism and intellectual realism. If it is difficult to distinguish in what sense the supposedly moral phenomena Piaget discusses cohere into a group or in what sense they are related to the question of externality, it is even more difficult to connect them with the still more remote phenomena Piaget discusses under intellectual realism. The characteristics of intellectual realism – the tendency to see names, thoughts, and so on as existing in the things they represent or as otherwise being material – involve construing something as an external, material reality that is in fact internal and nonmaterial. The reactions of moral realism differ in at least three significant respects.

First, the sense in which rules, responsibility, and so forth are internal is several steps removed from the sense in which thought, dreams, and even names are internal. Rules are something people make, through a decision to make them. A decision is an internal process; therefore, rules have an internal (i.e., mental) aspect. Similarly, to conceive of responsibility as a mental or internal phenomenon one must associate responsibility with intentions (doing something on purpose, etc.) and conceive of intentions as mental phenomena. Thought, however, just *is* an internal phenomenon.

Second, even if we disregard this first distinction and consider subjective responsibility (the idea of judging an act on the basis of the actor's intentions) to have an internal aspect in the same sense that thought has an internal aspect, there is a further, important disanalogy between the two cases in their relation to this internality. In the case of subjective responsibility, we are talking about whether intentions *ought* to be taken into account in assigning blame (degree of gravity, etc.) and hence about whether responsibility *ought* to be considered internal. In the case of thought, we are talking once again about whether the phenomenon in question *is* internal.

Third, children construe moral phenomena (rules, responsibility) to be external in a different sense than they consider psychological phenomena (thought, dreams, etc.) to be external. Children conceive of thought, dreams, and so on as existing on the outside and as being material. They do not think of rules, however, as existing somewhere out in reality (at least Piaget's studies did not concern such views). They think that rules are *imposed* from without. Similarly, although they may use criteria (i.e., consequences) that we recognize as external to judge responsibility, Piaget presents no evidence that children think of responsibility as an external entity.

There are, however, weaker analogies that Piaget might draw. The tendencies of moral realism could be likened to those of intellectual realism only to the degree that both involve conceptualizing phenomena or issues that are (or ought to be) in some way connected to the mind in a way that takes no account of mind. The trouble with this analogy, however, is that the paths from the two classes of phenomena to the mind are sufficiently different that it is difficult to see this small area of common ground as being central to children's – or adults' – conceptualization of either class.

Another possibility is to see the tendencies of moral realism as deriving from intellectual realism. The argument might be as follows: Rules will be regarded as related to the mind only insofar as they are seen as arising through people's decisions, and decisions are seen as something made with the mind. Similarly, subjective responsibility can arise only insofar as responsibility is associated with the intentions of the perpetrator of an act, and intentions are associated with the mind. We know from the data on intellectual realism that children have difficulty associating mental properties of all kinds – which would presumably include properties such as decisions and intentions – with the mind (where mind is defined more or less as adults would define it). Given that rules and responsibility can be associated with the mind only if they are associated with these properties (and children do not associate these properties with the mind), children will not associate rules and responsibility with the mind.

This alternative account poses two problems. The first is that the question of whether children see mental properties (e.g., intentions and decisions) as mental still does not tell us whether children will associate responsibility with intentions and (the origins of) rules with decisions. Children could associate responsibility (the gravity of an act, etc.) with the intentions of the actor (e.g., with whether someone did something on purpose) and associate the existence of a rule with a decision that someone made, without recognizing that intentions and decisions are psychological phenomena. Conversely, the belief that intentions and decisions are psychological phenomena would not necessarily move children any closer to assigning responsibility on the basis of intention or to having an "autonomous" conception of rules than they were before. They might still hold an "objective" conception of responsibility and a "heteronomous" view of rules.

The second problem is that the account depends on children's engaging in a complicated chain of inference, or at least in a complicated series of associations, in order both to hold the views they apparently do and to develop different views. We must again question, however, whether children's array of beliefs at any given stage or the development of new ideas arises in this way (see chapter 1, section 4 under Critique).

Piaget might, however, argue for a parallel between the two kinds of realism from the other side. In that case the two realisms would be unified not by the "independence of the mind" (MJ, p. 111), but by the reliance of each one on the notion that the phenomena in question (e.g., thought, dreams, rules, responsibility) were "self-subsistent" (p. 111). What Piaget meant by this in the case of moral realism was that things like duties, rules, and responsibility were considered and evaluated independently of any contextual factors whatsoever. It was as if these phenomena had a life of their own.

But now we have a problem that is the converse of the one we just dealt with. It is difficult to extend this idea of self-subsistence to the reactions that come under intellectual realism. To be sure, children express the view that thought is in the things to which it refers and that dreams come from the light and take place in the room, and so on. It is unclear, however, in what way, other than "independence from the mind," thought (dreams, etc.) is being taken to exist independently of any contextual factors whatever.

This statement simply does not describe anything children say, or anything their actions imply, about thought or other similar phenomena. It would seem equally inappropriate to say that it is as if these phenomena had a life of their own. All children are doing is locating dreams and thought in the outside world and failing to associate them with the mind. *We* are the ones who see the implication that these phenomena would therefore be free to take on a life of their own.

In general, the only clear points of correspondence between the two kinds of realism appear to be either highly specific, isolated areas of empirical overlap or else extremely abstract and arbitrary theoretical properties. As to the empirical correspondences, one can cite results such as the finding that children think that both names and (received) rules are divinely given or the finding that they think that rules that they themselves invent (this again in the game of marbles) are sent into their heads from without, just as they think that dreams are sent to them from without. As for the theoretical correspondence, Piaget argued that children's attitudes regarding so-called moral phenomena exemplified a broader tendency, characteristic of intellectual realism, to project mental contents onto the outside, or to "reify" them. There is no clear way in which Piaget's results on moral development exemplify this property.

2.4. Morality and the consciousness of self

There is a further step in Piaget's realism argument that is worth considering both in its own right and because its shortcomings suggest a major alternative viewpoint. Piaget theorized that realism, in whatever form he observed it, and the various phenomena that he associated directly with egocentrism (e.g., objective responsibility, the inconsistent application of rules, "naive selfishness") were to be explained ultimately by children's failure to distinguish a self. This is the thesis I now wish to consider. I take as my reference point Piaget's observations of Jacqueline, which he believed were explained exactly by this thesis. Piaget's treatment of these observations is revealing once again, both of the peculiar shortsightedness of his account and of a possible, if ironic alternative that might penetrate closer to the basic issues underlying early moral development.

The observations, again, are instances in which Jacqueline as a very young child (between the ages of 1 and 3 years) exhibited apparent signs of such sentiments as remorse and shame for acts that she committed but that she did not intend (or the results of which she did not intend). Piaget cited these examples for their documentation of objective responsibility, whereby the gravity of an act is measured by its consequences rather than by its intentions. Objective responsibility, in Piaget's theory, is explained ultimately by children's tendency toward egocentrism and realism, which in turn are explained by the absence of the consciousness of self.

There is another way to interpret these examples. Jacqueline is upset not just about the consequences of her actions, but about the consequences of *her* actions. One feels shame and remorse when one's own actions (or one's failure to act) have had a bad effect, not when just any action has had a bad effect. Intentions need not figure here. Authorship is what matters. To Jacqueline, then, what may have been significant is not simply that a bad thing happened, but that *she* did it. Thus, the very reaction that Piaget describes as exemplifying a lack of awareness of self might in a different and more basic way have precisely to do with self.

Children might still have a great deal to learn about self and about when it matters that this self is involved in something that happens. But the initial point at which self is held accountable at all may be deeply significant for moral development (see Sully, 1914, ch. 7 for a related argument). Piaget, despite himself, may have directed us to that point. His theory, however, not only fails to recognize this possibility, but explicitly denies it.

3. The development of full-blown morality

I conclude this critique with an attempt to draw the implications of the previous analyses for the question of how full-blown morality develops from the putative beginnings I have been discussing until now.

If moral egocentrism and moral realism cannot be established, we cannot argue that full-blown morality (as Piaget conceives it: autonomy, reciprocity, etc.) is explained by the decline in these tendencies. This leaves two possibilities, within Piaget's account. One is that the various phenomena described under moral egocentrism and moral realism are still important for the development of full-blown morality; however, Piaget has characterized them improperly. My first set of criticisms (see section 1 under Critique) addressed this possibility. I seriously questioned whether Piaget had indeed looked in the right place for the origins of morality.

The second possibility is that tendencies that are the opposite of what Piaget referred to as moral egocentrism and moral realism explain the development of full-blown morality (in Piaget's sense). These tendencies include the ability to appreciate other people's points of view, the disposition to be wary of possible intrusions of one's point of view in what one takes to be the objective truth, and so on. Presumably these tendencies would also include the desire and the attempt to cooperate.

Let us assume that Piaget is correct in thinking that these tendencies would produce the sort of morality he takes to be full-blown, that is, a morality with a conception of rules or duty as self-given, with the notion that rules have intrinsic reasons, and with a recognition of the centrality of cooperation and reciprocity to everyday life. It follows that qualities that are contrary to egocentrism provide one possible route to a true morality and (by Piaget's definition) are even partly constitutive of it. It does not follow that these qualities are fully constitutive of a true morality, that their cultivation and exercise are sufficient to prompt the development of that morality, or that their cultivation is necessary – or at least centrally necessary – for this development. Some of the tendencies that Piaget discusses might facilitate moral development, but possible facilitation is different from the determinative relation Piaget describes.

I have just been assuming, with Piaget, that the contra-egocentric tendencies he discusses would produce moral human beings. I now wish to question this assumption. The contra-egocentric agent Piaget describes would be an agent who cooperates and values cooperation, who participates in relations of mutual respect, who is sensitive to others' points of view, and who is aware of the potential intrusion of his or her own point of view into his or her perception of things. This still does not give us an agent who reflects consciously and reaches *moral* judgments and makes *moral* choices. At best it presupposes such an agent.

Alternatively, as Piaget himself remarks, many of the contra-egocentric tendencies he cites could lead to collective vice as well as to collective virtue. He notes as examples the honor among thieves or a band of young ruffians working together to play practical jokes on people (MJ, pp. 97–8). To deal with this problem Piaget says only that collective vice involves mutual *consent,* in which the anarchical tendencies of one individual simply converge with those of another, whereas collective virtue involves mutual *respect,* which involves "admiration for a personality precisely insofar as this personality subjects itself to rules" (p. 98). These would seem to be insufficient grounds for drawing the distinction. There could be mutual respect among thieves, who nonetheless are up to no good.

4

"The child's conception of number"

I have now considered, in various degrees of detail, three of Piaget's early works on children's thought: *The child's conception of the world, The language and thought of the child,* and *The moral judgment of the child.* Because these works form a natural unit, I will review some of the key points of the preceding critiques before turning to the remaining books, which were written later and are organized around somewhat different themes.

Piaget's central aim in these early works was to give a unified account of the primitive, childlike behavior he observed and to explain how more mature forms of behavior could arise. His egocentrism thesis plays a central role in this explanatory account. According to this thesis, children exhibit the behavior, beliefs, and attitudes they do because they engage in a special mode of thinking called egocentric thought. The predominant definition of children's egocentric thought is unconscious absorption in their own point of view. Mature behavior, beliefs, and attitudes arise, according to the same view, as this mode of thought declines and countervailing tendencies, such as confrontation with alternative points of view, increase.

This account and the arguments presented in its support posed several difficulties. Primarily, there seemed to be little warrant for the attribution of egocentrism to the behaviors that were supposed to be egocentric. The problem was not that children exhibited the opposite of egocentrism, namely, some kind of perspectivism, which was supposed to occur later. What was inappropriate was the whole application of the dimension of egocentric/nonegocentric to children's behavior. Time and time again, we found that to apply the label "egocentric" to children's behavior intelligibly we had to ask what the implications would be of an adult's behaving in the way children behaved. Even here the resulting attribution often seemed arbitrary, that is, from the point of view of adult logic.

At certain junctures it seemed as if Piaget were using the concept of egocentrism to refer not to the positive, or manifest, properties of so-called egocentric behavior, but to the absence of certain later-appearing properties that are self-evidently nonegocentric from our adult point of view. In their speech to others children eventually adopt the perspective of the listener, for example, in ways that they do not do so earlier. In considering the question of whether the sun follows them down the street, children will eventually be able to take account of the vantage point of several observers, whereas initially they do not even see the relevance of doing this. Sometimes "egocentric" seems to be simply a label for the absence of these distinctly nonegocentric qualities.

"Negative" observations of this kind can be useful. Knowledge of qualities that appear after a certain age and not before can reveal the significance of what older children have achieved. These data tell us which of children's behaviors *are* significant and demanding of an explanation. Many of the problems here arise, it seems, not from Piaget's negative observations themselves, but from the implications he draws from them.

Perhaps the most drastic and unwarranted of these derivations is Piaget's immediate conversion of some of the negative observations into positive theses about what younger children are doing instead. Piaget seems to think, for example, that younger children's failure to "take perspectives" on occasions in which they will later *means* that children have a special mode of thought or a special "tendency" that *prevents* them from doing this. But this need not be the case. Children's failure to take perspectives in a particular way at a given age may be best explained by their inability to appreciate the kinds of relationships or other complexities involved in taking perspectives in that way. As a result of this failure, they may perceive or judge the situation they are in differently from the way an adult would perceive or judge it (e.g., they may think the sun follows them). This does not in itself make them "egocentric," however, in the various positive senses Piaget tries to show they are (e.g., that they take their own point of view as absolute, consider their own perception to be part of external reality, or consider themselves to be the center of the world).

Some of the purely negative theses Piaget develops also have drawbacks, however. I refer in this regard to a position I eventually called Piaget's capacity argument (chapter 3, section 2.2 under Critique). Without repeating my entire analysis here, I will reiterate that Piaget invariably claims that when children *are not* doing something (e.g., taking the perspective of the doll in the three-mountains task, drawing a particular inner–outer distinction), they *cannot* do it. It is inappropriate, and above all misleading and uninformative, then to point out that children are failing to do something they cannot do – let alone that they are (positively) "confused" about the concept or distinction in question. "Failing" at the things to which Piaget alludes presupposes that one could in principle succeed at them (one could in principle take alternative points of view but remains instead trapped within one's own vantage point). The idea of egocentrism, even when stripped of its overt positive content (e.g., taking one's point of view as absolute, confusing the differentiae of undrawn distinctions), is a negative evaluation of this type.

As I argued earlier, when this kind of evaluation is attached to what is ultimately a claim about an incapacity, it ends up at best only restating the data without explaining them. The negation is too broad. It does not say what is really missing. Specifying the truly operative deficit in what children are doing requires a closer analysis of both the apparently missing capacity (e.g., to take perspectives, to lie with the full intent to deceive and hence be accountable for not lying) and the behaviors children exhibit instead. I have tried to give examples of this kind of analysis.

I want to be clear that I am not criticizing Piaget for arguing about the capacities and incapacities of children. To be able to specify what children can and cannot do at different ages and to do this in a theoretically enlightened way would seem to be one of the major goals of developmental psychology. I am criticizing what I take to be Piaget's abandonment of that goal at too early a stage of analysis and the highly inappropriate and essentially irrelevant inferences he draws from the potentially illuminating data he collected, namely, the developmental differences in children's behavior.

There is, finally, another weakness in both the negative and positive versions of Piaget's egocentrism thesis. It is that, even if children were lacking in all of the ways Piaget says they are (and that led him to describe them as egocentric), it is simply not clear whether the acquisition of skills and abilities associated with taking perspectives and coordinating points of view is central to psychological development. First of all, do children, either implicitly or explicitly, actually make the discovery that there are points of view other than their own, or do they mainly develop other understandings and strategies, the result of which is that their conceptions of things and their behavior take account of these points of view? Suppose that they do make this discovery, at some level, and suppose that Piaget is correct in asserting that in some instances it does materially affect the way children deal with a particular problem. Piaget seems to imply that children will generalize from this discovery to their whole way of viewing reality and interacting with it. At the very least we should be skeptical of such an assumption. It presupposes either that children's putative discovery is sufficiently abstract that it could generalize in this way, or that – as I argued on several occasions – developmental changes in children's outlook in different areas are brought about by complex processes of deduction and inference. Either presupposition is questionable.

The remaining works we shall consider invoke unifying constructs other than egocentrism. To prepare the transition to these works, we might consider the generic problems in Piaget's account thus far. These problems include a systematic, if ironic failure on Piaget's part to adopt the point of view of his subjects in developing cognitive accounts of their behavior, a designation of theoretical constructs at too abstract a level to account for the phenomena under consideration of their true interrelationships, and the possibility that in some cases (e.g., morality) Piaget has failed to address the basic issues. Related to these difficulties is Piaget's tendency to tie all of his observations into a single system, specifically into an extremely tight, virtually closed system. The developmental claims I just summarized regarding egocentrism are a case in point, as are Piaget's attempts to connect animism and realism, and moral realism and intellectual realism. In these and numerous other cases, the relationships among the phenomena in question turn out to be far more complex than Piaget allowed, and the common elements through which he attempted to connect them are based on a very arbitrary abstraction from the phenomena. In some cases (e.g., the attempt to connect animism and realism), the purported common element changes its character depending on which of the phenomena under investigation Piaget was considering.

A further problem, which I have not summarized here since it applies to only one of the works (CCW), is Piaget's account of children's conceptual development as a progressive "differentiation" of ideas. In that work Piaget persisted in maintaining a decidedly arbitrary and highly reified view of the relation of earlier and later behaviors to one another and of the process through which these behaviors come about. This problem, along with the others, will be pursued further in the works considered in this and the following chapter.

NUMBER: RECONSTRUCTION

1. "Operatory" thought

Piaget described the books we have just discussed as being concerned with the "verbal and conceptual aspects of the child's thought" (CCN, p. vii). They were directed at the content of children's thought or its "implicit tendencies" (CCW, p. 189). The majority of Piaget's works deal instead with what might be referred to as the structural properties of children's thought. What mental operations and what formal principles are presupposed by the different understandings and methods of problem solving that children exhibit? What, with respect to these questions, do the essential constructs of thought, for example, the concepts of space, time, cause, and number, consist of?

Piaget originally referred to this second line of work as dealing with the "operatory" aspects of thought. The term "operation" had a very particular meaning for Piaget. It concerned thinking that exemplifies the properties of a group in mathematics, that is, a formal structure exhibiting the properties of identity, negation, and inversion (expanded by Piaget to the more psychological concept of "reversibility"), among others. Piaget believed that operations in this sense were basic to thought. In studying operatory thought, Piaget was interested in determining when children's understanding of such essential concepts as space, time, cause, and number and their logical reasoning exhibited the grouplike properties to which I have just referred. He pursued this question because, as I will discuss shortly, he held the theoretical view that space, time, and so on were not really defined for an individual unless they were defined operationally, that is, unless the individual's way of thinking about the concept in question (or alternatively, his or her logical reasoning) exhibited the grouplike properties designated by Piaget.

In his later works Piaget began to analyze children's thinking from the point of view of formalisms other than the group (e.g., Piaget, Grize, Szeminska, & Vinh-Bang, 1968/1977). Also, he invoked different formalisms depending on whether he was considering the "concrete" thought of middle childhood (as in CCN; also Inhelder & Piaget, 1959/1966), or the "formal" thought of adolescents (Inhelder & Piaget, 1955/1958). I will use the term "operatory thought" to refer to the whole of Piaget's effort to identify the structural properties of children's thought, independent of the particular formalism(s) chosen as a point of reference.

Because my aim in this chapter is only to illustrate some of the ways in which work along this second line is related to the problems discussed in the preceding chapters, I will consider just one of Piaget's investigations, *The child's conception of number.* I selected this work both because it is one of the most comprehensible of Piaget's structural works and because it is programmatic. It was essentially the first of its kind in the Piagetian corpus.

Unlike the other topics discussed in this book, number is an area to which Piaget returned in his later work. Although he never retracted his account in *The child's conception of number,* his analysis does shift. The later studies replace the unifying theme of conservation, prominent in *Number,* with such notions as correspondence and "recurrence," which Piaget and his colleagues came to view as more primitive (e.g., Gréco, 1962; Inhelder & Piaget, 1963; Piaget, 1979; 1980a). In addition, some empirical studies completed by Piaget's group sought possible precursors of mathematical thinking in young children's spontaneous ordering and arranging of objects (e.g., Robert, Cellérier, & Sinclair, 1972), an emphasis notably absent in *Number.*

As I have already indicated, I discuss Piaget's original study of number here because it exemplifies the general way in which he approached the study of children's thinking in the majority of his empirical investigations. I am less interested in it for its specific claims about the way in which "number" develops. Nonetheless, it is worth pointing out that *Number* remains the basis of most contemporary research on children's concept of number (see, e.g., Flavell, 1985, for a review). Moreover, versions of some of the most basic ideas in *Number* appear in both Piaget's own later works and contemporary research (see chapter 6 of this book). These ideas include the notion that conceptual development involves the "differentiation" of ideas, the mechanism of change being the detection and resolution of contradiction.

Before I proceed with the discussion of *Number,* it will be helpful to clarify the three broad levels of knowing that Piaget distinguished and to which *Number* and subsequent works on operatory thought refer.

There are three different ways in which an individual can conceive of such qualities as number, space, and time. First and most primitively, one's actions can presuppose a certain concept of, say, space. Here no claim is made about one's conscious ideas about space. Rather, one's way of behaving implies certain assumptions about what space must be. Piaget calls this level of knowledge sensorimotor knowledge. It is the subject of the books on infancy and will be considered in chapter 5.

Second, Piaget distinguishes "intuitive" knowledge of number, cause, space, time, and so on. Here he is referring to a partial conceptual understanding of the notions in question. This understanding is more than sensorimotor knowledge (hence, more than something that is simply implied by the individual's action) but is not yet fully reflective insofar as the individual does not yet understand the rational basis of the notions.

Third, there is "operational" knowledge of number, cause space, time, and so on, whereby these concepts are clearly defined and their rational basis understood. Piaget came to distinguish "concrete" and "formal" operational knowledge. *Number* concerns only concrete operational knowledge.

In Piaget's view, these three forms of knowledge emerge sequentially in development, in the order just given, for any particular concept. Each form is progressively "constructed," at least in the sense that complete understanding at any of the three levels arises only gradually. Piaget makes the further assumption that the later developments, either within any one of the three levels or in the evolution across levels, build on the earlier developments.

The works on concrete operatory thought deal with the consolidation of intuitive knowledge and the transition to operatory thought.

2. "Conservation"

The child's conception of number covered a variety of topics, all seen by Piaget to be related to the concept of number. The work begins with analyses of children's ideas about the "conservation" of quantity, independent of the specific question of number. Piaget began with these analyses because, as I will discuss momentarily, he considered the idea of conservation to be central to all rational thought and to the question of number in particular. The remaining topics concern number more directly. These topics include children's construction of one-to-one correspondence relations and their conception of the implications of these relations for the equivalence of two sets. Additional topics include children's construction and understanding of serial order, class inclusion, and the additive composition of number (e.g., if on one day I have 4 sweets at lunch and 4 at dinner, and on the next day 2 at lunch and 6 at dinner, will I have had the same number of sweets on each day?).

In Piaget's treatment these topics build on one another. For instance, the studies of one-to-one correspondence center on the question of whether children "conserve" one-to-one correspondence or the equivalence that may be inferred from it. The studies of serial ordering are superimposed on problems in one-to-one correspondence and conservation and so on.

Because I am interested only in Piaget's general approach, I will consider only his studies of one-to-one correspondence and, through those, his account of conservation. I continue, in this section, with a discussion of his theoretical view that conservation is central to such concepts as number. In the next section I discuss his referral of the question of number to questions about one-to-one correspondence. A reconstruction of the empirical work follows.

In Piaget's writings, the concept of conservation is the notion that the quantity of a given substance (or, in the case of number, the number of elements in a set of discrete objects) remains invariant when other, nonquantitative aspects of the substance (or array of objects) in question undergo a change. The standard example is that, when liquid is poured from a wide container into a thin one (such that the level of the liquid visibly rises), the amount of liquid remains the same. In the case of number, the typical problem begins with two rows of counters that have been aligned exactly in one-to-one correspondence. One of these rows is either spread out or moved together, so that the length of the two rows is no longer the same. A "conserving" subject is one who recognizes that the number of counters in the two rows remains the same.

Under Piaget's definition of operational understanding, it is important that the subject not only find the right answer to the problems but that he or she also explain why that answer is right. The reasons the subject ought to give are principles from which it can be deduced that the change that occurred is irrelevant to the property in question (e.g., the height of the liquid, alone, does not signify that the amount of liquid has changed; the unequal length of the two rows of counters is irrelevant to whether the two rows still contain the same number of counters). These principles, in turn, are notions related directly or indirectly to the grouplike properties I alluded to earlier. These notions include, for example, identity (the liquid is the same body of liquid, or the counters are the same counters, as before), reversibility (if one poured the water back into the original container, it would come to the same height as before; if one moved the row back into place, it would come to the same length as before), and compensation (although the level of the liquid has risen, the width of the new container is narrower than before; although one row of counters is now longer than the other, the space between the individual counters in that row is now greater than it is in the other row).

Piaget's classic finding is that up until a certain age (around 7 years, although this varies with the problem and the population being tested) children appear not to appreciate the concept of conservation. When the water level rises in the liquids experiment, children will say there is more water. When one of the rows of counters is spread out in the number experiment, children will say there are now more counters in that row, even though they previously agreed that the number of counters in the two rows was the same. Gradually children come to see that the quantities in question remain the same, and eventually they spontaneously offer the appropriate reasons for this having to be the case.

Why, then, did Piaget think the idea of conservation was important, and how, exactly, does it figure in his account of the development of number? It is perhaps simplest to begin with a summary reconstruction of Piaget's argument regarding the development of the concept of number. I take that argument to have three steps:

1. The notion of conservation is central to all rational thought. It is central to the concept of number in particular.

2. The notion of conservation has to do specifically with the preservation of a thing or a quality across a possible set of changes related to that thing or quality. The set of changes to which Piaget refers the concept of number consists of changes in spatial arrangement or physical kind. The quality to be conserved is the "set" or the equivalence of sets.

3. According to the developmental argument, there is an early period during which in judging the numerosity of observed arrays of objects (specifically, in judging whether the number of elements in two rows is the same), children will offer a judgment of what we would describe as spatial extent. Even after having agreed that two rows contain the same number of objects, if one row is spread out, children will say that that row has more.

   During an intermediate period children may be able to construct rows of equal numbers of objects but will still deny their equivalence when one of the rows is spread out. Slightly later on, they may be unsure of the answer (or may get it right in some contexts but not in others) and may count the rows to establish their equivalence.

   Finally, children are able to draw a principled distinction between questions of numerosity and questions of spatial extent. They know that, if two rows of elements contain the same number and if one row is spread out, then the two rows must continue to have the same number. Eventually they will argue spontaneously that (a) the altered row contains the very same elements as it did before (identity); (b) if the row is longer by virtue of having been spread out, then there is, correspondingly, more space between the elements in it (compensation); (c) one could simply "undo" the spreading-out operation by moving the elements together (and without adding or subtracting anything) and produce exactly the same display that one had before (reversibility).

Piaget's conclusion is that the concept of number develops, and this development consists specifically of the progressive dissociation of judgments of number from judgments of spatial extent. This dissociation is motivated, in turn, by children's gradual understanding of arguments (a) through (c), which establish the necessity of the conservation.

I now give a more detailed reconstruction of Piaget's argument, taking each of these three steps in turn.

1. The notion of conservation is central to all rational thought. Piaget theorizes that any notion we have, whether in the realm of common sense or in the realm of scientific understanding, implicitly or explicitly presupposes a set of principles of conservation. Our notions would not be intelligible otherwise, and we could not under these circumstances use them in our thought.

The line of reasoning by which Piaget arrives at this position is complicated and obscure. The steps that seem to be involved are the following (this reconstruction is based primarily on Piaget's opening remarks in CCN, pp. 3–4): (a) For a concept or a notion (e.g., the concept "number") to exist at all, it must have a definition, and this definition must be intelligible. (b) To be intelligible the concept has to remain identical with itself. (c) For the concept to remain identical with itself, the objects or attributes it describes (e.g., the attribute "number") have to remain identical with themselves. (d) To remain identical with themselves, these objects or attributes have to remain unchanged across a given class of transformations, namely, all of those transformations that, according to the concept, are not supposed to change the identity of the objects or attributes defined by the concept. (e) The idea of identity across transformations is the idea of conservation. Thus, concepts such as "number" do not exist or are not intelligible unless they presuppose conservation of the actual attribute "number."

2. The particular class of transformations to which Piaget refers the concept of number consists of changes in the physical arrangement of parts (the elements to be counted). The attribute to be conserved is the "set" or (given Piaget's experimental procedure) the numerical equivalence of two sets.

Piaget says that an individual has the concept of number when that individual knows that the number of elements in some defined group of things remains the same when other physical attributes of those elements or of that group change. These changes include alterations in the spatial arrangement of the elements, alterations in physical kind, and (although not a physical transformation in the elements per se) differences in the order in which the elements are counted (five elements are five elements, regardless of where one starts counting them and regardless of the order in which one proceeds as one counts). Piaget focuses on the changes in spatial arrangement.

Conversely, if an individual cannot or does not preserve quantity across something like a change in the spatial arrangement of a group of objects, that individual does not have an intelligible concept of number. Number is being confused with something else, for example, the spatial extent of the group of things to be counted.

3. The developmental argument, the essentials of which have already been given, is that before a certain age, when asked to judge numerosity (specifically, the numerical equivalence of two rows of objects), children sometimes offer judgments that appear to be based on spatial extent (e.g., the row that is longer has more). Later, they make the numerical judgment reliably and can explain why the spatial transformation they have witnessed is irrelevant to number and hence why their answer must be correct. Piaget's general conclusion is that initially children confuse number with spatial extent and that the development of the concept of number consists of the progressive dissociation of number and spatial extent.

3. One-to-one correspondence

Piaget's emphasis on one-to-one correspondence derives from formal analyses of number, specifically the work of Cantor, who theorized that one-to-one correspondence was the fundamental notion of the concept of number (specifically the concept of integer). Cantor posed this view as an answer to the question "What do we understand by 'number'?," which he formulated as "What do we understand by the notion 'same number'?" At the most fundamental level, the notion "same number," according to Cantor's analysis, is the idea that the elements in two series correspond one for one.

From Cantor's formal argument Piaget extrapolated to the claim that one-to-one correspondence is also the psychological basis of the concept of number within the individual. It is "obviously the tool used by the mind in comparing two sets" (CCN, p. 41). Thus, to study how the individual mind develops the concept of number, Piaget studied how the mind comes to understand one-to-one correspondence. In studying how the mind comes to understand one-to-one correspondence, however, Piaget did not study whether children had any appreciation of one-to-one correspondence, but whether they understood that the one-to-one correspondence of the elements in two sets made those sets equivalent. Conversely, if confronted with the problem of having to choose the same number of elements as were in some presented group of objects, did children understand that one reliable method of achieving this result was selection by one-to-one correspondence?

These questions must be taken one step farther if we are to trace Piaget's inquiry back to the idea of conservation and if we are to understand his experimental procedure. Recall that for Piaget a concept is intelligible if the objects or attributes it describes satisfy certain conditions of identity (i.e., if it is "operational"). Therefore, according to this view, children's concept of number is intelligible (operational) if children think that the actual property, number (or, more precisely, the equivalence of two sets resulting from their one-to-one correspondence), remains identical with itself across "transformations" that do not affect number.

Thus, at least three questions are subsumed by Piaget's question of whether an individual has a (true) concept of number. First, does the individual have any appreciation of one-to-one correspondence? Second, does the individual understand that the one-to-one correspondence between two series of elements establishes the equivalence of those two series (or, conversely, does the individual understand that one-to-one correspondence is a means of constructing equivalent sets?). Third, does the individual "conserve" this equivalence across changes that do not in fact affect the one-to-one correspondence of the elements in the series and hence do not affect their number?

In Piaget's own formulation, the second of these questions becomes the third: To understand that one-to-one correspondence creates the equivalence between two series is to understand that it creates "lasting equivalence" (CCN, p. 42) between the sets in question, in the specific sense that the individual understands that changes that in fact have nothing to do with number do not change number. Piaget associates this understanding with the idea that the equivalence established by the correspondence is "necessary" (pp. 41–2).

4. Method

The tasks that emerge from these considerations are problems that assess subjects' ability both to construct a one-to-one correspondence between two groups of elements and their ability to preserve the equivalence established by this one-to-one correspondence when noticeable but irrelevant changes take place. In the experiments to be considered here, these irrelevant changes have to do with the spatial configuration of the concrete objects in question.

An important feature of these tasks is that the changes in attributes such as spatial extent must be sufficiently salient that a subject will be forced self-consciously to deal with them and consider whether or not number is affected by them. A subject who knows what number is (under Piaget's definition) should know that it is not affected and should know why it is not affected.

Piaget emphasizes that he is not interested in the situation where the constancy in amount can be "directly perceived" (CCN, p. 9), where there is nothing to counteract the judgment that the number is indeed the same. To establish constancy or equivalence under these conditions would be to exhibit only "intuitive" knowledge of number. It is only in the case where the subject consciously compensates for the potentially distorting effects of perception through an "effort of intellectual understanding" (p. 9) that the subject can be said to have an "operational" understanding of number.

I will discuss two of Piaget's tasks. The first and better known task was seen by Piaget as addressing the question of whether children would use one-to-one correspondence as a basis for inferring the ("necessary" and "lasting") equivalence of two sets. The procedure involved prompting children to construct a one-to-one correspondence between two groups of small objects (e.g., bottles and glasses, eggs and egg cups, flowers and vases; in the latter two cases the children began by putting the eggs, for example, in, rather than next to, the egg cups). The children were then questioned about the equivalence of the two rows when one of the rows was transformed spatially. For instance, after the children had agreed that the row of bottles and the row of glasses contained the same number of objects, the experimenter moved the glasses together (or, alternatively, spread them apart) and asked the children if there were as many glasses as bottles. If they said no, they were asked where there were more and why there were more. If they said yes, they were encouraged to elaborate their answers if they did not do so spontaneously. In a variation of the task, the children were prompted to exchange a group of objects (e.g., pennies for flowers) with the experimenter, were then asked to count their own collection, and, finally, to say how many objects the experimenter had. Piaget refers to the whole group of tasks as "provoked correspondence" tasks.

The second kind of task, called "spontaneous correspondence," was intended to address the converse question of whether the children would spontaneously use one-to-one correspondence as a means of establishing (or, more exactly, choosing) the "same number" of something. The children were presented with groups of counters arranged into spatial figures of different kinds and were asked simply to choose from a box the same number of counters as were in the figure. The purpose of presenting the different figures was to see if the children would select the method of one-to-one comparison of the objects over the alternative of attempting globally to reproduce the figure. Finally, those children who were able to produce a one-to-one correspondence were questioned about the numerical equivalence of the two displays under various spatial transformations, as in the provoked correspondence tasks.

The most important feature of the spontaneous correspondence tasks was that the children were never told to select or compare the elements one for one. They were told only to look at the figure in front of them and to choose the same number of counters.

Most of the children tested on either series of tasks (provoked vs.

spontaneous) were between 4 and 7 years of age. The "stages"[1] Piaget distinguishes for each task correspond roughly to age, within this range. For both the provoked and the spontaneous tasks, the results of the different versions of the basic task were generally consistent. The same types of response were seen with all versions, and they appeared in the same chronological sequence. The only differences were some local acceleration effects, all in the expected direction. Accordingly, in the ensuing presentation of results I will concentrate on the common trends.

5. Results: provoked correspondence

Piaget distinguished three broad stages in the children's responses to the provoked correspondence tasks. In the first stage the children could neither construct an exact correspondence themselves nor preserve the equivalence of the two sets of objects (after having agreed they were equivalent) once the rows were transformed spatially. In the second stage, the children could construct the one-to-one correspondence but did not conserve the equivalence of the two rows after the transformation. In the third stage the children both constructed exact correspondences and argued that the rows remained equivalent, even after they were transformed spatially. In the exchange version of the task, the children at the third stage immediately gave the correct number (when asked how many objects the experimenter had) upon counting their own group of objects. A more detailed description of these stages follows.

The children at the first stage were distinguished not only by their failure to produce an exact one-to-one correspondence, but by what they did instead. A common procedure was to take most or all of the glasses, eggs, and so forth, from the tray and align them in front of the corresponding objects so that the rows matched in length but not in number. Similarly, in the conservation part of the task, one child, who initially said there were more glasses (the row of glasses extended beyond the row of bottles at that point), spontaneously pushed the glasses together "because

---

[1] I am using "stage" here and elsewhere to refer to a type of response, not to the general status of the child across a variety of tasks or to all responses a child might make within the same task.

that makes them less" and then agreed that the two rows now had the same number of bottles (Car, 5;2, CCN, p. 43).[2] In the exchange problems as well, children at the first stage denied the equivalence of two groups of exchanged objects and were also unable to infer how many objects the experimenter had (they either guessed or said they did not know).

In the second stage the children easily made the one-to-one correspondence in the standard (nonexchange) problems. However, they denied the equivalence of the two rows of objects once one of the rows was spread out or moved together: "because [the vases] are spread out" (Sim, 5;7, CCN, p. 52), because "there are more where it's bigger" (Mul, 5;3, p. 45). At the same time, some of these children also agreed (in the flower–vase, egg–egg cups version of the task) that, if the flowers were returned to their vases or the eggs to their cups, they would correspond one for one, but they continued to deny the equivalence as long as the rows in front of them were of unequal length (Aud, 6;7, p. 59).

In the exchange tasks, children at this stage conducted an even exchange with the experimenter and could make the equivalence explicit: One could buy "three flowers . . . because there are three pennies" (Par, 5;2, CCN, p. 58). They also readily counted the correct number of objects with which they emerged at the end of the exchange. Nonetheless, they did not infer from this the number of flowers or other objects the experimenter had, and they denied the equivalence of the two exchanged groups of objects if the objects were not organized in parallel, even after they had correctly counted the two groups (Fur, 5;9, p. 58; Aug, 6;7, p. 59).

At the third stage the children not only preserved the equivalence of the different series of elements regardless of their rearrangement, but explained why the equivalence was lasting: "You've only put them close together, but it's still the same number [of glasses]" (Lau, 6;2, CCN, p. 47). In the flower–vase and egg–egg cups problems some of the children pointed out that one had only to put the flowers back in the vases (or the eggs back in the cups) to see that the number was the same. In the exchange task, the children defended their answer that the two groups of objects were the same or defended their estimate of how many

---

[2] The notation 5;2 denotes 5 years and 2 months of age.

objects the experimenter had either by appeal to the fact that one could pair the objects one for one (Ler, 5;8, p. 60) or through reference to the exchange that had actually occurred: They are the same, "because I gave you my pennies" (Clav, 5;8, p. 61).

In summary, when asked to produce a numerical equivalence (specifically, when asked to put out the same number of objects, one for one, as were in an already formed group of things or when asked to exchange a group of objects one for one), some children attempted to match the overall spatial form of the group of objects they saw, but not the exact number. An intermediate response ensued, in which children produced the numerical equivalence (specifically, a spatial one-to-one correspondence) but judged whether the rows were equivalent on the basis of spatial extent. In the final stage children judged equivalence numerically, that is, on the basis of counting or direct one-to-one correspondence. They also "conserved" numerical equivalence across changes in spatial configuration and could explain why this equivalence held: One only spread them out; if one put them back, they would match one for one.

Piaget draws two major conclusions from these results. First, he infers that initially children confuse number with other properties, such as the spatial extent of the group of entities to be counted. The development of number, according to this view, consists in the children's progressive extraction of number from this initial nondifferentiation. Second, Piaget believes he has documented that one-to-one correspondence is insufficient by itself to generate notions of numerical equivalence or cardinal number (he attributes the view that it is sufficient to various other authors). One-to-one correspondence (or one-for-one exchange) has to become "operational" (CCN, p. 61) for these notions to result.

The evidence for this conclusion is that children can produce and recognize one-to-one correspondences (stage II) before they use one-to-one correspondence as a basis for establishing the "necessary, lasting" (CCN, p. 65) equivalence of the sets being compared, that is, before they "conserve" the equivalence of the two sets after the spatial correspondence of the elements has been destroyed (stage III). On the basis of this progression of stages, Piaget argues that the latter understanding (necessary, lasting equivalence) arises not through the development of the idea of correspondence itself, but through a more advanced "operation" (pp. 56, 61). With this operation the children either "equalize the differences" (p. 56) that are created by the spatial transformations of the sets or insert the correspondence of the elements in a "reversible system of displacements and relations" (p. 61). In the latter case Piaget is referring to children's recognition that, once the spatial correspondence is destroyed, the objects can be put back in one-to-one correspondence and can thereby be shown to be equal in number.

6. Results: spontaneous correspondence

By Piaget's account, the results of the spontaneous correspondence task fall into three stages paralleling the stages of the provoked correspondence tasks. Children at the first stage tried only to reproduce the overall shape of the model figure. They did not match the objects in the figure one for one. When the model figure was a single row, for example, the children simply copied the length of the row. When questioned subsequently about whether the two figures (model and reproduction) had the same number of counters, they generally agreed that they did (provided that the overall length or shape was the same). If the experimenter intervened and changed the length or shape of the figures, the children denied the equivalence, even when the figures had been adjusted by the experimenter so that they had the same number.

At the second stage, the children selected the counters one for one in accordance with the model figure. However, they did this only in the context of attempting to copy the overall shape of the figure at the same time. Critically for Piaget, as soon as one of the configurations was altered, the children denied the equivalence of the number of counters in the two figures.

In the third stage not only did the children produce a one-for-one correspondence with ease, but they did not bother to copy the form of the model figure. In selecting the counters to match the number of counters in a model figure that was a single row, for example, some children simply placed the selected objects into a pile. Further, when dealing with complicated model figures (e.g., unfamiliar geometric forms, such as a rhombus, or badly structured figures), the children sometimes deformed the model (e.g., by aligning the objects in it two by two) to make the selection task easier. Finally, these children continued to insist on the equivalence of the two groups of objects after the experimenter spatially transformed them. Once again, they offered reasons such as "because you've put them closer together" (Fet, 5;5, CCN p. 82).

Piaget finds in this sequence confirmation of the theoretical view he elaborated on the basis of the provoked correspondence tasks. Children initially confuse number with properties of spatial configuration, and the development of number consists in the children's progressive extraction of number from these other properties. Piaget argues once again that the pivotal acquisition in this development is not the procedure of one-to-one correspondence per se, but the reversibility in thought that allows children to cancel the effects of changes in such properties as the length and density of an array.

He sees this reversibility in thought (and the resulting "compensation" between such factors as length and density) as coming about in the following way. After the initial period (stage I), in which children judge number by length or density alone, a period (stage II) ensues during which, Piaget thinks, children consider length and density simultaneously but in which this "coordination" (CCN, p. 81) is only perceptual.

The reason Piaget thinks that children now consider length and density simultaneously is that his subjects matched the elements one for one in reproducing the model figures. In addition, when the experimenter rearranged one of the rows spatially and the children thought the rows were no longer equivalent, the children at this stage frequently attempted to restore the equivalence by rearranging one of the groups and reproducing the spatial correspondence. For instance, if the experimenter spread out one row of objects, the children would spread out their row or else compress the experimenter's row. Piaget says that children who are otherwise classed at the first stage exhibit instead a tendency to add or subtract objects under the same circumstances (perusal of the protocols in the text suggests that both reactions actually appear at both stages).

The connection of these two developments (producing exact spatial correspondences and restoring apparent "nonequivalences" by spatial rearrangement) with the coordination of length and density appears to be as follows. In the first case (producing exact correspondences), paying attention to length or density alone is not enough to allow children to pair the elements one for one. Therefore, they must pay attention to both. In the second case (restoring apparent nonequivalences by spatial rearrangement), the same logic applies. If in rearranging the objects, children paid attention to length or density alone, they would not be able to restore the one-for-one correspondence between the objects in the two figures. An additional coordinative feature of this case is that children "reverse" the initial action that disrupted the correspondence in order to reproduce it.

Piaget thinks that this coordination of length and density is only perceptual at this stage for two reasons. One is that children produce the numerical correspondence only by reproducing the spatial figure. Thus, the idea of one-to-one (i.e., quantitative) correspondence is wedded to the idea of spatial correspondence. At the third stage, by comparison, children select the new objects one for one without necessarily reproducing the spatial form of the model figure and may even decompose the model figure in the process. Hence, at that stage numerical correspondence is independent of any spatial correspondence. The second reason Piaget thinks that the coordination of length and density at stage II is only perceptual is that, as soon as the spatial correspondence is disrupted (e.g., when the experimenter spreads out one of the rows), numerical correspondence and equivalence are denied, and, in effect, the coordination of length and density is denied. Children judge numerosity on the basis of length or density alone, rather than considering both together and possible compensations between them.

At the third stage the coordination between length and density becomes "operational." Not only are numerical correspondences produced independently of spatial arrangement, but it is understood both that any (spatially transforming) action can be undone by its inverse and that the (spatial) consequences of action in either direction compensate for one another. If a given row of objects is spread out so that it becomes longer than it was before (or longer than some corresponding row of objects), there is also a greater distance than there was before between the objects in the row. Thus, there is no reason, on this basis alone, to conclude that the number of objects in the row has changed (or has become different from the number of objects in the corresponding row).

Therefore, at the third stage, number has become detached from spatial considerations and has become embedded in a system of relationships that guarantees this independence.

NUMBER: CRITIQUE

I begin this critique with brief mention of a confusion in Piaget's initial framing of the problem of the concept of number. The confusion occurs in the original presentation of the notion of conservation.

On the one hand, Piaget says that "any attempt by thought to build up a system of notions requires a certain permanence in their definitions" (CCN, p. 3). This statement suggests that what must be "conserved" are the definitions of concepts or the concepts themselves, as opposed to the entities to which they refer. So the claim would be that, to think about "number" at all, one's definition of what a number is must remain invariant.

On the other hand, Piaget's entire discussion of conservation, in the *Number* book and elsewhere, presupposes that what must be conserved is not the individual's concept of number but the thing to which that concept refers. What is at stake is whether one thinks that "number" is itself a property that remains invariant across changes in other properties.

For the attribute "number" (or "quantity") to remain identical with itself is not the same thing as the concept or definition of number remaining identical with itself. I might grasp perfectly well the idea that the number of objects in an array remains the same across changes in the spatial arrangement of those objects and yet my concept of what a number is might be unstable or ill defined. Conversely, I might have a very stable concept of number and yet confound my judgment of numerosity with judgments of spatial extent.

It is clear from Piaget's writings that the problem Piaget actually investigated is the second one: How do children come to see that number is a property that remains invariant across certain changes either in the components of that property or in the contexts in which number is a matter of concern? As I indicated in my reconstruction of Piaget's argument about the centrality of conservation to thought, it appears that Piaget may have seen this problem as a particular instance of the problem about the conservation of concepts of definitions. I only wish to point out that this translation cannot be made, and certainly not a priori, as Piaget appears to have done.

For the remainder of the critique I will assume that Piaget is referring to this second sense of conservation, namely the conservation of the entities or attributes to which the concepts under question refer. Another of Piaget's prefatory remarks deserves mention, however, before I begin the critique proper.

Regarding the second sense of conservation, Piaget comments that "a set or collection is only conceivable if it remains unchanged irrespective of the changes occurring in the relationship between the elements. . . . A number is only intelligible if it remains identical with itself, whatever the distribution of the units of which it is composed" (CCN, p. 3).

Two problems immediately arise in connection with these comments. First, to the extent that Piaget is concerned with the conditions under which sets are "conceivable" or number is "intelligible," he would seem to be presupposing an agent who had some intuition of "set" and "number." Otherwise questions about the "intelligibility" of "set" and "number" could not be asked. It would seem that one main purpose of the study of the developmental origins of "number" would be precisely to discover when these intuitions can be said to be present and how they come about. So as eventually emerged in the study of morality, Piaget is potentially preparing the reader for an account that may bypass important foundational questions.

Second, the comments I have cited are misleading insofar as they refer to conservation across the permuting of mathematical entities, whereas Piaget's actual tasks involve the "permuting" of concrete objects that could be represented in terms of their "number." It is not clear what kind of connection there is, or ought to be, between an individual's understanding of the "permuting" of concrete objects and his or her understanding of the "permuting" of mathematical entities. There might be little or no connection, or else a very complicated one. In either case we would again have to question the relevance of Piaget's investigation to the development of the concept of number.

For the present, however, we can defer these abstract questions and examine Piaget's account. Do conservation and the other constructs and findings Piaget discusses illuminate children's development of the concept of number? I will argue that the account presupposes, rather than describes or explains, this development. In addition, Piaget's preoccupation with conservation leads him to overlook important pieces of numerical cognition that his own subjects appear to have demonstrated. I deal, in turn, with three topics to which these problems seem to apply: (a) children's understanding of the relation between correspondence and equivalence, (b) Piaget's developmental claim that the concept of number arises through children's dissociation of numerical and spatial judgments, and (c) a more detailed version of the second claim specifying the actual process through which changes in children's ideas would take place.

1. Correspondence and equivalence

As I described earlier, Piaget believed one-to-one correspondence was the foundation of the concept of number and therefore set out to examine (a) whether young children could arrange objects in a one-to-one correspondence and (b) whether they inferred from such arrangements that the number of elements in the corresponding sets was, or had to be, equivalent. With a few minor exceptions, however, Piaget generally transposed the second of these questions into a third: Having agreed with the experimenter that the number of elements in two spatially corresponding rows was the same, did his subjects *continue* to agree that the number was the same after one of the rows had been rearranged (spread out or pushed together) and the spatial correspondence thereby disrupted? Piaget reformulated the question in this way, it seems, because he thought that this reformulation addressed the issue of whether the children had established a "lasting equivalence" between the two rows. "Lasting" equivalence was important, in turn, because one-to-one correspondence was supposed to establish a "necessary" equivalence between two sets. If the children constructed a "lasting" equivalence (across changes in spatial arrangement), then, according to Piaget, this would be an indication that they understood that a one-to-one correspondence creates a necessary equivalence.

The difficulty with this formulation is that the question of whether the children sustained the *equivalence* across the changes in spatial arrangement may have little to do with whether they initially used the *correspondence* to establish this equivalence. It is presumably the question of whether the correspondence was used as a means of establishing the equivalence that is of primary importance to the concept of number, given Piaget's views about the concept of number.

Consider the concrete argument. Suppose children deny (as many of Piaget's subjects did) that the two rows remain equivalent in number after the transformations have taken place. Piaget concludes that the *"correspondence* is not adequate to give true equivalence" (CCN, p. 41, my emphasis). All that has happened, however, is that children no longer believe in the *equivalence.* There could be many reasons for this, only one of which is Piaget's: that children fail to appreciate the implications of the original correspondence (i.e., that it means that the two rows are, or have to be, equivalent). Children's difficulty could also be that they can no longer construct a correspondence (mentally) from the array, they have forgotten about the original correspondence, or if they are reminded of it they still cannot accept that the objects indeed correspond one for one (or that the rows are otherwise equivalent) at that moment.

Some of the reactions Piaget describes as supporting his thesis are at least as consistent with the alternative view that children do understand the implications of one-to-one correspondence and subsequently deny the equivalence of the two groups of objects for some other reason. Consider, for example, Piaget's reference to the stage I children who, after judging that the transformed rows were not equivalent, were surprised to find that the objects did correspond one for one when they were returned to their original positions (e.g., Zu, CCN, p. 51). This surprise reaction suggests that under the spatial transformation the children (or at least this child) thought that the objects did not correspond one for one. If the children thought that the objects did not correspond one for one, it would be appropriate for them to conclude that the number of objects in the two rows was not the same. That is, it would be appropriate under our conception of the relation between correspondence and equivalence. It would also be appropriate for them, under the same circumstances, to be surprised when the objects turned out not to correspond one for one.

Similarly, recall the protocols from the spontaneous correspondence tasks in which children at stages I and II (Piaget explicitly noted only the stage I cases, but the response seems to have occurred at both stages) added or subtracted elements when they erroneously concluded that the transformed rows were of unequal number. If the children actually thought that the number of objects in the two rows was unequal, they were correct (in our view) to add or subtract objects. The alternative would have been to elongate or collapse one of the rows, but this would not have changed the number.

Thus, in this as in the preceding example, the error children make seems to lie in their direct estimate of the numerosity (or one-to-one correspondence) of the concrete arrays with which they are dealing. It may not lie in the way they interrelate the operations that make use of these estimates, that is, operations that we associate with number.

So Piaget may be correct in claiming that the basis of children's estimates of whether two rows are equivalent may change, and in the way he describes. Initially, children may have a tendency to estimate number on the basis of spatial extent, and they may, as Piaget says, need to see a spatial one-to-one correspondence of elements in order to believe that those elements do in fact correspond one for one *and therefore come to the same number*. It may be wrong, however, to draw implications from these findings relating to the immediate *judgment* of numerosity to questions concerning children's *concept* of number, "concept" referring in this case to children's understanding of what one-to-one correspondence means.[3]

2. The development of number

This problem of the relation between numerical judgment and children's concept of number leads me to my second point of criticism. My concern here is with what Piaget claims is the developmental sequence of the concept of number in children. Piaget's argument is roughly as follows. Initially, children appear to confuse judgments of number with judgments of spatial extent. Later they judge number independently of considerations of spatial extent, and they can explain why considerations of spatial extent are irrelevant to that judgment. Piaget's conclusion is that initially children's concept of number involves a confusion of number with properties such as spatial extent, and the development of the

---

[3] Similar conclusions have been reached in empirical investigations of Piaget's results (e.g., Bryant, 1974; Gelman, 1972).

concept of number consists precisely (or in part, if one takes into account the other topics Piaget covers in his book, e.g., order, additivity) of the progressive dissociation of number from these other properties.

From the fact that children initially rely on spatial extent to judge numerosity, however, it does not follow that their concept of number, or their numerical reasoning, involves a confusion of number with spatial properties. All that has been shown, once again, is that children may use spatial extent as an indicator of numerosity. As I have just argued, the numerical inferences children draw from their numerical judgments may be properly "numerical" and perfectly logical but incorrect.

Similarly, it does not follow from the fact that children eventually resolve this confusion of spatial and numerical judgment that the *development* of the concept of number is the development of the ability to disentangle judgments of numerosity and judgments of spatial extent. We must ask first what the concept is behind the "numerical" judgment that children progressively disentangle and how *this concept* changes. Given children's tendency to conflate numerical and spatial judgments, to find out about this concept, we as analysts should perhaps rely exactly on spatial extent (and other cues) to draw out children's numerical concepts and intuitions. This is the opposite of what Piaget has done.[4]

Suppose, however, we accept that at some point one thing we will want to know about children's numerical abilities is the process through which children come to dissociate numerical and spatial (or other contextual) judgments, in other words, the problem Piaget investigated. Piaget has proposed some hypotheses regarding this developmental process, and it is these I now wish to

---

[4] In suggesting that we rely "exactly" on children's dependence on spatial cues in order to study their numerical thought, I have in mind numerical thought (e.g., the relation between one-to-one correspondence and equivalence) other than the "conservation" of number, or the discrimination of number from nonnumerical cues. Here Piaget quite convincingly points out that, if it is conservation understanding one wants to study, one must provide children with nonnumerical cues (i.e., "transformations") that will be salient enough that the children will have to deal with them. "Conservation" loses its meaning otherwise. My point is that this understanding is not unambiguously "numerical" and that if one wants to study cognition that is more clearly numerical, Piaget's results suggest a design opposite to the one he adopted.

examine. It appears here that Piaget has again drawn some quite arbitrary connections.

Piaget's question is, How do children come to sustain their judgments of numerical equality (or inequality) across purely spatial transformations in an array? His answer is that they eventually perceive the compensation between the length and density of the array or envision that the disrupted correspondence could be reinstated if one merely moved the objects back to their original positions.

The difficulty here is that, although children may be able to generate arguments of this sort when they are asked to justify their judgments, it does not follow that the judgments themselves were based on these justifications.[5] Over time, children may come simply to ignore the spatial configuration of arrays about which they are asked numerical questions and may consider only whether a one-to-one correspondence exists, whether anything has been added or taken away, and so forth. Indeed, to argue, as some of Piaget's subjects did, that "you only spread them out" may be only to argue that nothing has been added or taken away. Although the same children can *also* "equalize the differences" (e.g., between length and density), this may not be why they believe the rows are equivalent.

Piaget's argument about children at stage II poses a similar problem. This is the stage at which in both the spontaneous and provoked correspondence tasks children produce exact one-to-one correspondences. Children at this stage do not, however, judge two arrays to be equivalent once the correspondence is disrupted, and they may assert that there is an equivalence when the rows correspond in length but not in number. Further, in the reproduction tasks (spontaneous correspondence), any exact correspondence that Piaget's subjects achieved was accompanied by an exact reproduction of the spatial figure that served as a model. Piaget's argument is that the correspondences that children achieve at this stage must be the result of their ability to consider length and density simultaneously. The justification for this argument is essentially the opposing case: If children paid attention only to length or density alone (as do children at stage I), they would not be able to achieve these correspondences.

[5] See Halford (1982, ch. 8) for an illuminating discussion of some related points.

But from the fact that attention to length or density alone would preclude the correspondence, we cannot automatically conclude that children's ability to construct the correspondence depends on their ability to coordinate length and density. Instead children may focus on pairing the objects one for one, and when they do so they have simply stopped paying attention to such global factors as length and density. Indeed, it would probably be difficult to think about these factors while one is trying to match the objects one for one at the same time. It seems more plausible that children might *either* try to match the objects one for one *or* pay attention to length and density, but not both simultaneously.

Thus, Piaget has no clear grounds on which to argue, as he seems to do, that the actual process through which children come to produce one-to-one correspondences is a coordination of length and density. The *products* that result from this process (i.e., the actual one-to-one correspondence configurations) can be described as exhibiting this coordination, but that is not the same thing. Alternatively, Piaget may think that his thesis (that the products come about because children go through a process of coordinating length and density) is justified by the fact that there is an earlier stage of development in which children focus on length or density alone; the contrast is not merely hypothetical. To think that this justifies the coordination thesis, however, is to suppose, as Piaget also does in *Child's conception of the world,* that there is something that children must "undo" in order to move onward in development. But they need not do this to stop using length and density and start using one-to-one correspondence to align the rows. They may simply develop a new strategy that supersedes the old one, although they may fall back on the old one under certain circumstances (e.g., the actual conservation probe).

It will be useful to summarize this second point of criticism thus far. Piaget extracts three interrelated conclusions from the fact that children initially judge numerosity on the basis of spatial extent and so on and later separate their numerical and spatial evaluations. The first conclusion is that children's "concept" of number is initially fused with their apprehension of spatial properties. The second conclusion is that the development of the concept of number consists in developing the ability to separate numerical and spatial considerations. Third, this separation of numerical and spatial judgment comes about through children's growing ability to "cancel out" the spatial effects on the basis of which they have been making their judgments.

None of these conclusions seems warranted by the empirical sequence Piaget reports, and alternative hypotheses of equal or greater plausibility can be shown to be compatible with the data. Further, insofar as Piaget's questions (e.g., when do children "conserve" number across changes in spatial arrangement?) presuppose that certain basic mathematical intuitions are already in place (e.g., the intuition that one-to-one correspondence between two groups of elements means that the two groups have the same number), the "developmental" account tells us neither what these intuitions are nor how they come about.

Even if the data are inadequate, however, it is still plausible that children do not initially associate number with discrete quantity when they are first alerted to the idea of number through people's reference to it. When small children are first shown counting, or when they first hear that there are certain numbers of things ("There are two socks"), for example, they might, as Piaget's account suggests, connect number with something more vague than discrete quantity.[6] The attribute with which they connect it might be more closely related to global spatial extent or other spatial properties. Far simpler problems (or naturalistic observations) than Piaget's problems would be necessary to canvass the relevant possibilities. However, to explore the full consequences of Piaget's theory, I will next adopt the a priori assumption that children begin with the inchoate sense of number to which Piaget seems to allude, and follow out the account from there.

3. The development of number from inchoate origins

Piaget himself raises the possibility that initially such number terms as are used and "understood" by children refer not to discrete elements or discrete quantity, but to some indeterminate

---

[6] I merely note that this question is different from, and somewhat independent of, the question of whether infants and young children can discriminate what we would call discrete quantity, for example, in discrimination learning or habituation tasks. The latter question is frequently investigated by contemporary researchers (e.g., Starkey & Cooper, 1980). Even if infants and young children do discriminate "number" on these measures, they would not automatically attach number terms to discrete quantity when they are first exposed to them.

combination of numerosity and space occupied (CCN, p. 48). This position leads, however, to an immediate discrepancy with Piaget's account of the conservation results. I will discuss this problem briefly and then turn to the primary concern of this section, namely, how Piaget envisions that children develop beyond their initial inchoate sense of number.

If, as Piaget says, children's understanding of number is indeterminate as between quantity and space occupied, the "number" that is not conserved when the children deny the equivalence of the two rows in Piaget's experiments is only our sense of number. If the children actually think that "number" is tantamount to the space occupied, then they are not being inconsistent when they assert that the longer row has more than the shorter row. Under their concept of number, the rows are no longer equivalent. Hence (again under their concept of number), they cannot be said to be "failing to conserve the equivalence of the two rows."

Piaget might agree and point out that the conservation tasks were intended to demonstrate exactly this point. One can gauge what children's concept of number must be according to the conditions under which they will and will not conserve "number." This is a reasonable line of analysis, up to a point. As I argued in the two preceding sections, this procedure has distinct limitations, the most important of which is that it may lead one to overlook important numerical knowledge (e.g., the knowledge that two groups of elements contain the same number if the elements correspond one to one) the children actually have and demonstrate right within the conservation task.

Let us, however, pursue the implications of the possibility that initially children's concept of number is indeterminate as between spatial extent (mass, density, etc.) and what we would call quantity. How, then, are children to discover true quantity?

Piaget makes several suggestions. One is that insofar as children vacillate among different bases for judgment (e.g., density vs. length) they will generate contradictory results. The same row will be judged to have more, for example, when the judgment is based on length and less when the judgment is based on density. Alternatively, children will begin to see that, when the row gets longer, it also gets less dense. A third possibility is that children begin to see that actions that change the physical shape of the array (e.g., that lengthen it) can also be undone and the array returned to its original state.

Piaget thinks that by making these observations, children will eventually recognize the constancy of the set (CCN, p. 90) and hence extract quantity from the spatial form of the collection of elements to be enumerated (p. 89). I will now attempt to demonstrate that to argue for this thesis in the way he does, however, Piaget must either presuppose the end state he is trying to explain or else must fail to account for children's progress toward it.

Consider the first of the three motivating experiences I just enumerated: Children will judge the same row to have more and less, depending on the cue to which they are attending at that moment. This observation should bother them only if they have some reason to expect their judgment of the numerosity of the row to remain the same. What might this reason be? It would have to be some belief along the lines that the transformations of spreading things out and moving them together do not change number, or that nothing was added or taken away. But these are exactly the beliefs that are supposed to be developing. From children's vantage point (according to the "inchoate origins" theory) "spread out" *is* more, and "pushed together" *is* less.

Consider the second condition: Children will begin to see that when the row gets longer it also gets thinner. Presumably Piaget finds this potential observation pertinent because, if children are inclined to treat both length and density as indices of numerosity, they may find themselves attempting to conclude simultaneously that the same array has both more and less. This condition thus resolves into the first condition, which is that insofar as the basis of children's numerical judgments vacillates between length and density they will end up concluding that the same row has both more and less. Hence, the same objection applies: In order for the simultaneous (or sequential) conclusions of both "more" and "less" to bother them, children would have to have some reason to believe that the same row cannot have both more and less. The kinds of reasons that could form the basis of this belief would seem to be exactly the developments Piaget is trying to explain.

There is another, slightly different way in which Piaget might see the second condition as a potentially productive perturbation for children. Having decided that length and density compensate for one another, children might infer that the conclusion about numerosity that might have been reached on the basis of the one cue is canceled out on the basis of the other. Suppose children did make an abstract inference of this sort. What then? They would still have to deduce from this conclusion that therefore the actual number of things in the row would have to be the same. Alternatively, they would have to deduce that "number" must be neither length nor density but something else (presumably what we know to be discrete quantity). It is not at all clear, within the confines of the theory, how children would arrive at these deductions.

Finally, consider the third condition I cited as a potential catalyst for children's discovery of true quantity. This condition was that children will begin to appreciate that actions such as lengthening the array can be undone, with the result that the array will return to its original state. Again there is the problem of connecting this observation to judgments of numerosity. Children spread the row out and think that there are more. Then they push the row together and think that there are fewer. But they also notice that "pushing together" just reverses "spreading apart." Everything is back where it was before; the row looks just as it did before. Somehow this observation is supposed to change children's opinion about the number of things in the row.

How might this change come about? Maybe children see not only that "pushing together" just reverses "spreading apart" and brings everything back to where it was before, but that their judgment of "how many" returns to what it was before. For instance, if previously they thought the row in question had "fewer" than some comparison row, maybe they now see that they are again saying that it has "fewer." It would still remain for them, however, to draw the correct inference from *this* observation. They would still have to infer that therefore the number of things in the row has remained the same or that this return of their judgment to its previous state (e.g., "fewer") is more important for some ultimate judgment of numerosity than are the cues (such as length) to which they otherwise attend. That is, something has to convince them that in expanding and then contracting again the row did not just go from "fewer" to "more" to "fewer."

We could go on and differentiate ever finer "catalyzing" opportunities that children might have, and as Piaget (e.g., 1974/1980a, 1974/1980b, 1975/1985) did in some of his later work. The most this effort seems to accomplish, however, is a deferral of the central problem one more step (see chapter 6). For instance, we might attempt to salvage the third condition I discussed by attributing to children some concept of gross identity of the row of objects: The row is the same mass of material, regardless, for example, of the elongations and contractions it may undergo. This concept of gross identity might then be seen to give priority to judgments of "same number" as before or "same judgment of number as I made before" over fluctuating judgments of the same row (there are more if it is longer and fewer if it is shorter). There will still be the problem, however, of explaining how children would get from this notion of gross identity to the concept of discrete quantity, or the concept of constancy with respect to discrete quantity. Alternatively, if children really operate under a conception of gross identity, we would have to explain how they eventually decide that changes such as the addition and subtraction of an element, but not changes such as elongation and contraction (of the "mass" of things), alter the number of things in the array. Hence, Piaget would again be leaving us without an account of how true quantity arises.

The main problem here, as with the preceding accounts, is not that Piaget fails to provide a causal explanation for the development of "number." It is that, by construing what he is doing as attempting to provide this explanation, he is pushed more and more either to omit crucial analyses of what children understand or to make highly arbitrary assumptions about it. The more he differentiates the account in the way I have just demonstrated, the more abitrary these assumptions become. This general problem, which can be seen as an impoverishment of *description* in the theory, is the heart of my critique and the ultimate focus of the next chapter.

5

Infancy

Piaget wrote three works on infancy: *The origins of intelligence in children, The construction of reality in the child,* and *Play, dreams, and imitation in childhood.* Together, these books contain the richest and most thematic series of observations in the published literature on the cognitive development of children. Through the analysis of these observations Piaget attempts to give an account both of the infant's eye view of the world and of the development of this view from its ostensively meager beginnings at birth to the very considerable advances that appear to occur by 18 months of age.

Thus, we meet again the synchronic and diachronic programs that Piaget pursued in his works on children's thought. In a way the infancy works are the culmination of these two programs. With respect to the synchronic program, it is far more difficult to determine the infant's eye view of the world than it is to determine the child's eye view. Whereas one can simply ask children what they think or instruct them in such a way that they will reveal their thought, one must infer the whole nature of infants' mental life from their behavior. As for the diachronic program, although developmental change is, if anything, more clearly marked during infancy than it is during any other period in the life cycle, Piaget set himself a far more ambitious goal regarding development during infancy than he did regarding later development. That goal was to show how all of human intelligence could arise from the functioning of a few reflexes.

Even a more modest aim would have set the infancy work apart. The idea that some connection exists between child and adult thought is relatively uncontroversial. With infancy it is not as clear what sort of connection with adult thought one ought to look for or indeed whether one ought to seek any connection at all (some of Piaget's early critics voiced concerns of this type; see the preface to the second edition of OI and the introduction to PDI). Piaget insisted, however, that development in infancy involved essential preparation for adult thought, even though, he believed, infants do not think in the same sense that adults and children do.

In Piaget's view, what infants do is act. We have no reason to assume, according to Piaget, that reflective or discursive thought runs alongside this action or independently of it. Doing *is* thinking, insofar as it is appropriate to speak of thought at all. Piaget's central (diachronic) thesis regarding infancy is that this action lays the basis for reflective thought and constitutes its point of origin.

Piaget's central task, then, is to establish this connection between action and thought. He fails, and in a way that ultimately can be specified quite precisely. The account is no less fascinating for its failure, however. Further, as was the case in the preceding chapters, the analysis of Piaget's failure points the way toward some of the work remaining to be done.

I will discuss two of the three infancy works: *The origins of intelligence* and *The construction of reality*. These two works form a unit. In *Origins* Piaget attempted to describe the developing structure of intelligent action. How is infants' action in the world organized, and how does that organization change? In what way might these patterns be said to be intelligent, and how might the whole developmental sequence of patterns define a continuum of increasing (or increasingly higher order) intelligence? In *Construction of reality* Piaget examined what he considered to be the converse side of the problem of intelligent action, namely the question of how children interpret the world in which they act.

Origins is the more foundational work and was written first. However, I will consider the two books in reverse order, so that I will end with the more foundational questions. I will reconstruct each book in turn and then proceed to my critique.

RECONSTRUCTION

1. Reality

For Piaget, the question of how infants interpret their world had specifically to do with their conceptions of object, space, causality, and time. These are four basic categories of reality for the adult. They are basic, not in the sense that they are reflected on directly and consciously, but in the sense that our actions and reactions in the world and our ordinary discourse presuppose them. Our actions are such that we must assume, for example, that an object that is here one moment will not be gone the next, unless it has been moved. If it is moved such that it is no longer visible, we assume that it still exists somewhere and can in principle be found. We also assume that the object has a reverse side, and when we are viewing this reverse side we assume that we are dealing with the same object as before and not with some new object. Similarly, we assume that there are causes that are independent of our own action and therefore that events can come to pass without our intervention. Piaget's question was whether infants make the same assumptions about the world.

In asking whether infants make these assumptions, Piaget again was not asking whether infants have articulate or conscious concepts of object, space, and so forth; he was asking what concepts of object, space, and so forth are implicit in their ways of acting in the world. Given infants' total repertory of action patterns at a given stage, what minimal assumptions about object, space, and so forth do infants have to make to behave as they do?

Piaget's classic answer to this question was that initially infants do not make the same assumptions about object, space, causality, and time that adults do. Their world is not populated by substantial and permanent objects, and the "images" they do perceive are not located in a homogeneous space or within coherent temporal or causal series.

What infants experience, according to Piaget, is a "world of pictures each one of which can be known and analyzed but which disappear and reappear capriciously" (CR, pp. 3–4). These pictures are known by infants only in relation to their own activity. However, the pictures are indistinguishable from that activity, and the activity is indistinguishable from the pictures. There is, as Piaget would have it, a "radical egocentrism" (p. xiii), in which self and world are completely fused. At the same time there is a "phenomenalism" without self-perception (p. xiii), that is, a sense of the world that takes appearance for reality. In this world the subject's own activity and sensations count among the perceived appearances and as such are indistinguishable from what we know to be truly external objects and events.

Thus, the point of origin for the infant's reality is the motor and perceptual (Piaget would call it "sensorimotor") analogue of the point of origin of the child's reflective concept of reality, as described in *The child's conception of the world*. Piaget drew on this parallel in discussing the relation between infant intelligence and later thought. I will review this discussion at the end of the reconstruction of the two infancy works.

To continue with the account of infancy, if initially infants know a reality that comes to no more than what we know to be their activity, it is nonetheless through that very activity that they will construct a reality of (external and "objective") objects, space, causality, and time. More specifically, as infants grow older, their actions will both differentiate and become organized in new ways. Through this progressive differentiation and reorganization of their actions, they will be led, by around 18 months of age, to conceive a world of substantial objects and objective space, time, and causality. They will, in short, conceive a world that is independent of and external to themselves and, in parallel, conceive of themselves "from the outside," as elements within that world.

A footnote to this part of Piaget's argument is that the discussion is ambiguous about whether the differentiation and organization of action leads to, in the sense of causes, a growing awareness of an external world or whether it entails or implies that awareness. I will let the ambiguity stand for the purposes of this reconstruction and follow Piaget's usage wherever possible. In the critique I will argue that either reading makes crucial, unexplained assumptions.

Clearly transcending this and many other ambiguities and details, however, is Piaget's general view that the concepts of object, space, cause, and so forth are constructed at all, rather than pregiven either in our innate makeup or in experience. Thus, again, as in *The child's conception of the world,* Piaget saw himself as offering a major alternative to nativist and empiricist theories of the mind.

I proceed next with a reconstruction of Piaget's major results and arguments pertaining specifically to infants' concepts of object and causality. Piaget's treatment of these two concepts is more concrete and direct than is his treatment of space and time, which he self-consciously derived from his analyses of object and causality. The analyses of object and causality received considerable attention from researchers after Piaget.

1.1 The concept of object

To understand Piaget's analysis of infants' concept of object, one must be familiar with the account of the adult concept with which Piaget compared infants' behavior. Although Piaget develops his account of the adult concept throughout his discussion, the initial formulation is the notion that we "conceive and perceive" the elements of our experience "as objects that have substance, that are permanent and of constant dimensions" (CR, p. 3). Infants do not initially conceive and perceive things in this way. Piaget sets out to describe what they conceive and perceive instead and how they progressively converge over the first 18 months of life on a concept of object that is more or less like ours. He delineates six stages in this development, corresponding to the six stages in *Origins*.

In the reconstructions that follow I will use "stage," as I have in the preceding chapters, to refer to a type of response that Piaget associates with a given stage, not necessarily to the status of the whole child at any given time. Thus, in my usage, the expression "A child in Stage IV . . ." refers to a child in Stage IV with respect to the particular behavior, or group of behaviors, under study, not with respect to all possible, cognitively relevant behaviors. Nonetheless, it is useful to note the age ranges within which the behaviors Piaget described (in CR, OI, and PDI) tend first to appear. The approximate ranges, based on Piaget's account, are as follows:

Stage I: birth to 6 weeks
Stage II: 6 weeks to 5 months
Stage III: 5 to 9 months
Stage IV: 9 to 12 months
Stage V: 12 to 18 months
Stage VI: 18 to 24 months

The subjects for all three of the infancy works were Piaget's own three children. The data for the account of the concept of object consisted of the children's behavior with respect to objects undergoing changes that we as adults know leave those objects fully intact. These changes include simple visible movement from one place to another and simple disappearance, behind, under, or inside some other object. The observations were made during both purely natural events and structured experiments in which Piaget was attempting to determine the children's reaction to a particular kind of event, for example, the hiding of an object followed by another hiding of the object at a different location.

Thus, what Piaget was studying was infants' appreciation of the conditions under which an object remains identical with itself, or invariant. To appreciate the full class of conditions under which an object remains identical with itself is, in his view, to have a concept of object. Piaget's general thesis is that initially infants have a very limited grasp of this class. For only very few of the conditions under which we adults think an object remains the same object, and unaltered, do very young infants think an object remains the same and unaltered. Gradually, however, infants' appreciation of this class expands. The progression of the six stages of the object concept is a description of this gradual expansion.

A question arises, however: What is the nature of the "object" the identity of which infants are or are not conserving. I refer here to the issue of whether in perceiving or recognizing what we take to be objects, infants perceive or recognize entities of solidity, depth, and constant dimensions. Although Piaget does address these questions, he does so only intermittently and from a particular point of view. He says that he was not interested in object (or, as the case may be, space) perception. Here he seems to mean the question of whether infants discriminate the cues that to us would specify depth, solidity, and so on. He was interested instead in the question of whether infants see depth as depth, that is, whether they take the cues to mean the same thing that we do.

He addressed even this question only indirectly, however, for his interest lay in still more abstract issues. His whole definition of depth, form, and so on depends on his definition of the concept of object and of space in general. For example, if before a certain age infants do not turn over an upside-down bottle to find the nipple (when the nipple is initially out of view), Piaget would take this as evidence that they do not attribute the object with a "constant form." There is a more purely perceptual kind of form constancy that this distinctly conceptual criterion clearly ignores, the kind that is usually implied when researchers speak of perceptual constancies and related phenomena.

The discrepancy here would be tolerable were it not for the fact that Piaget often sounds as if he were drawing conclusions about mere perceptual discrimination or expectancy, when the data and theoretical description are addressed to more conceptual concerns, of the sort I just outlined. I will not attempt to resolve this problem here. Rather, I will try to follow Piaget's main line of analysis, which in the case of "object" concerns object identity and "permanence." I will discuss the more perceptual issues only to the extent that they bear on this analysis.

I continue, then, with Piaget's account of infants' concept of object, beginning with the first two stages, which Piaget treats together.

Stages I to II. From the first, infants have a concept of object, according to Piaget, insofar as they recognize certain recurrent impressions as familiar. Evidence of this recognition is the early differentiation of sucking, for example. From the second week of life Piaget's children were capable of finding the nipple when they were sucking to nurse and did not try to suck to nurse from the surrounding areas of the breast. From the fifth or sixth week the children's smiles indicated a recognition of familiar sounds and sights.

Piaget argues that these first recognitions are not recognitions of objects per se, that is, of substantial entities conceived of as external to infants. Rather the recognition reaction is one in which there is no clear, separate object. It is a response to a complex experience that we adults would divide into the perception of an external object (e.g., the nipple) and the infant's response (e.g., sucking) but that for the infant is not yet distinguished.

The basis for this argument is Piaget's observation that infants' reactions to things do not extend beyond the immediate excitations occasioned by those things. If, however, infants searched for the "images" that had vanished, Piaget reasons, we would have grounds for believing that they were granting those images an existence independent of, and hence external to, their immediate action or perception. This kind of search does not occur.

Additional evidence that there is no distinct "object," according to Piaget, is that there is no intercoordination of different actions involving objects. For example, what is lost from the mouth is not found by the eye and returned to the mouth under the guidance of the eye. What is lost from the mouth is at most sought by the mouth, if it is sought at all. Thus, theorizes Piaget, those recognitions that occur take place when the same particular action is extended or repeated. What is lost from the mouth must be found with the mouth, for recognition to occur. If the eye finds what the mouth lost, there is no recognition, at least not of any experience previously having to do with the mouth. In other words, in Piaget's view there is no cross-sensory recognition at the first stage.[1] That the recognition of what we know to involve an external object (e.g., the nipple) is synonymous with the infant's action on that object (e.g., sucking) is additional evidence for Piaget that recognition is of a total experience, and not of a discrete, external object.

Piaget makes the further claim that, recognition aside, direct perception is not at first a "perception of objects" (CR, p. 7). From various lines of evidence (some from his account of "space") he argues that, when confronted with a stationary object, infants do not, as we do, imagine the object's depth, its reverse side, possible displacements of it, or other characteristics that in his view make it an object. Nor are they able to distinguish an object in motion. They do not distinguish either a thing that moves, or a thing that moves and stops or is stationary and moves, as the same entity. If what infants experience is indeterminate as between their own reaction and things on the outside, they would have no basis on which to distinguish between what is "real" and what is "created by [their] own actions" (p. 7) or between the act of "following a moving image" and that of "creating it or making it last" (p. 104). Therefore, it would follow that an object that from our point of view is only changing location would be indistinguishable from a new object from infants' perspective.

Nonetheless, even from these earliest stages, according to Pia-

---

[1] The general subject of cross-sensory integration is taken up again later, in the discussion of *Origins*.

get, there are two kinds of patterns in which infants engage that seem to involve a beginning detachment of the object from absolutely immediate activity and that thereby confer at least a greater "continuity" (CR, p. 7) on it than would motor recognitions alone. One kind of pattern is the beginning coordination of actions in different modalities (e.g., hearing and looking, grasping and sucking, but not looking and grasping, which by Piaget's account follows later) and the other, rudimentary groping behavior and adjustments to things perceived.

From the second month Piaget's children turned to look at things they heard. Coordinations of this type have significant implications for the formation of object, he says, because they suggest that children expect (in this case) to see something before they actually perceive it. In that degree there is a dissociation of the thing perceived from the immediate experience of it.

Piaget hastens to point out, however, that infants do not, in these instances, conceive the visual and auditory images they perceive as coming from the same object (i.e., source). They simply try to see at the same time as they hear, and orient in the direction of perceived (in this case, heard) stimulation to do this. In trying to see at the same time as they hear, infants will still experience the image seen as an extension of their attempt to see, even though we as observers know that their perception of the sound is what instigated their attempt to look. Thus, in Piaget's view, the object has not advanced in externality, but only in (temporal) continuity. It is still tied directly to the infant's action. (Piaget's argument on this point will be reviewed in greater detail in the reconstruction of OI.)

The second group of patterns, groping and other accommodations, involves not only the anticipation of a perception (as when infants turn to look in the direction of a sound), but also the extension of an action relating to a vanished impression. Thus, on the second day of his life, Piaget's son, Laurent, gropes with his lips to find the breast, which has slipped away, and gropes more systematically as of the third day. After a month he gropes in the same way for his thumb after it has brushed against his mouth (Obs. 1).[2] Similarly, during the same period Laurent lets go of

---

[2] "Obs. 1" refers to Observation 1 in the text under consideration, in this case, *Construction of reality*.

and regrasps a sheet he is holding. (At this point he does not look at what he is doing or at least does not direct his grasping with his gaze in any obvious way [Obs. 4].)

The disappearance of visual impressions also leads to a certain kind of groping. At 2 months Jacqueline looks in the direction in which her mother disappeared, until her mother reappears. When Piaget continues to reappear at the same location next to Laurent's bassinet, Laurent continues to watch the same spot when Piaget disappears (Obs. 2). The children pursue noises heard in a similar way, according to Piaget. At 2 months Laurent looks at a kettle whose lid Piaget has shaken. When Piaget stops the noise, Laurent looks at Piaget and then at the kettle (Obs. 3).

Finally, Piaget notes a series of slightly more complex reactions, namely, instances in which the children themselves interrupt their action and return to it, as opposed to resuming an action following an outside interruption. Thus, at 3 months, Lucienne repeatedly returns to look at Piaget, who is on her extreme left, in between looking around the room at other things. Alternatively, when she is seated on his lap with her back to him, she turns around intermittently to look at him. Finally, she interrupts nursing every few minutes to look at Piaget and makes an expression that Piaget reports as "mingled disappointment and expectation" (CR, p. 11) when he withdraws (Obs. 5).

According to Piaget, there is an advance toward the concept of object in these examples insofar as the children's interest in something seems to continue even after the thing has disappeared. In some of the examples, the thing even seems actively to be sought (e.g., groping for the nipple).

Piaget emphasizes once again, however, that the "images" that are lost and regained do not have the status of substantial, permanent, and external objects. The reason is that the children do no more than repeat or directly extend the action previously in progress (or the posture previously adopted) once the valued image has gone away. If all the children are doing is either waiting in anticipation for the return of the image or merely extending the action previously associated with it, the image remains related to the children's action. The children simply preserve the "attitude" (CR, p. 11) of the earlier perception, and the image either reappears or it does not.

By contrast, says Piaget, if infants understood the object to be a substantial entity existing independently of their action, they "would actively search to find out where the thing could have been put" (CR, p. 11). By "active" or "true" (p. 11) search, Piaget means a search that involves movements that do not just extend the action that was interrupted. These movements might involve removing obstacles or changing the position of the objects at hand but could also involve purely visual search, reorienting of the infant's own position, and so on. Insofar as infants attempt only to extend their previous action or perception, what is to us an object may from their point of view be only an indissociated extension of action or perception.

Summarizing, Piaget says that the first two stages in the development of the concept of object are characterized by the absence of any special behavior connected with vanished objects. From this evidence and the positive reactions that he cites, Piaget infers that the "image" that disappears either sinks into "oblivion" or into an "affective void" (CR, p. 12) or else is regretted and desired. The only way infants can rediscover this desired image is through random crying or the repetition of their previous accommodating actions (e.g., looking in the place where the image disappeared or was last seen). Moreover, the image that they desire on these occasions is not "an object existing in space, remaining identical to itself and escaping sight, touch, and hearing because it has been displaced and is masked by various solid substances" (p. 12). It is an indeterminate, unlocalized complex that from our point of view contains a total experiential context, as well as the thing itself.

Stage III. Piaget marks the fourth stage as the beginning of the object concept, because that stage involves the beginning of the active search for vanished objects. In this context, Piaget thinks, the third stage assumes a special interest. It is then, he says, that children have the motoric means to engage in all the behaviors that are critical to the fourth stage (e.g., lifting a cover off a hidden object to retrieve the object); however, they do not use them. A group of intermediate reactions is seen, which Piaget interprets both as supporting his thesis that the concept of object is not pregiven and as supplying evidence of an important step on the way to the acquisition of that concept.

Children now reach for and grasp things they see (see the reconstruction under Stage II, OI; and section 2, following). This means they are motorically capable of lifting, say, a cloth that covers an object they desire. Piaget distinguishes as the third stage that period during which infants have mastered (and freely use) visually guided reaching but in which they do not engage in this or any other behavior to retrieve completely vanished objects. There are, however, five new patterns in which they do engage that suggest to Piaget that they are conferring both a greater externality and "permanence" on objects than they did during the first two stages.

The first pattern is visual accommodation to rapid movements. When an object moves too rapidly for its trajectory actually to be seen, Piaget's children look at the place where the object should end up, given its point of departure. Thus, for example, the children look to the ground in anticipation of the fall of objects dropped from a height. Earlier they just continue to stare straight ahead or else look around at other things as if they have forgotten the dropped object.

The second pattern parallels the first, but for grasping. If the children drop an object they were holding, they lower their arm for it. Alternatively, if someone takes something from them, they reach for it.

The third group of reactions involves activity with objects that is interrupted and to which the children then suddenly and of their own accord return. The activities come under the heading of "secondary circular reactions" (OI), which are repetitive actions carried out for their effects in the environment, as when infants bang, scratch, or swing something; they are to be contrasted with "primary circular reactions" (the hallmark of stage II in OI), which are repetitive actions carried out for their effects on the infant's own body (e.g., sucking). An example of an interrupted (or, as Piaget calls it, "deferred") circular reaction occurs when Lucienne stops scratching a powder box to look at Piaget and play with him and then suddenly turns back to her former position and resumes scratching the box (Obs. 18).

The fourth pattern is that of retrieving a partially hidden object. Thus, Laurent grasps a pencil when an inch or so, but not less than that, is showing (Obs. 21). Or Lucienne pulls back the cover over a new toy goose when its beak is showing, but not when it is completely covered (Obs. 23).

Finally, with the fifth pattern, the children remove a hand or other screen that is near their face and preventing them from seeing what is beyond.

Each of these reactions indicates, according to Piaget's interpretation, that the "object" extends at least somewhat beyond the immediate moment it is perceived and is distanced at least a little from the children's actions. If the children anticipate the future position of a falling object rather than look simply at the place where they perceived it, that object would seem to have an existence at least partly independent of the excitation caused by its perception. Similarly, if the children reach for something that they have dropped or turn to resume a former activity with an object, there is some presumption that the thing or the effect will be found. If they pull back the cloth that partly covers an object, then, according to the account, they must think that the rest of the object must be there, even when they do not see it. Finally, if the children remove obstacles blocking their view, they may be thinking that something exists beyond the obstacle.

At the same time, however, these reactions have definite limitations. It is on the basis of these limitations that Piaget will argue that the object remains heavily bound to the children's action at this stage and in that degree also remains nonenduring or, as he sometimes says, "insubstantial." In looking at or reaching for an object in a new place, his children extend only an action in progress or restrict their search to the observed trajectory of the object. If the object does not fall directly down, for example, or the children do not find it where they first look, they look back at the object's point of origin (e.g., the hand that dropped it) or give up searching altogether. As for the coverings of objects (the fourth pattern), the restriction here is well known. Although the children remove a cloth to retrieve an object when part of the object is showing, they do not, even in the next moment, lift the cloth if the object has been covered completely. In a related observation Piaget notes that his children at this stage do not turn the bottle over for the nipple when they are handed the bottom end and cannot see the nipple; as soon as the nipple comes into view, however, they turn the bottle the rest of the way. Finally, although they may remove a screen, for instance, a cushion that blocks their vision, they do not, again, remove a screen that blocks an object they are trying to see or use (Obs. 27).

Piaget draws two inferences from these limitations. First, from the finding that the children recover an object only by extending their initial movement of accommodation, Piaget infers that they must still be conceiving of the object as an extension of their action. If they had a concept that the object could move autonomously or existed independently of them, then, according to Piaget, they would interpolate other actions to bring themselves together with the object. That they do in fact remove obstacles blocking their view is not inconsistent with this account. Given that they remove only immediate obstructions of their view, Piaget infers that the children are attempting only to clear their vision rather to displace the obstacle in relation to the object it hides. Therefore, they are once again only extending an act of accommodation (adjusting their gaze, in effect).

Second, from his children's failure to search for completely hidden objects Piaget infers that objects that disappear from view cease to have a substantial existence for the children (e.g., CR, p. 32). In cases where the object is covered by something else, that is, when to our adult view it is hidden behind or underneath something, Piaget thinks that from the children's point of view the object is absorbed or "abolished" (p. 22) by the occluding object. When the children gaze expectantly at the place where the object disappeared or cry in distress over its departure, they think of the departed object as something that will somehow "emanate" (p. 32) from the thing in front of them. When and if the object emerges from its hiding place, the children regard it as arising from the screen that we know conceals it rather than as emerging from behind the screen or underneath it. Thus, from the children's point of view, says Piaget, an object both lacks substance (insofar as it can be absorbed by another object or is seen to "emanate" from it) and is alternately made and unmade (insofar as it is seen as abolished at one instant and reformed the next, when it reappears) (see especially pp. 31–2).

Stage IV. The hallmark of the fourth stage is that the children actively search for an object that has disappeared entirely. The search involves the interpolation of new movements (e.g., lifting the cloth that covers the object) rather than the extension of a movement of accommodation or the repetition of the action that was previously executed on the object. The fourth stage is also distinguished by an important limitation, however, namely, the children's persistence in searching for the object at the location where it first disappeared. Even if the object is moved within the children's view to a new location (Obs. 38) and even if it is fully visible (rather than hidden) at the new location (Obs. 39), the children search at the old location.

Piaget draws two main conclusions from this behavior. First, there is progress in the "objectification" (externalization) of the object, insofar as the children no longer conceive the object purely as part of their action. Nevertheless, they also see it as being "at disposal" at the location where the action has "made use of it" (CR, p. 50) and thus do not understand that it has a fully external and "substantial" (p. 50) existence.

The second conclusion is that, for the children, objects are not the individualized entities they are for us. Although specific objects might have "permanent" identities (e.g., Papa is Papa, wherever he is seen or imagined; a ball is a ball, regardless of where it is found), they nonetheless have multiple existences, each separate existence being embedded in its own particular location or context. There is Papa-at-his-window and Papa-in-front-of-oneself, or ball-under-the-sofa and ball-under-the-armchair. That the two different occurrences of Papa (or ball) are distinct existences for the children is suggested, according to Piaget, by the fact that, when an object is seen to disappear at one location, it is sought at the other. A single, unified, substantial object would be sought at the place where it disappeared.

Stage V. In the fifth stage the children search for objects at the location where they disappear rather than at a special location. Thus, even when unable to find Piaget's watch under a cushion where Piaget has hidden it (very far back), Jacqueline turns unnerved from the cushion and touches different things around her. Among the things she touches is the cushion under which Piaget had just previously hidden the watch; however, she does not turn it over (Obs. 53).

The restriction on this stage and the characteristic that distinguishes it from the next, is that the children do not know what to do when an object has been transferred while out of their view, for example, when Piaget puts a toy in his hand (last visible hiding), puts his hand under the rug and deposits the object (invisible hiding), and brings his hand out empty. Under this condition the children give up their search, search only at the place where they saw the object disappear (e.g., Piaget's hand) (Obs. 56), or toward the end of the stage, search at secondary hiding places where the object was previously located but are not the location of the object this time. After having allowed the children to find the toy under the rug, for instance, Piaget conducts a new trial in which he hides the toy in his hand and passes his hand under a pillow, depositing the object there. The children at Stage V search under the rug (Obs. 60, 62).

Piaget infers that his children at Stage V have "bestowed the quality of object" (CR, p. 78) on images and impressions in the perceptible universe. However, he says, they do not grant substantiality or permanence to objects that pass into spaces where they did not see them go or that follow a displacement they did not observe. Piaget believes that the children do not think of the latter objects as permanent because either they do not search for them, or if they search they look no farther than the place where they saw the objects disappear or places where they have previously found them. These objects are insubstantial insofar as, Piaget thinks, the children conceive of them as capable of turning up at locations that, from our "objective" point of view, they would have no way of getting to – that is, other than if they were multiple objects or were displaced by impossible means.

Stage VI. In the sixth stage the children systematically pursue an object through multiple hidden displacements. If an object has been hidden first in a container and the container is then carried to different locations and returned empty, they immediately search at a location to which the container has gone. If they do not find the object right away, they persevere in their search, checking other "possible" locations, namely those along the trajectory of the moving container (Obs. 65, 66). Moreover, they are not lured away from this pursuit by locations of past or customary success.

Piaget's central conclusion is that the children are now "imagining" the "whole of the object's itinerary, including the series of invisible displacements" (CR, p. 83). He also speaks of the new search pattern as involving an itinerary that is "deduced" (p. 85) insofar as the children search not only where they have not seen the object go, but at locations they have never visibly associated with it.

Extrapolating from this conclusion, Piaget infers that the "object" is now fully constituted. At least with regard to objects near at hand (as opposed, e.g., to celestial bodies), the object is now permanent and substantial under the ordinary conditions of the children's experience (appearances, disappearances, and other simple movements through space) and is a spatialized whole when it disappears. With all this, it is a body whose existence and movements have become independent of the self.

1.2. Causality

Piaget saw children's concept of causality as evolving through a series of stages analogous to those pertaining to the concept of object. He does not present any new observations for the first two stages in the development of causality but derives an account from the observations of subsequent stages and from his analysis of the first two stages of object and space.

Stages I to II. The account begins from the premise, elaborated under the discussion of object, that anything Piaget's children experience they do so through their own activity (where, as before, activity includes looking and hearing, as well as more obvious actions such as sucking, touching, and manipulating). But, the argument continues, at these very early stages, the children's activity is indistinguishable from the things it is directed toward, as well as from the feelings of effort and expectation that accompany it. Two consequences follow. One is that the children must not perceive or conceive causal relations between external events, because the only perception or conception they can have is of something in relation to themselves. Second, this relation between self and things (or between the activity and effort of self and the movement of things) does not in itself involve any separation of cause and effect. Although we as observers might distinguish that the act of sucking brings (the sensation of) milk, from infants' point of view the kinesthetic sensation of sucking and the gustatory impression of milk are all one continuum. If neither is distinguishable, neither can be cause, and neither effect.

The only "causality" infants can experience, according to this account, is thus a diffuse feeling of efficacy, connected with their activity, this feeling of efficacy (which combines the kinesthetic sensations of the activity itself and the sensations of effort, expectation, and desire that go along with it) being essentially indistinguishable from the results (e.g., contact with milk) to which it leads. The feeling of efficacy is not, however, "localized" (CR, p. 228) within a self, because the internal world has not yet been distinguished. If it can be said to be localized anywhere, it is localized in those "perceptual aggregates" that constitute infants' experience, namely their "fused" awareness of self, world, activity, and effort.

Out of this "indissoluble union" (p. 228) of efficacy and what Piaget calls "phenomenalism" (meaning the localization of the feeling of cause in the world) will come internal causation, or intention, on the one hand, and external or physical causality, on the other.

Stage III. Piaget dates a "systematic interest in causal relations" (CR, p. 229) from the third stage. The primary basis for this characterization is the hallmark of the third stage in general intelligence (OI), the "secondary circular reaction." This reaction, the reader will recall, involves the repetition of simple, unitary actions that are associated with what we would distinguish as extrinsic effects, where infants' interest is in these extrinsic effects as opposed to in some internal (e.g., kinesthetic) effect of the action. Infants now pull a string to make the rattles overhead move rather than pull the string for the pleasurable sensation of pulling it.

From the point of view of causality, Piaget says, infants have "placed into relationship" (CR, p. 229) certain movements and certain results. The question is how they conceive this relationship. Piaget's answer is that, on the one hand, whereas cause and effect were previously fused into a single mass, they have now begun to separate, insofar as infants' actions have become more purposive. This greater purposiveness, in Piaget's view, attends the interest in more distant, or extrinsic, effects. For example, an infant who sees an object he or she wants will have to mobilize reaching for the object before obtaining it. An infant who sees hanging rattles and wants to swing them will have to procure and shake the string before the rattles can be swung. In acting with greater purpose infants have become aware of a goal or desire that precedes a particular result of their action, as distinct from the result itself.

On the other hand, the only kind of causality infants can conceive is still that of mixed "efficacy" and "phenomenalism." In other words, the so-called causal effects they perceive are (in their view) connected with their own activity. Their own activity, however, is still not identified as their own (hence, the phenomenalism), and their behavior in these settings seems to presuppose that all they need to do is act, and the effect in question will result (hence, the efficacy).

Piaget uses as evidence for this view his analysis of his own children's reactions to three kinds of causal events that the children appear to deal with at this stage. The purpose of Piaget's demonstration is to show that, although these events are distinct from our perspective, they are equivalent from the children's point of view. They are equivalent insofar as they are all conceived as involving the "magicophenomenalistic" causality I just described.

The first of these events involves the children's observation of their own body movements, for example, their tendency to watch the movements of their hands or feet. By the third stage the children seem to bring their hands before their eyes intentionally and then to move them about in different ways while they watch them. On the basis of examples that I will not detail or evaluate here, Piaget thinks that the children are interested on these occasions in their power over the movements they see, in the fact that they can change and augment the spectacle before them, and do so reliably.

From circumstantial evidence in the analyses of object, space, and aspects of imitation (PDI), Piaget infers that the children cannot be recognizing the role of self in these episodes, either as mover or as that which is moved. Thus, there is awareness of purpose, of desire and effort – and to that degree a consciousness of cause – in these episodes and an effect associated with this cause. Rather than being localized in a self, however, the cause is "immanent" (CR, p. 233) in immediate reality, and the "effect" is no different from any other (e.g., external) phenomenon the children might witness.

The second group of causal events Piaget considers involves

(what we know to be) the children's direct action on external things, in other words, the episodes characteristic of the secondary circular reactions, which I described earlier. Piaget's argument here is that, from the children's point of view, these episodes are no different from those in which the children watch their hands and (as Piaget interprets it) try to make the spectacle move. It is only we, who in watching a child shake a string to make a rattle go, distinguish the rattle, the string, and the hand that pulls the string. The child simply engages in an efficacious gesture that goes along with the rattle's swinging.

To document this account Piaget cites the fact that when his children are confronted with a fortuitous result that they seem to like (e.g., the shaking of the rattle), they repeat only the action that seemed to lead to the result (e.g., shaking the hand or the string). Most critically, in Piaget's view, they do not ensure that there is physical contact between cause and effect. They do not have the concept of an intermediary. For instance, rather than hit the hanging dolls with her feet to make them swing, Jacqueline simply shakes her legs and looks expectantly at the dolls (Obs. 131). That the children might come reliably to shake the string (in the earlier example) to make the rattles move, as opposed to waving at the empty air, does not disconfirm this account. From the children's point of view, grasping and holding the string could simply be a contingency that has to be observed to make the rattles move. The learning of this contingency need not be accompanied by the understanding that the string must be held because it is connected to the rattles.

Piaget offers what he considers to be still more compelling evidence that the relationship the children envision between cause and effect is an efficacious-phenomenalistic one. Referring to *Origins,* he cites numerous cases in which the children's secondary circular reactions "generalized" (CR, p. 237) to remote effects. Thus, for instance, after having learned to pull the string hanging from her bassinet to move the rattles overhead, Jacqueline pulled the string when Piaget alternately swung and stopped swinging a book or a bottle at a distance (OI, p. 113).

Piaget sees in these examples evidence that the children are establishing an "immediate link" (CR, p. 236) between their movements (and the associated feelings of effort, etc.) and their final result. He thinks that these instances of (objectively) remote connections are telling in this respect, because the children cannot have analyzed the cause–effect relations that actually operate in these situations. The only relation that could conceivably be "intelligible" (p. 240) to them is that between their action (or effort) and the observed phenomenon. The situation is thus analogous to the children's movement of their limbs. There Piaget would also argue that the children are connecting their impressions of effort and the image of their limbs directly, "as though the former acted magically and without intermediaries upon the latter" (p. 236).

Finally, regarding both cases, Piaget emphasizes again that this feeling of efficacy is located not in a self but "in reality midway between the internal and the external" (CR, p. 241). Given that the children do not, in Piaget's view, distinguish internal impressions from external realities, they would have no basis on which to locate a cause within themselves. Nor could they conceive of their action purely "externally" as a material cause, because they do not understand what makes the action effective. They have no concept of the need for material contact with the object to be affected.

The third class of causal phenomena concerns episodes that to an adult involve causal relations that are external to the children, for example, when Piaget taps on a tin box and thereby produces a particular sound. Piaget's question was whether these events were conceived by the children as involving the action of an external causal agent, or whether they, too, were regarded as having been caused by the children's own action, if they were regarded as having been "caused" at all.

Piaget tested these hypotheses by observing what his children did when a given causal sequence (e.g., Piaget drums on a tin box or scratches a cushion, thus producing a sound) that was occurring close at hand was discontinued. He theorized that, if the children acted directly on the causal agent (e.g., Piaget's hand) at this juncture and not on the recipient object (e.g., the tin box), there was tentative support for the hypothesis that the children were viewing this causal agent as the operative causal agent in the situation. If, however, the children acted directly on the recipient object or on the causal and recipient objects together, there was support for the hypothesis that the children regarded the effect in question as dependent on, or else as extending, their own activity.

Piaget added one more condition to the first of these possible reactions (acting directly on the causal agent). The evidence for the children's conception of an autonomous causal connection would be most compelling, he reasoned, if they acted on the causal agent specifically by pushing it gently toward the recipient object, for example, nudging Piaget's hand back toward the tin box, rather than pushing it forcefully. The more delicate behavior would indicate that the children regarded the mediating object as capable of carrying out an action, or producing an effect, at least partly on its own. If, alternatively, the children were to wave this mediating object around as though it were an extension of their own hands, the evidence would be stronger that they were, once again, subordinating the desired effect to their own action, and not to that of an outside agent.

The children responded in either of two ways. One was to act directly on the causal agent (e.g., Piaget's hand), but only by beating or striking it, not by guiding it into motion. The second and more frequent response was to act directly on the recipient object (e.g., the tin box), shaking or striking it if it were within reach, or by engaging in the remote "procedures" (pulling strings, waving arms, etc.) described under the second group of events.

Regarding the first of these two reactions, Piaget maintains that the children were treating the hand (or other mediating object) as an appendage of their own bodies. In the case of the second reaction, in which the children acted directly on the recipient object, Piaget infers that the children considered the effect in question to be "one of the many phenomena which extend [their] own action and not as the product of a process independent of that activity" (CR, p. 247). Piaget rejects the hypothesis that infants perceive no causal relation in these situations, because from the first stage their very perceptions are accompanied by feelings of pleasure, expectation, and other impressions that go along with the attempt to "assimilate" things. In the early stages their experience is therefore "infused" (p. 248) with their activity. By the third stage Piaget thinks, this sense of dynamism has developed into infants' impression that perceived effects "depend on" (p. 248) their own movements.

Thus, according to Piaget, this third group of causal events (causal sequences that are in fact independent of infants) can be classed with the first two groups. In all three kinds of events, he thinks, infants have a conception that observed effects are linked more or less directly to their own activity. The link, however, is a purely phenomenalistic one.

Piaget examines one last form of causality, namely causality by imitation, which is first seen at this stage but which he considers to overlap the three types of events just discussed and so treats separately. I include it here because it is a particularly clear example of Piaget's overall approach to infant causality. Piaget reports numerous episodes in which his children imitate someone else's actions, in his view to make that person continue his or her actions. From the fact that the children intensify the action when the other person pauses, Piaget infers that the children are trying to make the other person continue. The question for Piaget is not, then, whether the children are trying to cause something to happen, but whether "the use of imitation as a causal procedure" (CR, p. 251) involves an implicit efficacy and phenomenalism (as in the other reactions at this stage) or whether the children are attributing to the persons they imitate a causality independent of their own action.

Piaget argues that the children are likely to deem other people more lively centers of causality than physical objects. The children seem to wait for events to occur in the presence of a person, whereas they seem immediately to try to bring them about when objects are concerned. Nonetheless, Piaget thinks that, although persons may be endowed with a certain spontaneity, in the main, infants regard their action as contingent upon, if not continuous with, their own activity.

He cites in support of the latter thesis the early and repeated responsiveness of adults to infants, which he thinks cultivates in infants the notion that the activity of persons is under their direct influence (in the magicophenomenalistic sense). Moreover, when it finally does develop, reciprocal imitation can be compared, Piaget thinks, with other "procedures" by which the children try to make (what we would describe as) a remote display continue through direct action. Finally, when imitating another person (presumably to get that person to continue some action), the children often look concertedly and "expectantly" at the part of the other person's body whose movements they are imitating. They do not look at the person (Obs. 137, 138; also CR, p. 306). In Piaget's view, this again supports the hypothesis that in imitating others the children are trying to act directly (without intermediaries) on a thing rather than indirectly on a causal agent.

Thus, in reciprocal imitation, as with the other purported causal series Piaget describes for this stage, there is magicophenomenalistic causality. The children think, in Piaget's view, that the events they desire will not occur unless they act, and act directly, that is, without intermediaries. In acting "directly" in this way, the children act purely "efficaciously," in Piaget's view, insofar as they do not appreciate the need for physical contact between a causal agent or instrument (in this case themselves) and the body on which it acts.

Piaget's treatment of causality at the three remaining stages (IV through VI) deals with three issues: the externalization or "objectification" of causality (meaning the ascription of causality to an external body regarded as moving independently of the children), the spatialization of causality (the children's appreciation of the necessity for spatial contact between elements in a [physical] causal relation), and the reconstruction of absent causes or effects. The third problem, of reconstruction, concerns only Stage VI. Piaget's discussion of Stages IV and V centers on the other two issues (externalization and spatialization). Within this context, Piaget conceives the fourth stage as transitional to true externalization and spatialization of causality but as not quite constitutive of them.

Stage IV. At Stage III, says Piaget, the causal connections that the children establish link only a global attitude of efficacy, experienced from within but not identified as internal, with a perceived effect. According to this view, the children neither understand their own body movements to be objective displacements that impart the effects produced nor appreciate the intermediaries that sometimes intervene to produce these effects or how precisely these intermediaries operate. The children act, and something is supposed to happen. In Piaget's view, the children think that things can happen *only* if they (the children) act.

At Stage IV the children begin to attribute some autonomous movement to objects; however, they do not conceive of this movement as entirely free of their influence. In addition, they begin to understand the need to put interacting bodies into contact but do not understand these connections completely. Piaget likens these advances to Stage IV of the object concept, which is when the children grant "permanence" to objects, but only in those positions connected in some way with the children's activity. "Causality," similarly, is detached from the children's activity, "without being attributed once and for all to objects independent of the self" (CR, p. 257).

Piaget gives as the first clear instances of objectified and spatialized causality the children's attempts to push someone else's hand back toward the location where it was producing an interesting result. Thus, whereas at Stage III Jacqueline would attempt to get her mother to swing the flounce again through "efficacious" procedures (e.g., beating her legs, swinging her hands, or even imitating the swinging motion), she now pushes her mother's hand gently toward the flounce. Similarly, she pushes Piaget's hand against a singing doll that she cannot activate herself (Obs. 142).

Piaget sees these examples as instances of the utilization of "active instruments" (CR, p. 259) or, alternatively, as instances of the treatment of the intermediaries in question as "independent sources of action by contact" (p. 260). The children are setting these tools in motion rather than determining every movement of the tools as though they were extensions of their own hands.

Thus, there is objectification insofar as the other person's body (or body part) is deemed capable of some autonomous movement. There is spatialization insofar as the children no longer act on the person or object through "efficacy" (CR, p. 262), but push the hand or other body part toward the desired place or, if it does not go the rest of the way itself, may put it there themselves.

Why, then, are the objectification and spatialization of causality incomplete at the fourth stage? Piaget's answer seems to be that, although the children use some procedures that involve spatial contact and that accord some autonomy to the object acted upon, they continue to use the secondary procedures of the third stage, which operate by efficacy or, as we might put it instead, by remote contact. To the extent that the children continue to engage in these procedures (e.g., of arching themselves, waving their hands in the presence of interesting spectacles), Piaget thinks that they continue to behave "as though someone else's

acts depended merely on [the children's] own desires and movements" (CR, p. 264).

There is a parallel change, in Piaget's view, in the children's
interactions with the purely physical environment (as opposed to
their interactions with people). The children now appear in part
to wait for things to happen, whereas previously they acted only
so that things would happen. Piaget notes in this connection the
appearance of attenuated secondary circular reactions in which
the children slow down their action, for example, beating a swinging toy, and watch carefully as the object comes and goes on its
own. Alternatively, they may watch an object closely that has
moved unexpectedly and then push it gingerly as if to see what it
will do next. In contrast to the following stages, however, they do
not look for a possible (external) cause of the movement (e.g., a
hidden string, an internal mechanism) and engage in classic secondary procedures (beating the legs, etc.) if they get no results.

Piaget's general conclusion regarding this stage is that the children have begun to center in objects and people a "causality" that
was previously "reserved" (CR, p. 271) for their own activity.
Nonetheless, the account continues, the movements of these external bodies remain partly "subordinated" (p. 266) to the children's action insofar as the children believe, in Piaget's view, that
they can intervene directly in this activity and, through "efficacy,"
cause it to continue (p. 269).

Stage V. With the advent of the fifth stage, according to Piaget,
the children conceive of causes completely independent of themselves (objectification or externalization of causality), and they
fully appreciate the need for physical contact between bodies that
are to act causally on one another (spatialization of causality). I
will consider each of these advances in turn.

Regarding objectification, the children now position physical
objects in such a way that the objects put themselves in motion.
Alternatively, they orient themselves or the things on which they
want some action executed in such a way that other people will
perform the desired action. Instances involving purely physical
causality include dropping things from a given height to watch
them fall or bounce, pushing objects to the edge of a surface so
they will fall, and releasing a ball at the top of an incline so that it

will roll down. Further, although a certain amount of active apprenticeship is required, they master fairly readily the movement
of giving a slight push to a ball that rests on level ground, so that
the ball will roll (Obs. 148, 150). As for interactions with people,
after Piaget has blown on Jacqueline's hair, for example, Jacqueline positions her head beneath Piaget in the same way as before
and waits for him to resume. In the earlier stages she would either
have used efficacious procedures (Stage III) or the maneuver of
pushing on Piaget's arms or lips (Stage IV) to induce him to
continue (Obs. 152).

Thus, according to Piaget, whereas earlier the children seemed
to see the need to impart movement themselves to anything they
wanted to move, as of the fifth stage they attribute autonomous
movement to things and persons. In that degree they acknowledge causal centers outside themselves.

Piaget addresses the possible objection that the children might
have been granting this kind of autonomy either to persons or to
some indeterminate agent in earlier stages, when, for example,
they would cry (but engage in no further "direct" action) for their
meal and eventually get it. He dismisses this view on the grounds
that in the early stages the children regarded the movements of
other bodies only as extending their own action and effort. It is
only we who appreciate the indirect connection between the
baby's cries and the arrival of food. If the children experience the
movement of others (the arrival of food, etc.) as an extension of
their own activity, then, he reasons, they do not view that activity
as external to themselves and cannot, in principle, view it as
externally and independently caused.

Regarding spatialization, Piaget maintains that, until this stage,
relations between causes and effects have been phenomenalistic
from the children's point of view. Whether "cause" (or the cause,
in a given situation) was construed as the children's own activity
(Stage III) or, in a rudimentary way, as the action of an intermediary (Stage IV), what the children seemed to understand was the
correlation between a given action and a given effect, not the true
nature of the connection between the action and the effect. Thus,
even as late as Stage IV, when the children could use intermediaries such as strings or supports to draw objects toward them, they
would on occasion use these intermediaries if they were in the
vicinity of the goal object but not in spatial contact with it (e.g., if

the goal object–say Piaget's watch–was being held above a cushion but not on it). The major advance of the fifth stage is that the children now intentionally and accurately put the goal and intermediate objects into spatial contact. They see the need for doing this. For instance, they will not pull a cushion forward to retrieve a watch unless the watch is on top of the cushion. (The examples Piaget cites here are from *Origins,* Stage V.)

These reactions have limitations, however. Although the children may know, for example, that to move an object with a stick one has to put the stick in contact with the object, they may fail to appreciate either that further movements are necessary or what these movements must be (Obs. 154). As a result, Piaget infers, although the children have begun to externalize and spatialize causes, these relations are not yet "analyzed intellectually" (CR, p. 286). They remain governed by immediate perception and hence are phenomenalistic.

Insofar as the children now conceive of external causes and understand some of the conditions (e.g., spatial contact) of their operation, Piaget speculates, they should also begin to see themselves as subject to these external causes. He notes in this connection that, whereas Jacqueline used to keep herself in motion in order to keep her swing moving, she now gathers momentum and then lets herself swing until the swing stops. In his view she is "submitting to the effect of causes independent of herself" (CR, p. 291).

Stage VI. With the sixth stage the children begin to reconstruct causes that they cannot perceive and to anticipate the effects of a possible source of action that is not yet in motion. Until now the children could reconstruct causes and effects only from what was given in perception. (Piaget refers to the difference as representing causality vs. merely perceiving it [CR, p. 294].)

The kind of reconstruction Piaget has in mind regarding absent causes and effects involves connections the children infer or create for the first time, as opposed to "sensorimotor" (CR, p. 294) anticipations based on past experience. Placing the ball on the floor and waiting for it to roll would be an example of a sensorimotor (i.e., familiar) anticipation. As an example of the reconstruction of a cause given an observed effect Piaget cites an episode in which he moved Laurent's carriage with his foot, while he otherwise appeared to be disengaged by reading. Laurent leaned over the side of the carriage and smiled when he saw Piaget's foot (Obs. 150). The idea is that Laurent had not seen Piaget put his foot under the carriage and did not know from past experience that Piaget could move the carriage with his foot. For an instance of the anticipation of an effect given (the projected operation of) a cause, Piaget cites an occasion on which Jacqueline pretended she had to relieve herself when what she wanted was to be let out of her playpen to resume a game she had been playing on the floor (Obs. 160).

Piaget believes that in the absence of represented causality in the strong sense connoted by these examples the universe would be, from the children's point of view, a series of "creations and annihilations" rather than a universe that "endures" (CR, p. 294). The enduring universe is constructed from the sixth stage onward, at least with regard to the immediate environment.

2. Intelligence

According to Piaget, infants gradually construct their reality. This construction occurs, the theory holds, through the development of their action, as its reverse side. It is through infants' very basic tendency to attempt to reproduce their experience, for example, that the first feelings of (inchoate) cause arise. At the same time, by virtue of the fact that infants' action is initially limited to this attempt at reproduction, Piaget argues, their reality must consist of no more than indeterminate extensions of this action and the effort (expectation, desire, etc.) associated with it. Further, the *development* of this reality is linked to the elaboration of action. Once infants begin to adjust their actions to the exigencies of reproduction, once the kinds of action they perform proliferate, and once they begin to intercoordinate these actions, says Piaget, they can begin to distinguish a world apart from themselves. Through the continued elaboration of action, the structure of this world develops further, and the world expands.

In the light of contemporary emphasis on the alleged conservatism of Piaget's measures of children's conceptual development (see, e.g., Bullock, Gelman & Baillargeon, 1982; Carey, 1983), one is likely to attend to the side of Piaget's argument that says that the concepts he discusses will not appear *unless* infants are engaging in the sorts of actions he delineates as criteria for those concepts. There is, however, another side to the argument. It is that along with the progressive elaboration of action in the world there must come an elaboration of the universe, in the terms that Piaget describes: "the formation of a world of objects and spatial relationships, in short, the elaboration of a solid and permanent universe" (CR, p. xii). That is, these developing actions either lead to or entail the construction of a reality as we know it, the construction of object, space, time, and cause as we know them and as Piaget thinks emerges in children's behavior.

But it is not obvious that corresponding to the development of activity per se (e.g., the adjustment of sucking to the nipple, the coordination of eye and hand movements, the use of intermediaries) there would be a progressive construction of a reality. There might simply be a development of activity, without all the gains in understanding or experiencing that Piaget ascribes to children. Given action in the world, there does not need to be the experience of a reality, regardless of the way in which we might construe that reality from the subject's point of view. Piaget seems rather to *assume* that there will be this experience. He speaks, for example, of a "consciousness" that is at first protoplasmic and then differentiates into a self and a not-self (CR, p. 355). Given the assumption that some reality will be experienced, he then turns to his children's action patterns for evidence of what that reality might be.

In other words, the analyses we have discussed thus far presuppose that we are dealing with an intelligent subject. However, none of the argumentation we have considered establishes that we indeed have an intelligent subject. *The origins of intelligence,* however, addressed this point.

2.1. Piaget's approach to intelligence

In the most general terms, Piaget saw intelligence as an adaptation, specifically the adaptation of thought to things. Piaget used "adaptation" in its biological sense: the intake, or "assimilation," of input by the organism, combined with the adjustment, or "accommodation," of the organism to that input. An important constraint on these processes is that the organism can assimilate input only to its existing "structures," which in Piaget's analysis of intelligence refers to the organism's existing means of coming to know or understand things. *Origins* can be seen as a study of the development of these means.

Clearly, however, there is more to intelligence than adaptation (seen as assimilation and accommodation and the general principles of their functioning). Otherwise we could not distinguish intelligence from other forms of biological adaptation, for example, from the organic reactions of amoebas or of humans themselves. It is rather that Piaget looked at intelligence from the particular point of view of adaptation. This still leaves us, however, with the problem of identifying some aspect of life that we will call intelligence, the adaptational mechanisms of which will be studied.

Piaget deals with this problem in two ways, each addressed to a somewhat different point. First, he grants a "specific heredity" to humans that admits the attainment of levels of intelligence superior to the level attained by other species (OI, p. 2). He goes on to say, however, that the "functional activity of reason" (p. 2) is connected not with this specific heredity but with the fact merely of being a living organism, and it is this functional activity of reason that he will study. Thus, at one level, Piaget simply assumes the existence of "intelligence" and proceeds to study its functional properties in the terms he specifies.

There is a second way, however, in which *Origins* can be seen exactly as a treatise on the question, What is "intelligent"? It can be seen as mapping out a continuum – as opposed to any single criterion – of what it is to act intelligently or with intelligence. We can view the depictions of each stage as attempts to specify that which is peculiarly intelligent, or perhaps that which is the closest approximation to intelligence, at that stage. I will present the book from this second vantage point.

Origins describes the stages through which intelligence becomes manifest in the human infant. In this context, Piaget believed that there is a "sensorimotor" intelligence, that is, behavior that is intelligent and that in being intelligent is to be distinguished from pure reflex or habit. In being sensorimotor, however, it is also to be distinguished from verbal or cogitative intelligence, which Piaget held marks the end of infancy (about 18 months).

Piaget believed that these different levels of activity were "functionally continuous." Verbal or cogitative intelligence (alternately called representational intelligence) was based on sensorimotor intelligence, sensorimotor intelligence on acquired associations and habits, and acquired associations and habits on reflexes. Piaget regarded the reflexes, in turn, as continuous with purely biological levels of functioning; however, *Origins* does not deal with these levels.

At least three different forms of continuity can be distinguished in Piaget's discussion. I refer to the first, which Piaget emphasizes, as functional continuity in the strict sense (I call it simply functional continuity). Functional continuity in this sense is the notion that the actual principles of functioning are the same at the different levels of activity just outlined. These principles are "assimilation," or the incorporation of input by the organism, "accommodation," or the modification of the organism given that input, and "organization," or the tendency toward internal coherence. Sometimes Piaget refers to these processes as "invariant functions."

I call the second form of continuity historical, or material, continuity: Successively higher forms of adaptation (e.g., intelligence vs. physiological organization; successively higher stages within intelligence) "develop" lower forms. They do not simply appear after the lower forms in development and do not simply exhibit the same principles of functioning (functional invariants). Conversely, the lower forms are necessary conditions for the higher forms, in that the higher forms would not develop if the organism did not realize the lower forms first.

I call the third kind of continuity structural continuity: Piaget asserts that the higher forms of adaptation are "imminent" within the lower forms. Sometimes this relation of imminence, in Piaget's usage, seems to be just another expression for the first (functional) form of continuity. An example is Piaget's statement that the formation of the first habitual (or "acquired") reactions in infancy involves assimilation and accommodation in the same way that more clearly intelligent behavior patterns do. On other occasions Piaget seems to be implying something more, that the process through which infants come to form habits is nearly, but not quite, intelligent. On still other occasions the intended connection seems to be even stronger: The process of habit formation actually contains the properties of intelligence; however, these properties do not mediate infants' behavior. For example, in the discussion of the second stage of sensorimotor development (the first acquired associations, or habits), Piaget describes intention, which becomes manifest in the third and fourth stages, as "imminent" in the behavior of the first and second stages but unaware of itself and hence unable to "differentiate behavior" (OI, p. 47). Similarly, at the end of the volume, Piaget comments that invention, which he regards as criterial of the sixth stage, arises by construction, and since construction occurs from the beginning of life, invention must be "in bud" from the outset (p. 418). As has been my practice up to this point, in reconstructing Piaget's account I will follow his usages as closely as possible, letting ambiguities stand where they may, and attempt to resolve those issues of relevance to my analysis in the critique.

I digress to note two different senses in which Piaget saw more primitive forms as constituting necessary conditions for higher forms (the relation of necessary condition is historical continuity). These are two reasonably well demarcated meanings; they are not an ambiguity in Piaget's usage. First, the more primitive forms furnish the content, originally the specific behaviors (or, as Piaget says, "action schemes"), for the higher forms. For example, Piaget describes spontaneous action cycles at his second stage in which infants repeat actions that incorporate initially incidental or accidental features of previous actions (e.g., repeating not only the act of sucking, but sucking plus systematically allowing the tongue to protrude). The first stage, which is the reflex stage, furnishes a necessary condition for this development insofar as, according to Piaget, these Stage II (acquired) reactions must be based in an existing reflex cycle (e.g., sucking).

The second sense in which the earlier form is a necessary condition for the later one is that the abstract organization embodied by the later form (the repetitive sucking plus tongue protrusion) would not arise except insofar as it builds incrementally from progressively simpler forms of organization. We might call this second sense of necessary condition a structural, as opposed to content, requirement.

These considerations regarding necessary conditions raise the further question of the transition process itself. Piaget argues that successively higher forms arise through the operation of the same "functional invariants" (i.e., assimilation, accommodation, and organization) that characterize all of activity. For instance, some of the initially "accidental features" that infants begin to incorporate into their action cycles during the second stage turn out to be, as Piaget says, "heterogeneous" behaviors (i.e., behaviors involving different sensorimotor modalities) that previously functioned autonomously. Examples include putting the thumb in the mouth and sucking, or looking at an object and simultaneously grasping something that happens to be the same object. Through what is initially an effort only to reproduce (i.e., to "assimilate") an "interesting result" of an old behavior pattern, infants acquire a new and more complex pattern.

Thus far we have considered some of the central ways in which Piaget regarded intelligence as continuous with other forms of activity of the organism and ultimately with biological organization itself. Indeed, the primary aim of *Origins* is to analyze intelligence in terms of these continuities. Nonetheless, the problem remains of how Piaget distinguished intelligence from other forms of adaptation such that he might study it in this way. He singled out two general properties that he believed were virtually definitional of intelligence and to which I have already alluded in passing. One of these properties was intention, which Piaget believed was a necessary component of intelligence at any level (i.e., sensorimotor or reflective). The other property was invention, which he regarded as a property only of reflective intelligence.

According to Piaget, neither of these properties exists at lower levels of functioning of the organism. In his account, habits, for example, do not exhibit either intention or invention and therefore are not (yet) intelligent. Nonetheless, Piaget also says that the *process* through which infants form their first habits is related to intentional action in the three ways described earlier. It is functionally analogous to intentional action insofar as both activities involve assimilation and accommodation and the same complex of interactions between these processes (functional continuity). Its results (namely the acquired habits) are a necessary condition for the development of more intentional behavior (historical continuity). Finally, intention is "imminent" within it (structural continuity). Manifest intention (and ultimately invention), moreover, will develop from these more primitive reactions, insofar as the ordinary exercise of these reactions will lead to their progressive "enlargement" or "complication" into more complex forms.

The thrust of Piaget's theorizing can be best appreciated if we take account of the positions Piaget considered to oppose his general view. He distinguished four such opposing positions. The first was the empiricist-associationist position, which, in Piaget's view, held that intelligence is the result of external pressure from the environment ("pure" experience) and has its origins in habits, which are a primary fact. The second position, which Piaget coins "vitalistic intellectualism" (and associates with Buytendijk and Maine de Biran), attributes to children what Piaget describes as an "intelligence faculty" from birth. Both habit and intelligence are derived from this faculty. Although the faculty does not contain the specific structures of later thought (the apriorist, and third, position), it consists of a motive force that resembles reason and emanates from an experiencing self. The third, apriorist position gives children not only an intelligence faculty, but the "structures" through which intelligence will be realized (Piaget had in mind the Gestaltists). The fourth position was Piaget's reading of what he termed the "pragmatist" view. In this view intelligence was the result neither of the direct impress of experience nor of any preformed endogenous factor. It was constructed by the organism through its actions on the environment, these actions consisting of a series of gropings controlled largely from without, by chance contacts.

Piaget's alternative is his theory of assimilation, which has been outlined in the preceding pages. According to this theory, intelligence arises through the development of assimilatory activity, that is, the basic attempt of the organism to incorporate input and reproduce (or, as Piaget sometimes says, rediscover) its experience. Experience (first position) plays a central role in this process, but only as mediated by the assimilating activity of the subject. In contrast to the second view (intellectualism), intelligence is elaborated little by little. One of the products of this elaboration is the formation of a self, which develops correlatively with children's concept of the external environment. In contradistinction to the third (apriorist) position, the specific structures of intelligence are also elaborated little by little, each one developing from the one before it, on the basis of the subject's structuring activity (assimilation and accommodation). Hence, it is the structuring activity that is given, not the structures. Finally, although Piaget's position overlaps significantly with the fourth view, which emphasizes activity, it differs in that it conceives the "gropings" of the subject as directed (by the attempt to assimilate) and specifies the nature of that direction.

Although I will follow Piaget's fivefold classification of possible theoretical positions no farther, I will mention that far from presenting a genuine alternative to the four rejected views, Piaget in fact falls prey to, and invites, the very kind of error he claims they are subject to (see Critique).

2.2. The stages of sensorimotor intelligence

I proceed next with the six stages of infant intelligence that Piaget describes. The sequence begins with reflexive reactions (Stage I) and ends with behaviors that Piaget regarded as indicative of the beginning of cogitative or reflective intelligence (Stage VI). In between are the stages involving the first acquired reactions, or habits (Stage II), and the stages of sensorimotor intelligence proper (Stages III through V).

The six stages again extend from birth to approximately 18 months of age and correspond to the stages delineated in *Construction of reality*. Given that there is overlap in the behaviors used as reference points, the age ranges for each stage are the same. The stages are based as before on Piaget's observations of his three children when the children were engaged in purely spontaneous activity, in natural functions such as feeding, or in impromptu experiments.

Piaget sees the six stages as comprising characteristic patterns of increasing complexity more than properly demarcated periods in development. Especially within the first two stages, Piaget says, development from one pattern to another can be quite rapid for any given behavior, and indefinitely many intermediate steps can be identified (see OI, pp. 150 and 331, for relevant discussion). I therefore present the sequence of stages with Piaget's qualification in mind.

Stage I. The first stage, as I have said, consists of the use of reflexes. Although Piaget does not consider the functioning of a reflex itself to be intelligent, there are two aspects of the use of some reflexes that Piaget sees as functionally analogous to intelligent activity and as its point of origin. One of these is the tendency of his children to repeat their behavior, which Piaget infers involves an attempt to reproduce the experience that was just perceived or felt (CR, p. 310). This is essentially what Piaget means by intellectual, or psychological, "assimilation." The second aspect is the tendency of these reactions to be elaborated. The reactions extend either to different kinds of input or to different conditions of excitation. For instance, although the sucking reflex initially requires some kind of contact with the inner membrane, sucking is soon triggered by contact with the lips, then the cheek, and so on. The babies' behavior also differentiates, either in the precise nature or in the exact circumstances of its execution. Sucking to nurse, for example, quickly becomes restricted to contact with the nipple. Finally, the behavior becomes more complicated, which in the reflex stage means incorporating a primitive kind of groping and other adjustments. These kinds of elaboration are the result, in Piaget's view, of accommodation or, alternatively, of the interplay of assimilation and accommodation.

The clearest examples of developmental progress in the reflex stage involve sucking. Here Piaget notes a minute progression in Laurent's sucking reactions. As early as the second day, Laurent seizes the nipple with his mouth as he sucks; he no longer needs to have it held there. He also engages in limited groping movements to retrieve the nipple when it slips from his mouth. In the ensuing days, contact of an object with the lips, and eventually with the cheeks, is sufficient to set off combined groping and sucking. The groping itself also develops in that it becomes increasingly systematic. For example, Laurent searches with his lips for the nipple only on the side of his face where the nipple touched his cheek. Initially he searched on both sides. Finally, there is a gradual differentiation of both the sucking and searching patterns, such that sucking to nurse, for example, occurs only with the nipple (and when Laurent is hungry he rejects other inputs) and nonnutritive sucking with a variety of other things (OI, Obs. 1 through 10).

In addition to these elaborations, Piaget notes a kind of "empty" sucking that appears to occur repetitively for its own sake. It is not stimulated by any input from the outside and does not appear to be a reflexive response to stimulation within the mouth. It seems to function instead through a kind of autoexcitation as do other bouts of nonnutritive sucking that the children engage in.

The ingredients that Piaget takes as the point of departure for intelligence are evident in these examples. They include the need for repetition, the progressive complication of the reaction through the need to adjust the gradual extension of the reaction to new circumstances, and its progressive differentiation in both form and application. In the last case, progressive differentiation, Piaget speaks of the beginnings of motor recognition.

Stage II. The demarcation point between the first and second stages is that in the course of the repetitive cycles involving reflexive actions (e.g., sucking), the children begin to retain certain movements external to the reflex and repeat these movements as well. Thus, rather than repeat mere "empty" sucking, for example, an infant may come to repeat a whole cycle that involves sucking, protruding the tongue, accumulating saliva, swallowing, licking the lips, and so on (Obs. 11–14). Similarly, Piaget notes occasions on which his children seem to take notice of the sharp cry that ends a cry of rage and then keep it up for its own sake (Obs. 40).

Piaget uses the term "circular reaction" (following J. M. Baldwin) for these repetitive cycles that, rather than being inborn, are actually acquired by the children. As I already noted, the circular reaction associated with the second stage is the "primary" circular reaction, which involves the repetition of actions for their effects on the children's own bodies. Important for circular reactions of all types, in Piaget's treatment, is that the so-called effects that are being reproduced have accompanied the behaviors in question from the first, or at least could have done so in principle. What demarcates the different stages is whether the children notice and attempt systematically to reproduce these effects.

Along the same lines, Piaget says that, as of the second stage, the repetitive cycles in which the children engage are directed by the new results to which they lead. The circular reaction is thus to be distinguished from the repetitive reflex cycle of the first stage, in which the reaction continues on essentially fed by itself. The reflex cycle may be intensified or exacerbated by the intermittent "effects" on which the children capitalize at the second stage; however, it is not materially altered by them. Thus, whereas at the first stage accidental protrusion of the tongue might simply lead either to sucking or to an increase in the animation of sucking already in progress, at the second stage the whole reaction will become substantively modified to incorporate this movement (OI, p. 138).

As I mentioned earlier, a second kind of reaction develops during this stage, namely the coordination of actions that were previously executed separately. Piaget discusses three patterns in particular: finger or thumb sucking (i.e., systematically bringing the fingers to the mouth to suck them, as opposed to sucking the fingers if they happen to graze the mouth or otherwise end up in it), turning to look at sound sources (this being a coordination of hearing and looking), and reaching for things seen (a coordination of looking and grasping). Piaget's central claim is that these patterns come about through a mechanism similar to that involved in the formation of the primary circular reactions. The initial coordination of actions is "accidental." For instance, the children look by chance at the hand that grasps. They then attempt to reproduce this result, and the reproduction is accomplished through the reciprocal "enlargement" (alternatively referred to as "reciprocal assimilation") of the two actions in question. I will discuss Piaget's treatment of hearing and looking and looking and reaching in some detail, because these analyses are Piaget's most focused and detailed efforts anywhere to account for developmental transitions. As I will discuss in chapter 6, his later (e.g., Piaget, 1974/1980b, 1975/1985) accounts of the transition process depend entirely on the account described here.

The analysis of the coordination of hearing and looking is of interest primarily for Piaget's theory of why (psychologically) the children turn to look at a sound source. This theory leads directly into Piaget's account of the transition to the fully coordinated behavior. The account of the developmental transition is elaborated more fully for looking and reaching than for hearing and looking. Hence I will reserve my main reconstruction of the transition argument for the presentation of looking and reaching.

To continue, then, with looking and hearing, Piaget observes that within the first two months of life his children pointedly turn to look at sound sources. Most of Piaget's examples involve sound sources that are difficult to locate, so as to rule out the possibility that the children are turning their heads merely to hear the sound more distinctly. In these more elusive instances, the children engage in active visual search and eventually stop at the target. When Piaget knocks his pipe on a piece of wood, for example, Laurent continues to look until he comes precisely to the point of contact (Obs. 49).

On the basis of various considerations, Piaget argues that, in turning to the sound source, the children are not turning to see the source from which the sound emanates. They are not looking for the "thing" they heard, because, as specified by the account of children's object concept at this stage, they have no concept of "thing" defined independently of the modality that perceives it. Instead, according to Piaget, all that has happened is that one system (auditory) has been stimulated, and this prompts the other systems to orient and seek stimulation as well. (Piaget notes that the children may begin to suck as well as look when they hear a sound; however, the sucking is likely to conflict with attentive looking.) So although we might say that the children are trying to look *at the same time as* (or *when*) they hear, we would not say that they are trying to look at *what* they hear.

Thus, at its inception, this "coordination" of hearing and looking introduces no real novelty. But insofar as turning to look "when" something is heard produces an interesting visual image, the children will try to reproduce this experience. In this way, hearing will come to provoke looking, just as starting to suck comes to provoke squirting saliva. The real transition – to looking at "what" is heard – follows. By virtue of the fact that the same "sensorial image" is at the point of "intersection" of several simultaneous currents of assimilation, Piaget says, that image will tend to become solidified and projected into an external, coherent universe (OI, p. 143; see also my earlier reconstruction of Piaget's account of the object concept).

As I said, Piaget treats the transition process more extensively in his account of the coordination of looking and reaching. The problem, in Piaget's view, is to understand how the children advance from the point where they look on the one hand and grasp on the other, to the point where they grasp the thing they see. Piaget's general argument is again that the transition begins to occur when the children begin to grasp *when* they see. Attempts to reproduce the resulting experience will lead them to grasp *what* they see. I next discuss the account in more detail.

Piaget distinguishes five substages in the development from purely reflexive grasping to coordinated looking and grasping. Two of these substages stand out as critical. One is the moment when the eye begins to direct the movement of the hand at all, regardless of whether any external object is involved. The other is when the eye begins to direct specifically the grasping of an object. These are the third and fourth substages, respectively.

During the first substage the children both exhibit a grasping reflex when contact is made with the palm and engage in impulsive movements of the arms and legs, which may or may not be related to the use of the reflex. There is no coordination of any of these movements with vision. The children do not direct their eyes to their manual activity (they have barely begun to direct their glance at all), and they do not bring what they grasp to their eyes.

In the second substage two novel patterns appear. One is circular reactions relating to grasping, for example, scratching the sheet, grasping it, and letting it go (all without looking) (Obs. 53). Related to these reactions involving grasping for its own sake is the observation that the children grasp objects not just when the objects touch the palm, but when they touch the tip of the finger. Groping upon the loss of an object from the hand, however, is limited and unsystematic. The second novel pattern of this substage is that the children watch the movements of their hands and fingers when they enter the visual field. However, although the children follow these movements with their eyes, they do not in any obvious way adjust these movements to accommodate their glance. They do not, for example, appear to hold their hands in the visual field or alter their activity in any other clear way, once the hands are seen (Obs. 60 to 61).

In the third substage the children begin actually to direct the movements of the hand with the glance, or at least one might say that the movements of the hand become responsive to the glance. Piaget cites as examples occasions on which the children happened to have grasped objects outside the visual field and (in most cases) were on their way to carrying these objects to the mouth, when the hand (plus object) came into the visual field. On these occasions the children stopped the movement toward the mouth in midflight and looked at the hand. Then they continued the movement to the mouth. Lucienne, on one occasion, went so far as to move the object back a distance once she started to look at it. She also took it out of her mouth to look at it after she began sucking (Obs. 68). Piaget notes that Lucienne made no attempt to grasp the object when it was simply presented to her visually. It had to touch her fingers first.

Piaget cites a fourth substage during which the children actually grasp an object that is seen but not touched. At this point, however, they grasp the object only if both hand and object are in the visual field. This grasping is often preceded by the children's alternately looking back and forth between the hand and the object (e.g., Obs. 79).

In the fifth substage the children grasp what they see, whether or not they see their hand at the same time. Conversely, they bring into the visual field things they have grasped.

I noted before that the third and fourth substages were critical. Let us see how Piaget accounts for them. The third substage involves holding the hand (or otherwise adjusting it) in the visual field once it is seen. Before coming to the question of the mechanism of this change per se, Piaget attempts to explain what it is that has developed. He thinks that, whereas in the second stage the eye simply attempted to follow what the hand did, now, in the third substage, the hand will try to preserve what the eye sees. This is not, in Piaget's view, a true coordination of the two patterns, because the children as yet neither grasp what they see nor bring into the visual field that which they grasp. There is only a conjoining, or a "reciprocal assimilation," of the two patterns. The children are simply attempting to preserve a reaction.

The mechanism of this conjoining is as follows. The children attempt to conserve both the activity of their hands and what they see, although these are initially separate impulses. Thus, when they initially see their hand, they will want both to continue to see this spectacle and to continue the motor and kinesthetic sensation of moving their hand. To begin with, they attempt to follow the sight with their eyes. Then, however, according to Piaget, a critical discovery occurs. The children find that in moving their hand in a particular way (moving it back, moving it more slowly, etc.), they can preserve the interesting image for their sight. At the same time, preserving the image for their sight becomes an impetus, or stimulus, for the activity of the hand, whereas previously only tactile stimuli affected its activity. Thus, there is a tendency to preserve (repeat and accommodate) the whole cycle (OI, pp. 108–9).

Piaget hastens to point out that this initial conjoining (reciprocal assimilation) of the tactile and visual patterns does not of itself result in an "identification" of the tactile with the visual image, or of the visual with the tactile image. This step, however, will follow as a matter of course, as in the crossing of two converging lines. The conjoining of the two patterns through reciprocal assimilation is the beginning of this convergence. As I have discussed with reference to other points, Piaget's idea here is that the simultaneous application of different actions to the same object will tend to externalize and solidify that object (OI, p. 108).

Piaget explains the transition to the fourth substage in a similar way. If the hand is already under the influence of the eye, it is but a small step, he says, for the hand to grasp what the eye sees. As it is, the hand already continues or intensifies its action in progress once it is seen, or it alters its action (e.g., becomes immobilized) to facilitate or augment the viewing experience. Sooner or later, according to the account, the hand will grasp an object while the eye watches. This grasping will become one of the many actions that the children reproduce for their sight. Reciprocally, moving the visual image will become one of the many actions that the hand reproduces for itself. Thus, says Piaget, "the hand takes hold of what the eye observes, just as the eye tends to look at that which the hand grasps" (OI, p. 119). The fifth substage (in which the children both grasp what they see whether or not their hand is simultaneously visible and bring objects that are grasped into the visual field), in Piaget's view, is only a generalization of the fourth substage. The basis for this generalization is that the behavior patterns of the fourth substage have "taught the child that [grasping what the eye looks at] was possible when the hand is perceived at the same time as the object" (p. 119).

As with the coordination at the third substage, this meeting of the children's actions ("schemata") on a common object, combined with the children's attempt to adjust those actions to each other and to the object, will tend to externalize the object. Another factor that contributes to this externalization is the development of grasping itself. Here Piaget notes that, whereas the children initially have only a "functional" interest in grasping (i.e., grasping as mere exercise), grasping becomes applied to increasingly diverse kinds of objects in increasingly diverse circumstances and is progressively differentiated to suit these different objects and circumstances. This diversification and differentiation, says Piaget, gradually focus the children's interest on the things grasped rather than on the grasping itself. This changed interest, in and of itself, tends to externalize the universe that is serving as "aliment" for the children's activity.

If, in this sense, objects are becoming externalized, the children not only will come to grasp *when* they see, or grasp toward the source at which seeing is stimulated, but will come to grasp *what* they see. The case thus parallels that of hearing and looking.

In summary, as far as the structure of action is concerned, the main development at the second stage is the incorporation of novel elements into the children's behavior cycles, these cycles being based on the reflexive reactions of the first stage. These novel elements arise through "experience," that is, through the exercise of the reflex actions themselves. From the point of view of the external observer, these elements are present all along as intermittent concomitants of the children's behavior. Now, however, the children begin to notice them and to attempt systematically to reproduce them. All of the "elements" or "effects" that the children notice and attempt to incorporate at this stage are immediate sensorial (or "corporeal") effects of the actions in progress rather than effects on things.

This limitation of the children's activity to immediate effects is what prompts Piaget to maintain that behavior at this second stage is not yet intentional and hence not yet intelligent. It is instead "acquired association" or "habit" (OI, p. 47). For a behavior to be intentional, in Piaget's view, it must be directed toward a goal that is detached from the immediate action. In the reactions of Stage II, goal and action are virtually indistinguishable. The end result of protruding the tongue is inherent in the act of protruding the tongue.

Stage III. Stage III is marked by the advent of the secondary circular reaction, through which the children's actions are brought to bear on things. Having achieved a particular result "fortuitously," as Piaget would say, the children attempt to rediscover the action that brought the result about and hence to reproduce the result. Classic examples include shaking noise-making objects so that they make a sound. Here the children shake by chance an object they have grasped. They then attempt to reproduce the sound, and this attempt involves rediscovering the action that led to the sound. Gradually they come to differentiate the action with increasing degrees of precision, such that the sound is reliably reproduced.

I note in passing that shaking an object could also be a "primary" (i.e., Stage II) circular reaction, if its focus were the movement itself and the kinesthetic impressions it creates. As Piaget's examples suggest, one can distinguish empirically whether the reaction is primary or secondary by comparing the attitude that attends the children's action, as well as the specific aspects of the action (e.g., sound or simply movement) that came to be systematically repeated (see Obs. 94 and 102).

Piaget theorized that the secondary circular reactions come about in the same way as the primary circular reactions. Just as the primary circular reactions are grafted onto reflex reactions, the secondary circular reactions are grafted onto primary reactions, that is, onto various "acquired" behaviors that function as primary circular reactions. Piaget notes, for example, that in the secondary reaction in which Lucienne ended up beating her legs to make the dolls swing (Obs. 94), the moving of the legs began as a primary schema, namely an action carried out for its own sake (or its immediate kinesthetic effects), and not for any extrinsic effect it might produce.

Piaget's account of the actual transition to the secondary reaction is that two "primary" schemata come together in much the same manner in which visually guided reaching is acquired. Thus, to continue the preceding example, before Lucienne herself connected the movements of her legs with the swinging of the dolls, she would already have been looking at and listening to the dolls as they swung. At this point she would have tended, separately, to "conserve" the activity of the legs and the spectacle before her eyes, but the eyes would merely have tried to conserve what they saw by continuing to listen, and the legs to conserve what they felt by continuing to move.

Insofar as these activities might co-occur (e.g., the legs continuing their action while the eyes continue theirs), they would tend to become "reciprocally assimilated" (OI, p. 175) in the manner described for the coordinations at the second stage. At the outset of this process Piaget would say of Lucienne that she was beating her legs "at the same time as" she was watching the dolls (as opposed to saying that she was beating her legs "in order to" make the dolls swing). But then as soon as this reciprocal assimilation were formed, Piaget thinks, it would follow as a matter of course that Lucienne would understand that the results she was observing depended on her action. From there she would attempt to "rediscover" the actions that led to these interesting results, and the cycle of the secondary circular reaction would be established.

Piaget considers the secondary circular reaction to be very nearly intentional insofar as it involves, in his view, a greater separation of means and ends than do the primary circular reactions. The separation is greater, he thinks, both because the rediscovery of the actions that led to the desired result requires more active and complex apprenticeship than does the rediscovery of actions for the primary circular reactions and because the reactions are focused on an element that is external to them. It is not just that we, as observers, know that an external object is involved. The object is known (it is seen and is associated with swinging) by the children before they attempt to swing it. In comparison, says Piaget, the thumb is not known, in the same sense, before the act of thumb sucking (thumb sucking is a typical primary circular reaction in Piaget's account).

Nonetheless, the secondary circular reactions are not fully intentional, according to Piaget, for two reasons. First, there is no real intermediary between the action and its result. The children do one thing (e.g., beat their legs) and anticipate a certain result (the swinging of the dolls). They do not do one thing in order to do another or in order to have another done. Second, these reactions are not adaptations to new situations. They are attempts to reproduce an already given result; they involve a differentiation of means and ends after the event rather than before it. The behavior patterns of the fourth stage will surpass those of the third in both ways and will thus mark the advent of truly intentional behavior, in Piaget's view.

Stage IV. The advances of Stage IV are pivotal in Piaget's account, as well as pivotal in development according to that account. The unifying feature of the fourth stage, according to Piaget, is the intercoordination of secondary "schemata" (by which Piaget means acquired patterns that arose through secondary circular reaction) and their application to new situations. The most important advance here is the development of means–ends behavior, in which means are unambiguously distinguished from ends and in which the children know the end to be achieved before the action takes place. Means and ends are unambiguously distinguished in the specific sense that intermediate actions that do not themselves realize the children's goal are introduced before the goal is reached. The end is known before the action takes place insofar as, rather than seek to rediscover a result previously obtained by chance, the children now pursue an end that has not yet been attained. Although this end is suggested by the immediately perceptible surroundings (rather than by an internal plan), circumstances prevent the children from realizing it directly. If the children want to attain it, they must seek alternative and indirect means.

Thus, another novel feature of this first explicit form of means–ends organization is that a certain amount of improvisation takes place in order to find the means. Earlier the "means" that the children used to realize primary or secondary "effects" arose from the attempt only to rediscover the action that had previously led to the desired result. The improvisations at this stage are restricted, however, to an application of existing action patterns (modified, however, to suit the circumstances). At the fifth stage the children will truly innovate.

Piaget discusses three main kinds of means–ends, behavior. The first includes instances that Piaget considers intermediate between the third and fourth stages, in which the children pull a string to obtain something that is out of reach. In one case, Piaget has offered Laurent a piece of paper and then placed it on the basinet hood, just where the hood is joined by a string connecting the hood to the bassinet handle. First Laurent tries to reach for the paper directly. After a while, it seems to Piaget, he looks for the string. He then grasps the string and pulls it harder and harder. When the paper is about to fall, he releases the string and catches the paper. Piaget considers this example an intermediate case, because the paper was placed at the location (the hood) Laurent already associated with pulling the string. Therefore, he might have pulled the string not in order to get the paper, but instead of trying to get it. He pulled the string only to do with the paper what he normally does with the hood (or with things hanging from it); however, the action had the fortunate consequence of making the paper fall (Obs. 120; also Obs. 121).

The second kind of behavior Piaget describes involves the removal of obstacles blocking an object the children want. Laurent, for example, strikes a cushion (or Piaget's hand, depending on the experiment) out of the way to get the object beyond it (Obs. 122–3).

The third kind of behavior involves the use of an intermediary to achieve some further result. As mentioned earlier regarding causality, Jacqueline pushes her mother's hand back toward a flounce her mother had been swinging in order to get her to do it again (Obs. 127). Alternatively, she places objects on the floor in order to kick them (Obs. 129).

The transition mechanism that Piaget posits to account for these different patterns is again the reciprocal assimilation of the component action patterns (schemata) involved. He explains Laurent's eventual retrieval of the paper via the string (Obs. 120) as follows. After having failed to grasp the paper directly, Laurent begins instead to "assimilate" the paper to the schema of pulling the string. That is, he pulls the string at first not with the intention of making the paper fall, but to provoke the usual effect that pulling the string creates, namely shaking, or movement. Here, as I noted, Piaget points out that the paper was situated at a location that Laurent already associated with pulling the string in order to create movement. At the same time, however, theorizes Piaget, Laurent continues all the while to "apply" the schema of grasping the paper, in the sense that he continues to desire to grasp it. As a result of this "double assimilation" (OI, p. 231) and the fact that the paper eventually does fall, pulling the string becomes a means of grasping the paper.

The other two cases I described (obstacle removal and the use of an intermediary) are more complicated, because the objects they involve are not already in a relationship, as are the string and the paper. Mother's hand is not attached to the flounce, and the "obstacle" that is in the way must be put out of the way. Piaget theorizes that the children arrive at the idea of these relationships first by attempting to assimilate one object to the other. In effect, they transfer to the object they can reach (mother's hand, the obstacle) the actions they wish to perform, or wish to have performed, on the more distant object (OI, pp. 233, 235). But, Piaget continues, simple assimilation will not work. Beating mother's hand as one would like to have the flounce beaten will not result in the beating of the flounce. Mother's hand has to be maneuvered in a particular way in order to accomplish the result. This particular way must take into account both the fact that the object is a hand (i.e., a thing that is responsive to some movements and not others and that, by the fourth stage, is appreciated as the center of a certain amount of causal activity) and the requirements of the objective (i.e., the hand must be propelled not just in any direction, but specifically toward the flounce).

What all this means, according to Piaget, is that reciprocal assimilation no longer works by simple "fusion" of the schemata being combined as it did previously. It now operates through the "inclusion" of one schema in the other, in conjunction with the elaboration of the necessary spatial, causal, and temporal relations among the objects on which the schemata bear (OI, p. 234).

Stage V. In Piaget's theory, the central developments of Stages V and VI elaborate the basic means–ends framework established in Stage IV. My treatment of these two remaining stages will therefore be brief, given that the essential explanatory tenets of the theory are presented in Piaget's discussion of the earlier stages, and the account becomes more descriptive thereafter.

In Stage V, the children, confronted by a novel and initially insoluble problem, devise completely novel means to solve it. This behavior contrasts with that of Stage IV, in which the children's improvisation extends only to the application of familiar means (e.g., striking something) to a novel situation (removing an obstacle to retrieve a more distant object).

The novel means are constructed by a process Piaget describes as cumulative groping. With this process the children capitalize on the chance effects of their unsuccessful attempts to solve a problem. The effects that are exploited in this way are singled out because the children have in their repertoire action patterns (schemata) that will produce those effects. First the children recognize that a particular accidental effect is both a result that moves them closer to their goal and a result that they can produce. They then set about attempting to produce it or other accidental effects arising from that attempt, until they solve the problem at hand. The new procedure thus devised then becomes consolidated and more finely adapted through further use.

Piaget gives as an early example of this process a case in which Laurent is trying to retrieve a toy from the far end of a circular tier of a table. He is accustomed in similar circumstances to drawing the support object (in this case the tier) directly toward him in a straight line. This will not work in this instance, however, because the support can be moved only laterally or in a circular motion, given that it pivots about an axis. After repeated, unsuccessful attempts to draw the tier forward, Laurent seems to observe that it has moved sideways by small degrees. He then starts to apply the action of pushing, which is one of the ways he has come to displace objects sideways (Obs. 148 "repeated").

Faced with a more difficult problem, Jacqueline tries to pull a large, irregular cardboard rooster through the playpen bars. At first she tries to pull it directly, and it gets stuck. During some of these attempts, however, the rooster falls down, and in retrieving it, Jacqueline happens to tilt it up before it reaches the bars. The lowering, raising, and tilting are sufficient to get the rooster through the bars. After a while Jacqueline seems to have developed the procedure of letting the rooster drop intentionally, so that she can pick it up and pull it through. Later she modifies this procedure into a lowering motion that does not involve letting go (Obs. 165).

Piaget gives no systematic account of a transition process into this stage, except insofar as he traces the historical roots of the schemata the children bring into play. He does note in passing, however, that the mechanism by which the children devise their new procedures, namely the tertiary circular reaction, shares with the more primitive (primary and secondary) circular reactions the attempt essentially to "reproduce experience." It differs, however, in that the children no longer attempt only to repeat a previous effect but to gradate and vary it.[3]

---

[3] As with the secondary circular reaction, which forms the basis of the means–ends behavior of the fourth stage, the tertiary circular reaction (i.e., the process of repetition with systematic variations) is frequently seen outside explicit goal pursuit. A typical example is dropping or throwing things at different angles to watch their trajectories.

Stage VI. The sixth stage, which ends the sensorimotor period, contains the beginnings of "representational" or "systematic" intelligence, that is, discursive thought. In the present context, namely the consideration of intelligent action, the advance of interest is that of invention through "mental combination" or "deduction" (OI, p. 331). In speaking of invention in this way Piaget is trying to distinguish invention from the "discoveries" that arise as a result of the cumulative groping of the fifth stage.

Essentially, Piaget views invention through mental combination as a speeded and internalized cumulative groping. So in some sense, the problem-solving process in which the children engage is the same as in the fifth stage, only the process is taking place in their heads.

Most of the examples Piaget presents for this stage consist of the children's solutions to problems that were discussed in connection with the fifth stage. The same problems appear, because one or more of the children did not solve them until the sixth stage. Either they were not interested in them or Piaget did not present them earlier.

The main difference with the Stage V solutions is that the solutions of the sixth stage are almost immediate. Thus, a child of Stage VI attempting to pull the rooster through the bars for the first time would, perhaps after one or two false starts, lower the rooster from the bars before rotating it and drawing it forward. The lowering would no longer have to happen accidentally for the child to recognize that this was a necessary or advantageous middle step in solving the problem. The child would foresee its consequences and its potential utility (see Obs. 178 for a similar comparison).

Piaget stresses that solutions of this kind are sudden, or immediate, only in the sense that they are rapid, not in the sense that they are in any way pregiven. Piaget thus intends to distinguish the kind of insight the children demonstrate at this stage from the "sudden insight" or "sudden structurization" (OI, p. 332) described by Gestaltists (such as Köhler). Insofar as the children appear to be suddenly restructuring the perceptual field, this is not the result of the application of an innate organization to the data of perception. It is the outcome of a process whereby the children mentally apply, in sequence, possible courses of action.

The possible courses of action (schemata) the children will try out are completely conditioned by their individual histories, as in the fourth and fifth stages. In Stage VI, however, the schemata that are aroused in this way remain in a state of "latent activity" (p. 347) rather than being materially applied. In that latent state they intercombine with other latent schemata, as opposed to being "reciprocally assimilated" through actual action.

3. Later development

Piaget's primary motivation for studying infancy was his belief that the origins of mental life were indeed to be found there. Therefore, I conclude this reconstruction of Piaget's treatment of infancy with a summary of his view of the relation between infant intelligence (and "reality") and child thought. Piaget's most detailed discussion of this topic is contained in the concluding chapter of *Construction of reality*. I draw primarily from that discussion in the following overview.

As can be seen in the account of Stage VI of sensorimotor intelligence, Piaget thinks that the same kinds of "continuity" exist between "sensorimotor" and "representational" intelligence (i.e., thought proper) as exist between the different stages of sensorimotor intelligence. There is functional continuity (in the strict sense I designated earlier) insofar as reflective thought operates by the same principles of assimilation, accommodation, and organization as sensorimotor intelligence. There is historical or material continuity both in the sense that sensorimotor intelligence is a necessary precondition for reflective thought and insofar as the specific schemata that children have elaborated over the sensorimotor period continue to be a source for interpreting experience (a pail is something to put things in, whether you actually carry out the action or only think it). Finally, there is structural continuity, Piaget thinks, insofar as the very organization of a deduction, or the very substance of a causal judgment, spatial intuition, and so on, in reflective thought is exactly a reconstruction of the organizations and understandings that were achieved in infancy at the sensorimotor level.

A special problem arises, however, in this transition to later thought. It would seem, Piaget says, that by the time children reach the later stages of sensorimotor intelligence, they have succeeded in developing a mental life that borders on rational thought. As of the fourth stage, he claims, children have developed a system of schemata capable virtually of unlimited combination, a property also associated with logical concepts and relations. By the sixth stage children appear to be capable even of internal regroupings of these schemata. Piaget likens this capacity to mental deduction and construction. Further, by the end of the sensorimotor period, children would appear to have elaborated a coherent and objective universe of objects, space, time, and causality.

One might think, therefore, continues Piaget, that once children are capable of representational thought (Stage VI and beyond), this thought would simply extend the whole complex of sensorimotor operations and understandings more or less directly, thereby exhibiting the rationality and objectivity that these operations and understandings seem to embody implicitly. According to Piaget, thought at its outset, however, does not do this but exhibits properties of the earlier – not the later – stages of sensorimotor intelligence. It involves a subjectivity (egocentrism) unaware of itself and only a juxtaposition of ideas rather than true deduction. Piaget's discussion of the relation between infant and child thought is above all else an attempt to account for this alleged incongruity.

Piaget gives two reasons for the disparity. One is that in practical intelligence alone, which continues to develop through the highest stages of reflective intelligence, "residues" of the earlier stages of sensorimotor intelligence appear when especially complex problems are encountered. Citing a series of experiments by A. Rey (1934) involving children between 3 and 8 years of age, Piaget notes an early phase during which, when confronted by a practical problem that eludes their comprehension, children resort simply to repeating the act they think should be performed. They do not adapt this act to the circumstances of the problem or establish the proper relations among the elements of the problem. Their behavior therefore resembles that of the third or fourth stage of sensorimotor intelligence insofar as, according to Piaget's account, they confer on their gestures a kind of "absolute value." They do this, Piaget thinks, because they have a "residual belief" in the power of their activity (CR, p. 358). He reasons further that this conferral of power is tantamount to children's having forgotten momentarily that things in the world are permanent substances, organized in space and time, and capable of acting on one another causally.

The second and more important reason Piaget gives for the apparent regression of early child thought is that the transition to representational thought presents specific obstacles. The only way children can surmount these obstacles, he says, is precisely to repeat on the representational "plane" the same progressive series of adaptations that were carried out on the sensorimotor plane.

Piaget discusses two obstacles in particular. The first is a change in aim: Whereas sensorimotor intelligence aims only at "utilization" and "success," conceptual thought aims for knowledge and, in aiming for knowledge, places the highest value on truth (as opposed to success) (CR, p. 359). Its primary characteristics therefore include such processes as judgment and proof. The very ideas of judgment and proof are foreign to the infant, however, even to the infant engaged in clearly goal-directed activity (Stage IV and beyond) or to the infant who systematically "experiments" with his or her actions in order to "see" their results (Stage V). Equally alien, notes Piaget, is the idea of explaining phenomena, as opposed simply to foreseeing them (p. 377).

The second obstacle is that, whereas sensorimotor intelligence is at most "adapted" to another person, conceptual thought is genuinely socialized. Infants can imitate others or anticipate their actions. However, this is not the same thing as subordinating thought to collective norms or exchanging ideas, both essential characteristics of a socialized intellect.

Piaget sees these two innovations of conceptual thought as deeply interconnected. The collective nature of thought (second innovation) motivates the search for truth, explanation, and proof (first innovation). Alternatively, as long as children's aim is only to utilize reality or exert influence on it rather than to represent it as a thing in itself (i.e., to discover the "truth"), they have no reason to go beyond elaborating a system of relations between things in the world and themselves, or between one (external) thing and another, but viewed from their own perspective. Once there is an aim to communicate or to obtain information from someone else, however, it will become necessary to envision how the world might appear from a different point of view. The truth, so to speak, will depend on coordinating different possible points of view.

In earlier chapters I reviewed Piaget's attempt to show how difficult this coordination of perspectives purportedly is for young children. Children are much more easily "led to satisfy [their] desires," he thought, and to judge things from their own perspective than to anticipate the perspective of others and hence arrive at an "objective" point of view (CR, p. 363). They also exhibit an allegedly complementary tendency toward docility regarding the social environment. They tend to mimic what they hear and to imitate, without understanding, the attitudes they observe. In the context of the comparison with infant intelligence these two tendencies suggest to Piaget a lack of coordination (or "equilibrium") between assimilation and accommodation.

Early reasonings, too, he thinks, exhibit the same structural properties as infants' first coordinations of sensorimotor schemata. Children assimilate one concept or one idea to the next rather than properly subordinate one to the other. Logical deduction requires this subordination.

Regarding "reality," although by 2 years of age children may have externalized and substantialized objects and events in the immediate environment, they become egocentric all over again in their attempt to understand more distant phenomena. Mother may move of her own accord and along her own trajectory; however, the sun and moon follow children around. Near objects may be regarded as having constant form and dimensions; however, on a country drive children will say that the mountains are moving and changing shape. Therefore, says Piaget, the mountains are not objects, because they lack permanence of form and mass. Similarly, just as the Stage IV infant's behavior with vanishing objects suggests a belief in the existence of multiple objects or in some uneasy compromise between the individual and the multiple, so too does children's belief that the sun follows them presuppose the existence of many suns.

To this list Piaget adds young children's difficulty with "conservation" problems. Just as infants, he thinks, believe that objects "return to the void" (CR, p. 371) when they are no longer seen, so do young children think that the quantity of a substance "augments or diminishes according to the form [it] takes, and that a substance which dissolves [e.g., sugar in water] is completely anni-hilated" (p. 371).

As for causality, Piaget believes that a direct extension of senso-rimotor magicophenomenalist "efficacy" can be found in occur-rences of child magic. Here, in moments of anxiety or desire, according to Piaget, children resurrect their belief in the efficacy of their own activity through phenomenalistic connections arising from chance comparisons. Further, although children may under-stand at a practical level that they cannot control the movement of either adults or various physical phenomena (e.g., the sun, stars, rain, wind, clouds), when it is a matter of explaining how things operate they may represent the universe as a large machine cre-ated by humans and designed for their well-being. At the same time, children may endow the individual things in the universe with a will and a sense of purpose, all because children, in Piaget's view, cannot conceive of an action that does not have a conscious goal. Thus, if children do not themselves control the movements of the external world directly, those movements are either influ-enced by them indirectly or are at least modeled in their image.

And so, Piaget concludes, the formation of intelligence and the construction of reality continue throughout development. Sensori-motor intelligence, or intelligence in infancy, prepares this devel-opment but also constrains it. It constrains it, because conceptual thought introduces new realities to which children must adapt, realities that are opposed in some sense by the very nature of sensorimotor intelligence. These new realities include the goal of discovering the truth, as opposed to desire or success, and the need for coordination among individual minds. In the initial state of disadaptation, children's "represented" universe exists in a state of chaotic undifferentiation – between things in the universe and between these things and the self – as did the neonate's practi-cal universe. Differentiation, or understanding, begins with chil-dren's crude attempts both to reduce phenomena to their per-sonal activity or to concepts inspired by it and to "accommodate" in superficial ways to these phenomena. This differentiation or understanding proceeds gradually from the surface of things to their interior as children experiment with the realities they know, seek regularities in them, and construct systems of relations in which to embed them.

Thus, theorizes Piaget, the development of reason, which is "outlined" in sensorimotor intelligence, follows the same "laws" as the development of sensorimotor intelligence "once social life and reflective thought have been formed" (CR, p. 386). This recapitulatory process is for Piaget the central connection between development in infancy and child thought.

CRITIQUE

Piaget elaborates three distinct theories in *Construction of reality* and *Origins:* a theory of infants' conception of reality, a theory of intelligence and how it develops, and a theory about the relation between infants' intelligence and their conception of reality. The theory of infants' conception of reality is parallel, mostly by design, to the theory of children's conception of the world, which I analyzed earlier. Most of its weaknesses, which I will discuss, parallel the problems I raised earlier in reference to the childhood works. Because I have already discussed these problems at length, I will give only illustrations of the shortcomings of the theory of infants' reality. I begin with that overview and then proceed with the second and third theories, which are the focus of the critique.

1. Reality

As with *The child's conception of the world,* one can distinguish stronger and weaker versions of Piaget's claims about infants' reality. At times Piaget appears to say that infants simply do not distinguish elements of their experience that we would distinguish. He claims, for example, that when babies at Stage I recognize something, they recognize not a thing perceived, but a complex experience in which external objects and the babies' response to these objects cannot be distinguished. This is the weak version of the theory, one that we might say attributes to infants an indeterminate or inchoate sense of object, cause, and so forth.

At other times Piaget seems to attribute not a lack of differentiation among elements that we would distinguish, but a confusion of these differentiae. An example of this kind of attribution would be the claim that infants consider (what we know to be) external objects *as* extensions of their activity, or that they take what is "real" to be "created by [their] own actions" (CR, p. 7). As I discussed in earlier chapters, claims of this stronger type presuppose the differentiae that are being conflated, whereas the weaker claims deny their existence. I will discuss the stronger claims first.

The stronger claims are scattered throughout Piaget's treatment of both object and cause. Like the equivalent claims in *The child's conception of the world,* they exhibit unwarranted intrusions of the observer's point of view, presupposition of the end state under inquiry, and various other unexplained assumptions. I consider next the account of magicophenomenalistic causality (Stage III) as a case in point.

Piaget's claim is that, when in the face of an appealing spectacle infants simply repeat gestures that we know are only remotely connected with the spectacle, they envision that they are causing the phenomenon directly. If they envision that they are causing the phenomenon directly and yet do not ensure that there is physical contact between the causally interacting bodies, they must construe the gesture to be efficacious or magical.

But this notion of a direct connection, from which the idea of efficacy follows, would seem to be an observer construction. Children may have only a diffuse concept of the connection between their action and the observed effect, for example, "I wave my hand *and* Daddy waves the book (or the book waves)," as opposed to "The waving of my hand *makes* Daddy wave the book (or makes the book wave)."

Piaget's account raises two other problems, each implied by this general criticism. The first is that the account presupposes the end state it is trying to explain. To speak of direct or efficacious (i.e., magical) causation is to presuppose a contrast with mediated ("spatialized") causality. Magic is causation in the absence of this connection. Hence, for infants to perceive that their behavior "magically" produces a result would seem to presuppose that they understand both that there is no connection between their behavior and its alleged result and that (physical) causation normally involves such connections.

The second problem is that Piaget appears to be making hasty, if not altogether unwarranted, assumptions about infants' intentions in acting as they do. To raise the question of whether infants ascribe a magical versus mediated effect to their behavior presupposes that they intend an instrumental connection of some kind.

As noted in the example of the book, it is not clear that they intend this. These understandings are supposed to be precisely what develops over the six stages. There is the further possibility that they may have no causal intent at all.

In the vast majority of examples that Piaget gives, the children's intent is ambiguous. It is ambiguous to the observer (i.e., it is difficult to interpret), and it may actually *be* ambiguous or indeterminate from the children's point of view. Insofar as we might speculate about the more differentiated intentions behind the children's behavior, however, we do not need, even then, to infer an intent to cause anything. On some occasions the children may only be exhibiting their pleasure. On others they may be doing something closer to expressing a wish or a hope that something might continue. On still others they might be trying in a diffuse way to influence or incite the adult (or, more vaguely, the situation) to occasion the continuation of the desired spectacle.

Relevant to the last possibility – that the children may be trying in a general way to influence the adult – is the fact that, in most of the examples Piaget describes as involving "efficacy," an adult is present and is visible to, or otherwise detectable by, the children. This includes many of those episodes that Piaget classifies as having to do with the children's interaction with physical objects, for instance, the observation in which Piaget waves the book at the end of Jacqueline's crib. If the children's aim is (either diffusely or pointedly) to influence the adult, physical contact is not only unnecessary but, by adult standards, inappropriate.

Piaget attempts to refute some of these counterinterpretations of the children's intent by noting such observations as the children's tendency to intensify their movements the longer the desired effect is suspended or to appear disappointed and expectant when the effect is not reproduced. These reactions are at least as consistent with simple desire and frustration, however, as they are with the intent specifically to cause something. Even if the children were to appear confused or disappointed at the nonrecurrence of the event, this confusion or disappointment could arise from the observation that something that was happening (and happening perhaps in conjunction with the children's actions) is now no longer happening. Alternatively, they might simply be at a loss for what to do.

Piaget could counter again that the only kind of link the children know between their activity and various outcomes is a direct link. The children cry, and mother comes. They have no further concept of how mother's arrival is brought about or how, exactly, their crying is connected with it. Nonetheless, it is still a leap from the notion that mother *does* arrive in conjunction with the children's crying to the notion that the crying "causes" mother to come.

Sometimes, however, Piaget speaks in a slightly different way about the connection the children envision here that does not specifically ascribe a notion of (instrumental) causation. He attributes to the children the idea that mother will appear *only* if they cry, and it will *suffice* to cry for mother to come.

These attributions are also arbitrary. It may be, as Piaget says, that the only way the children respond when they want something to occur is either by crying or by repeating the action previously connected with the desired event. It does not follow from this limitation, however, that the children think that the desired event will not come to pass "unless" they act or that their actions are "sufficient" to bring the event about. They may simply not know how to do anything else. They *cannot* do anything else. To say that they think their action is sufficient, for example, is to presuppose that they think there is something else that they could do (or that could be done) but that they do not "have" to do (or that does not have to be done). Piaget's own theory denies such a possibility.

Piaget's entire argument on this point seems to be another instance of the kind of "negative–positive" error that I discussed in earlier chapters. Piaget has observed ("negatively") that these very young infants do not insert intermediaries or do not ensure that there is spatial contact between movements that he interprets to be causal movements and the bodies to be affected. They only cry or repeat their (empty) gestures. From here Piaget seems to infer ("positively") that the children think they do not "have" to do anything other than what they do (cry or repeat their gestures), that they "must" do what they do, or that it will "suffice" to do it. None of these "positive" inferences is warranted. That the children do not insert intermediaries or ensure spatial contact and that they are limited to crying or repeating their previous behavior can be explained by their failure to understand any connection beyond the correlation between their activity and the desired outcome. Crying or repeating a previous gesture because of a failure to understand any aspects of the situation beyond this correlation is not the same as endowing the crying or the gestures with a special power or explicitly denying that power to anything but this behavior.

Most of the foregoing comments would apply equally to Piaget's account of the later stages of infant causality, for example, to the claim that children at Stage V who place a ball on the ground and merely wait for it to roll or touch a distant object with a stick (rather than displace the object with the stick) think that these actions are "sufficient" to engender the movement of these objects (e.g., CR, Obs. 154). Again, rather than thinking that their action is (necessarily) sufficient or otherwise harboring bizarre ideas about causal interactions, children could be doing as much as they know how to do on the basis of the relationships they understand. Alternatively, they might (as Piaget suggests) be generalizing astutely from other contexts in which these actions have turned out to be sufficient (e.g., when a ball is placed on an incline, it is sufficient simply to place it for it to roll). But in this case we are again left more with the sense that there are gaps in children's understanding than that they hold odd generic beliefs from which these gaps would follow.

Similar problems appear in the account of the object concept. Consider the claim regarding Stages I through II of the object concept, a claim related to the account of Stages I through II of causality: Infants initially conceive (what we know to be) objects as extensions of their own activity and effort. This claim derives principally from the observation that, when an object either vanishes or is displaced out of the immediate line of action, the most infants will do is repeat or directly extend the action that was in progress when the object was present. Alternatively, they resume the position they held when this action took place. Piaget infers that if infants' only way of rediscovering the lost "image" is either to hold their position or repeat (or extend) the action in progress, they must consider the object to be continuous with their activity.

The operative basis of Piaget's inference is that infants are not engaging in any behavior that takes account of the autonomous trajectory of the object, that is, its potential to move independently of their (original) action. Insofar as they do indeed fail to engage in any action that takes account of the autonomy of the object, however, this does not necessarily mean that infants assume that the object's movement is the opposite of autonomous. Nor do they have to assume that the object is somehow dependent on their action or is part of it. As Piaget says, at least in some cases infants may have no concept of whether the object still exists and no concept of it as an independent body moving through space. This "negative" account is different from the "positive" thesis either that infants think the object is *not* independent of their action or that it *is* dependent on it (or is an extension of it).

To put this point somewhat differently, it might be correct to say that the only "reality" Stage I infants can perceive either is, or could be, construed as continuous with their activity. Piaget goes farther and ascribes to infants the view that "anything that is, is an extension of my activity (is caused by me, etc.)." The most it would seem we could attribute to them, however, on the basis of Piaget's evidence, is the notion that things just are, and we as external observers know that the only "things" to which children will grant an existence are those that could in principle be perceived to be continuous with their activity. In other words, whatever reality Stage I infants do perceive, they perceive through their activity, and this activity is severely limited, for instance, to mere repetitions of certain kinds of actions. Either a cause or a consequence of this severe limitation may be infants' very limited grasp of the external (or internal) world. But these gaps need not be filled with "positive" mistakes either about the nature of that world or about the status of the self in that world.

Parallel problems appear in Piaget's arguments regarding Stages III and IV of the object concept. Consider Stage III. Here Piaget's children actively pursue objects when they are visible or even partly hidden (in which case the children may go so far as to raise and discard the partly occluding screen). When objects are completely hidden, however, the children exhibit various signs of noncomprehension or distress. Alternatively, they appear to have given up all interest in the object as if it no longer existed. Piaget theorizes that at this stage the children do not understand that one thing can be behind another. Not recognizing this possibility, they stop pursuing the object. But Piaget also attempts to describe an alternative physics that the children are observing. The one object is "absorbed" or "abolished" by the other. If it subsequently reappears, it is seen to have arisen from the thing that (we know) masked it.

The children may, as Piaget says, fail to understand that one object could be behind another. They might be mystified as to what has happened or even suppose the object to be irreparably gone. They do not, however, have to have an alternative theory to explain the facts before them. Indeed, they may not even notice the same "facts" that we do. From their point of view, the comings and goings of the object may have nothing to do with the screen. Hence, they would have no reason to have a theory regarding the screen. When things reappear they just *are*. They do not have to have appeared by "arising" or "emanating" from the things that (we know) hid them.

Consider, finally, the reaction at Stage IV. Here the children return to search for a missing object at hiding places where they have previously found the object, after they have seen the object disappear at a different location. In addition to theorizing that the object thus remains tied, in the children's view, in some way to their action, Piaget depicts the children's world as consisting of objects that are "at disposal" in the places where they have previously been found. The world also consists of multiple objects where there is in fact only one object.

To begin with, Piaget assumes that when the children search at these former hiding places they are expecting to find the object there. They could, however, be inspecting these locations for some other reason, for example, to affirm that the object is not there or to establish something about the hiding place as opposed to something about the object. Especially in the later "residual" reactions that Piaget describes (e.g., Lucienne's inspection, at $3\frac{1}{2}$ years of age, of her godfather's room after she had just said goodbye to him and seen him drive away in his car [CR, Obs. 51]), if not in the original reactions, this assumption would seem questionable. Let us grant the assumption for the sake of argument, however, and proceed with Piaget's account.

Suppose, then, that when the children erroneously search at former hiding places they think they will find the object there. The notion that objects must therefore be mysteriously attached to locations or must exist in multiple copies are particular abstract consequences that Piaget draws himself regarding the children's behavior. Under the set of physical assumptions that *he* makes about the world, there is no other way the object could possibly be in the locations at which the children search. One of these assumptions is that an object that disappears at location x must be at x, unless it is known to have gone elsewhere. Piaget states explicitly, however, that the children do not share these assumptions. They do not assume that an object that disappears in one place must be in that place, and they do not, according to the theory, understand how objects move from one place to another. If they do not understand these things, they could easily believe that the object they are searching for at a formerly successful location is a single object. Alternatively, they might not have any thoughts about the matter one way or the other. In either case, not understanding the object's movements, they might try to remember particular places where they have found it before.

These are, then, characteristic "strong" claims that Piaget makes about infants' reality. For each claim I have considered, the observer's point of view has intruded beyond the amount of adultomorphizing that must take place given that we look at the infant through adult eyes. Piaget ends up attributing to the children specific, differentiated beliefs based on unwarranted assumptions. If it makes sense to attribute any kind of belief at all in these cases, something more inchoate, and certainly less dogmatic, would seem appropriate. (In speaking of dogmatism I refer to Piaget's ascriptions to the children of the notions that their behavior is necessary or sufficient to bring about particular results.)

In fairness to Piaget, the account does contain instances of these more inchoate, indeterminate descriptions, as well as the stronger claims I have been discussing. The trouble is that the two kinds of descriptions are not the same, as Piaget seems to imply they are.

There are other, less formal reasons for questioning the strong version of the reality thesis. Many of the beliefs ascribed under this thesis can be traced in one way or another to the view that babies see the world as being under their control or at their disposal (i.e., the egocentrism thesis). It would seem at least as plausible, however, that babies regard the world as being anything but under their control or at their disposal (see Watson,

1977, for a pertinent discussion). Hunger occurs and is not immediately satisfied, discomfort arises and is not immediately alleviated, nipples slip away and are not recovered, interesting "images" appear (to the eyes, hand, mouth, or ears) and are not rediscovered. Moreover, if Piaget is at all correct about children's early concept of object, we must add that objects continually disappear in incomprehensible and seemingly irreparable ways.

These considerations raise the possibility that, contrary to the egocentrism thesis and its variations, the development of "reality" in infancy might best be studied from the point of view of infants' progressive gain, rather than their progressive abandonment, of their perceived control over things. At the very least, some attempt ought to be made to reconcile these quite contrary impressions that Piaget, if not most observers, attribute to the infant's reality.

A similar point is that if, according to the weaker version of the reality thesis (wherein infants are attributed with unformed and inchoate beliefs), infants do not start out with the idea that they are "causing" anything, the question arises as to when they may be said to have this idea. When do infants have the perception that they actually can bring about desired (or, for that matter, undesired) events, and what is the evidence that indicates that this is so? Similarly (with reference to the discussion of object), when, from their point of view, is it accurate to say that infants are actually "searching" for something that has disappeared? When do they recognize that a lost object is a thing about which they can do something? These questions are not so far from some of the points that Piaget addressed, and portions of his data might profitably be used by others to examine them. However, Piaget never squarely confronts them, and he clearly raises other issues that obscure and contradict them.

For the remainder of the critique I will consider the weaker (inchoate beliefs) version of the theory of infants' reality. The main problem with this version is that, given Piaget's views about intelligence and its development, it is unclear how infants could ever get beyond the undifferentiated beliefs with which Piaget says they begin development. This brings me to the critique of the second and third theories in the infancy works: the theory of intelligence (and its development) and the theory of the relation between infants' intelligence and their conception of reality.

2. Intelligence

My central criticism is that, rather than give a description and explanation of intelligence and its development, Piaget ends up presupposing the very thing he is trying to explain. As a result, he also ends up presupposing rather than explaining how children form a conception of reality.

Piaget's official view suggests that the relation between *Construction of reality* and *Origins of intelligence* is one of increasing specificity. That is, in *Construction of reality* Piaget describes a parallelism in development between children's conception of reality and their "general intelligence" and claims that the development of intelligence is the motor that drives the changes in children's conception of reality. He thus raises the clear expectation that in *Origins* he will explain the mechanism by which intelligence develops.

On a careful reading, however, it turns out that *Origins* does not offer a new and more fundamental specification of the nature of intelligence and the mechanism by which it develops. Rather, it merely reproduces in the purported realm of intelligence the same parallelism between the conception of the world (or such considerations as "intention" and "interests") and action described in *Construction of reality*. In the following discussion, therefore, I will refer to only one parallelism (described variously as that between thought and action, or intelligence and action), with the understanding that I am tracking the argument in both books and hence what I have called Piaget's second and third theories: the theory of intelligence and the theory of the relation between intelligence and conceptions of reality.

Piaget's whole discussion of infants' intelligence and their conception of reality depends on a basic assumption – that there is an inherent connection between the way infants conceive of the world (i.e., between "thought") and the way they act in the world. Exactly which inherent connection Piaget intends here is unclear. His allusions to the connection are incomplete and inconsistent, as well as vague. Usually he retreats into metaphor without even attempting any systematic description, and the metaphors leave critical points unspecified. Hence, a certain amount of vagueness in my discussion of this basic issue is unavoidable.

Nonetheless, we can distinguish two slightly different models of a connection, which appear in Piaget's discussion at different times. Piaget sometimes speaks as if children's thought and action, which are inherently connected to one another, are, as he says, just two sides of the same coin. This seems to mean, alternately, that they are two parts of the same thing or two ways of looking at the same thing (see, e.g., the introduction to CR). At other times he suggests that children's thought and action are two separate spheres or domains, which stand, however, in a relation of continual mutual influence.

There is an obvious sense in which thought cannot simply be the reverse side of action. One can envision cases in which a certain kind of action is produced without the thought that normally accompanies it. Such cases would include, for example, an animal that has been trained to produce mechanically a certain kind of behavior or a machine that has been programmed to generate the behavior. These considerations would seem to argue that the more charitable interpretation of Piaget's account of the interconnection between thought and action is the second account I just described. Thought and action are two spheres that stand in a relation of continuing mutual influence.

Piaget and his commentators often use the metaphor of a spiral to describe this relation of thought and action in development. According to this view, initial features of children's conception of the world bring about particular modes of activity. These modes of activity develop in such a way as to bring about increasingly sophisticated conceptions. These increasingly sophisticated conceptions, in turn, bring about further turns in the spiral.

Although Piaget does not define precisely the nature of the interrelation between thought and action, he has definite views about the mechanism of development. After all, if there is a process of development in which thought and action progress in tandem, each influencing the other, we want to know how that process gets started, what makes it continue, and what makes it continue in the direction of increasing sophistication. Piaget's answer to these questions lies in his theory of assimilation or, more broadly, his theory of "functional invariants." Alternatively, insofar as Piaget argues that children's conception of reality (their "thought" or their "intelligence") is the reverse side of their action, this relationship holds, in his view, when we take "action" to mean the assimilating activity that Piaget thinks is involved in the action. Thus, regardless of the way in which Piaget intended us to understand the relation between thought and action, assimilation (and, by extension, the other functional invariants) is a crucial middle term in his account.[4]

Piaget's purported functional invariants raise several difficulties. The most basic of these is that they are not invariant. Their meaning shifts. Assimilation, for example, is sometimes an extremely rudimentary and undifferentiated notion meaning a tendency simply to *act*. At other times it is slightly more complicated and refers to a tendency to *repeat* action. This meaning, in turn, sometimes becomes the more interpretive or intellective notion that children have a drive, so to speak, to "*rediscover* an effect identical to that which was just perceived or felt" (CR, p. 310, my emphasis). Further, juxtaposed with these different meanings is an ambiguity between whether Piaget is referring to the organism's "attempt" to carry out the processes I have just described (e.g., its "attempt" to reproduce its experience) or to the fact merely that it *does* carry them out (in which case we might refer simply to a "tendency" to reproduce experience). Finally, as I will discuss shortly in connection with Piaget's account of Stage IV (means–ends coordination), "assimilation" sometimes refers to processes that are much more sophisticated, highly differentiated, and specific than any of the processes I have just enumerated.

The main difficulty is not just that Piaget shifts the senses of his terms, but that these shifts correspond to shifts in development that the functional invariants are supposed to explain. When Piaget appears unable to generate the characteristics of the "next stage" solely through the operation of the functional invariants on the products of the previous stage, he seems to resort either to assuming the change in question or to altering the nature of the functional invariants. As I will attempt to demonstrate, at certain critical junctures Piaget seems to read into the concept of assimilation precisely those properties that define the empirical state to be explained.

What is most objectionable in this process is not that it fails to

---

[4] See section 2.1 under Reconstruction for a summary reconstruction of the theory of functional invariants.

yield an explanation. That in itself would be no terrible flaw.[5] The problem is the paucity and arbitrariness of description. Either Piaget makes unarticulated and unexplained assumptions about infants' mental states, or his account is empty. His purportedly theoretical claims, those statements that explain infants' behavior with reference to assimilation, accommodation, and so forth, at best only redescribe the data and do so extremely abstractly. The presumed empirical descriptions that are supposed to be the focus of these explanations are also necessarily abstract, so as to be explicable within the theory. They give the appearance of being descriptions of mental states but either do not describe any mental state at all, or else introduce major assumptions about one.

In the remainder of the critique I will attempt to elaborate and document these points. I begin with some brief remarks about the implications of Piaget's shifting concept of assimilation for the characterization of the original state of the organism.

2.1. The original state

For the moment assume, as I think Piaget would like us to do, that all of the meanings of assimilation that I delineated above except the last (the sophisticated and differentiated process to be discussed in connection with Stage IV) apply to babies at birth. Considerations of the following sort arise:

Piaget is making a major assumption about newborn infants in saying that their intellective functioning is such that it is appropriate to speak of them as "attempting" to do something in anything other than a metaphoric sense, for instance, beyond the sense in which an amoeba "attempts" to assimilate particles. He makes another major assumption of a similar sort when he describes

---

[5] In a well-known statement, Fodor (1975) criticizes Piaget for his failure to provide an explanation of stage change. Fodor claims that Piaget's theory is inconsistent insofar as Piaget argues both that children's conceptual system is increasing in "power" and that the mechanism by which these increases come about amounts in the end to simple learning. Under Fodor's definition of what learning involves, the organism could not "learn" a new concept (for our purposes, come to the intellectual advances under question) unless the organism were already capable in principle of appreciating that concept. I will not deal with Fodor's criticism here, because it already presupposes resolution of the point that I find problematic, namely the poverty of *description* in the theory.

repetitions of action that are seen from birth (or, for that matter, from any given point thereafter) as either tendencies or attempts to "rediscover an effect identical to that which was just perceived or felt." Both the concept of "rediscovery" (or attempted rediscovery) and the idea of a comparison such that one effect can be appreciated as being "identical to" another convey a level of intellectual functioning that is neither trivial nor obvious.

It might be true that any or all of these descriptions apply to babies at birth, as Piaget claims. But then they are absolutely central to his argument about the "origins of intelligence." Reflexive action and assimilation in the broad, biological sense that Piaget discusses are decidedly secondary, according to this account.

We are then led to ask *why* Piaget thinks he needs to make these attributions at birth (or ever). What set of facts or abstract considerations led him (or would lead one) to these ascriptions? Do we need to make the same starting assumptions for all species that develop intelligent-looking behavior or that develop any behavior at all? Piaget seems to imply (introduction to OI) that the only difference between humans and animals lies in the extent of their development. In theory, if humans and animals progress through superficially similar stages for part of their development, they have the same "intelligence" and the same concept of "reality" during that period. It is not clear whether we should make this assumption. More to the point for human development, which specifically intellective forms of functioning do we need to attribute at birth, or at specific points thereafter, to account for human behavior? What kinds of attributions do we need to make even to raise the kinds of questions (e.g., about "concepts" of causality, etc.) that Piaget and his successors have investigated?

I proceed next with the main part of my argument, which deals with stage transitions. I use for my demonstration those stage transitions for which Piaget attempted most systematically to generate the developments in question from the operation of the functional invariants. These accounts are, in turn, the analyses of the coordinations of actions that purportedly arise at the end of Stage II (hearing and looking, and looking and reaching) and early Stage III (the secondary circular reaction) and the advance to Stage IV (means–ends coordination).

2.2. *The coordination of "heterogeneous" schemata*

The critical development of the second stage (regarding the coordination of actions) is that infants turn to look at "what" they hear and reach to grasp "what" they see. These *experiences* go along with the *behavior* of looking in the direction of a sound source and the behavior of reaching toward a target that we, as external observers, know is the same target that is seen. But the experience and the behavior are not the same thing. Piaget knows this and attempts to deal with the difference. For the theory to succeed, for it to be a theory either of intelligence or of infants' conception of reality, it must account for the *experience* of looking at what is heard or grasping what is seen.

Initially, according to the theory, infants at most look only "while" they hear or grasp only "while" they see. They do not look at "what" they hear or grasp "what" they see. What is seen is experienced only as an extension of seeing. It is not experienced as external to that looking and therefore cannot be seen as the thing that was heard. Through a process that Piaget calls reciprocal assimilation, these joint action patterns may intensify, because turning in the direction of a sound source has the consequence of producing a new visual image, and grasping a thing (that we know to be the thing) that is seen, or otherwise moving the hand, may have the consequence of prolonging an interesting visual image. Nonetheless, and Piaget emphasizes this, the mutual stimulation of these different action patterns does not in itself result in the identification of the one (e.g., the heard) image with the other (the seen image).

However, this further step (of grasping "what" is seen or looking at "what" is heard) is unproblematic in Piaget's view. Once the two action patterns (looking and grasping, or hearing and looking) are being applied to what is in fact the same "sensorial image" (OI, p. 143), the identification of the one image with the other will follow as a matter of course, as the "geometric point of crossing lines" (p. 108).

But this development is not at all inevitable in the way that Piaget implies. Merely by virtue of being at the "intersection" (OI, p. 143) of several action patterns simultaneously, he says, the object will tend to become external to any one of those action patterns. The thing that is grasped while seen can no longer be viewed by infants as an extension merely of seeing, because it is also grasped. However, to come to the resolution that the thing that is seen is not just an extension of seeing, infants would have to know that the very same thing is also being grasped or is graspable. In other words, they would have to be identifying the image seen with the image felt. But this identification is precisely what Piaget is trying to explain.

Piaget has other arguments, however, that might appear to break the circularity that is evident so far. One of these appeals to developments that, in theory, have occurred within the individual action patterns that are being brought together. Piaget describes how in due course these individual patterns (e.g., looking and grasping) tend to differentiate as a result of contact with increasingly diverse circumstances. For instance, infants grasp things increasingly from different positions and through the use of different arm movements, to the point where they adjust their grasp differently in anticipation when given, say, a handkerchief versus a pencil. This diversification, says Piaget, results in their gradually shifting from a purely functional interest in grasping to an interest in the objects grasped. This change in interest is in its own way an externalization of the universe (OI, p. 120). If grasping now comes to converge with looking, the argument presumably continues, what has been combined with looking is not just a compulsion to grasp, but an interest in grasping *things* that are separable in some measure from the act of grasping itself. If the infant who grasps is more interested in what is grasped than in the act of grasping, then, when grasping is combined with looking, grasping should be bringing to this situation a "thing" that is already partly detached from the experience of grasping.

This argument still leaves us with the problem, however, of determining how that which is differentiated from the grasp is identified with that which is seen. Moreover, within the experience of grasping by itself, it is not clear how the differentiations Piaget describes would lead to a perception specifically of the externality of the thing grasped, in any case. It is compatible with the data, and with the theory, that infants would just be differentiating grasping such that each variant of the action would be continuous with the thing grasped from the infants' point of view.

Piaget might appeal, alternatively, to the tendency of the organism toward "organization." As I outlined earlier, Piaget's view is that, from the beginning even of the reflex stage, infants tend over time to systematize the accommodatory movements that they make in connection with their actions and that allow those actions to continue when they have been impeded. It might be argued that babies' transition from grasping "when" they see to grasping "what" they see reflects the same tendency toward internal organization, this time on a more mental level. To argue this point, however, would be to commit the unaccounted for shift in levels I alluded to earlier. If there is a tendency toward organization analogous to that of the first stage (i.e., if we keep the function of organization truly "invariant"), the tendency toward organization at this stage would add only the likelihood that grasping while seeing would become systematic or habitual. It would not become the psychologically new experience of grasping what is seen.

To summarize to this point, it appears that in significant respects the idea of grasping things seen or of looking at what is heard remains outside Piaget's theory. The theory can explain the convergence of the behavior patterns, and even their systematization, but seems to leave the imputed psychological advance to a set of extratheoretic assumptions. Alternatively, the theory raises rather than solves the question of when in development babies can be said (from their point of view) to reach for things they see or turn to look at things they hear.

The unaccounted for assumption, or alternatively the open question, is not trivial, because by Piaget's own account the acquisition that is important for intelligence is that of grasping what is seen, not grasping while seeing. Similarly, insofar as the formation of a concept of object (or in more general terms the externalization of the universe) depends on developments that from infants' point of view involve a convergence of different action patterns on the same object, then the theory also has not shown how the concept of object moves beyond the initial (undifferentiated) state. The action patterns have come together on what we know to be the same object. Under a strict reading of the theory, however, babies do not know this. Rather, as each action is applied to the object, the object is experienced as an extension of that action.

Piaget might have accepted this conclusion at least in part and pointed out that the concept of, say, object was only beginning at this stage. True objectification and externalization of reality would require all six sensorimotor stages to become complete. This argument does not solve the problem, however. To begin with, my claim is not that the concept of object has not come as far as one might think at this stage, but that it has not progressed at all. Further, although Piaget might agree in principle that the experience of reaching for that which you see might not be formed until later, the whole discussion of the immediately following stage (Stage III, secondary circular reactions) presupposes that infants are exactly reaching for things they see (with the caveat that the things that are simultaneously seen and grasped are not fully formed objects in the sense of the later stages).

2.3. Creating effects in the environment

The next major transition Piaget describes is the onset of the secondary circular reaction (Stage III). At the most external level of description, the main development here is that, whereas previously infants repeat actions for their inherent effects on their own bodies (i.e., primary circular reactions), they now repeat actions to bring about (what we know to be) an external effect. From their point of view, according to the account, two previously separate action patterns (schemata) have become coordinated. So, for example, infants now *shake* something to *hear* it sound or *strike* something to *see* it swing. Previously they would have shaken something only for the immediate sensation to the hand and arm and, as a distinctly separate activity, might also have listened attentively to the noise produced. They would have struck things, again for the immediate kinesthetic sensation of doing so and at the same time, but as a separate act, might have watched the interesting sight that also occurred.

From a psychological point of view, the description of the secondary circular reaction at this most external level presents two novelties relative to the earlier reactions with which Piaget compares it. First, the thing struck is identified with the thing that is observed to swing. Second, infants conceive that they are bringing about the result they observe.

Let us now examine the account of how these changes come about. Piaget again theorizes that there is a reciprocal assimilation of the two converging action patterns. Initially there is a fortuitous co-occurrence of striking something while looking at it, for example. At that point, babies attempt to "conserve" the result for their eyes by continuing to look at the spectacle and conserve the (tactile) sensation to the hand by continuing to strike. But, says Piaget, as soon as the two patterns have converged on the same object and same event in this way, the babies discover that by moving their hands they can conserve the image for their sight. It follows as a matter of course, he argues, both that the infants will perceive little by little that the image they observe to move is the same image that they move with their hands and that this visually observed movement depends on their manual activity (OI, p. 175).

It might indeed come to pass empirically that infants arrive at these two realizations, and it might be the case that an intermediate step of reciprocal assimilation, or something like it, makes this transition possible. Once again, however, the realizations themselves (that the image seen is the image grasped, that the movement observed is caused by the action of the hand) neither follow as natural consequences of reciprocal assimilation, nor, as *is* implied by the idea of reciprocal assimilation, are necessary to motivate the coordination of the behaviors. On a strict reading of the account, infants could go on beating objects and watching them swing without ever knowing that they are beating the things they observe or that the movement they observe depends on their manual activity.

The point of departure for all the remaining stages, however, is exactly that babies can act on the things they see. Thus, there is already a serious gap in the argument concerning the next (fourth) stage. We shall find, however, that even if we grant Piaget's unaccounted for point of departure and thus close this gap, Piaget leaves others.

2.4. Means and ends

The central acquisition of the fourth stage is, according to Piaget, the coordination of two "secondary" patterns in a means–ends relationship. His children now do one thing (e.g., move an object, pull a string) in order to do another (retrieve a different object) or in order to effect some more distant end indirectly (e.g., pushing mother's hand to the flounce so that it will shake it). Previously, in Stage III, the children would have performed any one of these actions as ends in themselves, not as means to some further end.

Like the coordinations of the previous stages, the subordination of actions at the fourth stage is theorized to arise by reciprocal assimilation, except, Piaget says, that reciprocal assimilation will now assume a new form. The process Piaget outlines has two components. On the one hand, the relevant actions have to come together (e.g., pulling the string and retrieving the object). On the other hand, the relevant objects have to be put into the proper relationship.

Regarding the actions, there is initially a co-occurrence of what will turn out to be the goal and intermediate ("means") patterns. This co-occurrence, however, comes about not through a purely accidental convergence in the manner of the earlier stages, but through a process whereby one action is initially replaced by the other. The subordination of one action to the other arises from the results of this replacement.

Recall the following example (OI, Obs. 120; analysis on p. 231). Laurent wants to grasp the paper that Piaget has placed on the bassinet hood so that Laurent cannot reach it. Laurent proceeds to pull the string that is attached to the hood, not, according to Piaget, because he thinks that this will enable him to retrieve the paper, but because having failed to do what he wanted to do, this is something else he can do with overhead objects. Laurent does not, however, abandon his desire for the paper, according to the account, so that when the paper finally falls, he grasps it. There is reciprocal assimilation of the actions insofar as Laurent initially pulls the string "at the same time as" he desires to grasp the paper. At least in theory (Piaget concedes that this example is ambiguous on this point), the reaction subsequently becomes pulling the string "in order to" grasp the paper.

The process by which the objects involved in means–ends maneuvers are placed in the proper relationship also begins as a simple assimilation. Desiring some presently unattainable objective, the children, according to the theory, act on a more accessible object in the way that they would have liked to have acted on the more distant objective. Not able to act on the flounce, for example, Jacqueline (Obs. 127) acts on (pushes) her mother's hand, which is both closer to Jacqueline than the flounce is and, in her view, associated with the flounce (because earlier she had seen it joined with the flounce). The flounce has thus been "assimilated" to the hand, in the sense that the hand is replacing the flounce.

In complex cases such as this, in which the intermediate object is not already connected with the goal object, this simple assimilation of one object to the other does not by itself bring the children their true objective. A special action, or special accommodation, will be required to ensure that the necessary relationship is effected. Here Piaget simply asserts that the children will maintain the distinctiveness of the two objects and interrelate them rather than "fuse" them completely. He then describes how the children have within their existing repertoires action patterns that, when properly "accommodated" to the circumstances, will meet these requirements.

The main weakness in this account is, as Piaget himself seems to recognize, that the idea of reciprocal assimilation (engaging in action A "at the same time as" action B) does not produce the critical advances at this stage. One action must be subordinated to the other, not simply "fused" with it. Moreover, insofar as one object is being used as a means to accomplish some end involving a different object, the necessary relationships among these objects must be established. Piaget's solution, at the most superficial level, seems to be that reciprocal assimilation will simply take on these two new features: "Reciprocal assimilation works no longer by fusion but by virtue of an inclusion of one of the schemata in the other," and this coordination is "accompanied by a physical connection established between the objects" (OI, p. 234). This solution, however, only restates the facts.

Nonetheless, Piaget does attempt some further analysis, as I have already shown, in describing how the children, beginning with a process similar to the kind of reciprocal assimilation applicable at the earlier stages, proceed to a more complicated organization. The attempt is worth reviewing, for like those connected with the preceding stages, it enables us to locate Piaget's truly pivotal assumptions.

Piaget seems to have the idea that, on some occasions, if the children do one thing in place of another, their original goal will unintentionally be accomplished. In shaking the string rather than (and as a substitute for) grasping the paper, Laurent occasioned the fall of the paper and was able to grasp it. Once this fortuitous result had been obtained, he was then able to attempt simply to reproduce the action that led to the result, as in a secondary circular reaction. He could then grasp the paper.

In order for us to say that Laurent pulled the string "in order to" get the paper we must attribute to him the desire to obtain the paper throughout his pulling of the string, as well as the *aim* of getting the paper by means of pulling the string. Piaget recognizes this. He therefore introduces the idea that initially Laurent, who does not yet coordinate discrete actions, will continue to *desire* to grasp the paper while he engages in the alternative, unrelated action of pulling the string. If the paper then becomes accessible (by falling), the original schema can reassert itself. Later, through further repetitions of the same circumstances, the pulling action can be undertaken intentionally, for the purpose of occasioning the fall of the object and hence the feasibility of grasping it.

With this account it seems that Piaget is trying to solve the problem of how, given that the children have some long-term (or unreachable) goal, they will come to discover a way of reaching that goal. The central advance of Stage IV was supposed to be, however, precisely that of having long-term goals, or acting with intention. It seems that what Piaget has done is described how such intentionality becomes visible in the children's behavior. Then, to explain how this behavior comes about, he presupposes the very advance it is supposed to signify.

To come to the more specific difficulty, the transition process that Piaget outlines for Laurent contains an important novel element. This element is the notion that Laurent has continued to desire to grasp the paper, even though he is not, in his view, striving to grasp it and is in fact engaging in (what is again in his view) an unrelated action. If this is what children begin to do at some point, it is very unlike anything they have done before. There is a shift from *applying* schemata to *wanting* to apply them. This is major. The difficulty with Piaget's treatment is less that he does not motivate this advance (which he does not) than that he fails to articulate and describe it. Having introduced the notion of continuing to desire to apply a schema, he quickly reduces this notion to the idea of applying the schema and then proceeds to discuss how this schema becomes coordinated with other schemata (OI, p. 231).

Inasmuch as Piaget's discussion of this transitional example poses difficulties, the account of the central Stage IV examples – those in which the relation between the intermediate and goal objects is not given but must be constructed – is all the more problematic. It will suffice to reiterate that Piaget only asserts, with no further analysis, that the children will construct the necessary relationships, because otherwise the means–ends organization would not work.

In Piaget's account, the acquisitions of the fifth and sixth stages are presented as fairly direct elaborations of the acquisitions of the earlier stages. The analysis also becomes more purely descriptive and less interpretive or explanatory than it was at the earlier stages, as I have said. Because a discussion of these stages would add little to the present argument, I will move directly to Piaget's account of the relation between infant intelligence and child thought.

3. Later development

In a way, Piaget's treatment of the relation between infant intelligence and child thought is most revealing of the kinds of gaps I have attempted to illustrate thus far. Correspondingly, this analysis points to some of the major questions that would have to be addressed in a theory of the origins of intelligence.

For Piaget, the central problem concerning the transition to conceptual thought was the question of how children would adapt to the new "realities" that conceptual thought imposed. He singled out two such realities: the socialization of the intellect and the characteristically different "aim" of conceptual thought. Conceptual thought "aims" at the acquisition of knowledge or truth, as opposed to the attainment of practical success, and it involves the novel processes of judgment, proof, and explanation, through which that aim is pursued. Piaget's thesis was that these realities are sufficiently novel that a whole new process of intellectual adaptation must take place. In this readaptation children must repeat all the work of coordinating assimilation and accommodation already completed at the sensorimotor level.

Suppose we were to grant the correctness of the analyses of both conceptual and sensorimotor thought that would allow these parallels to be drawn (it is precisely these analyses that I have questioned). We would see that Piaget once again presupposes the very thing most in need of explanation. He virtually says so himself, when, at the end of *Construction of reality,* he concludes that "the development of reason, outlined on the sensorimotor level, follows the same laws, once social life and reflective thought have been formed" (p. 386). What *are* social life and reflective thought, and how do they come about? What is true of the agent who can be said to be judging or trying to prove something or who can be said to be seeking an explanation or seeking the truth? How or when do these properties first take their characteristic forms? This, however, was not what Piaget asked but what he assumed we already knew.

6

The later Piaget

I have argued that there is no satisfactory account of mind or of development in the early Piaget. Whether he was attempting to describe children's thought at a given stage of development or the developmental process itself, Piaget continually imposed either the adult observer's perspective or some other arbitrary framework on children's behavior.

These problems persist in Piaget's later work. In this chapter I discuss three major emphases of that work: Piaget's structuralism, his account of biology and knowledge, and his theory of equilibration. In between the second and third of these themes I also discuss a comparatively late application of the "differentiation" model of development that also appears in some of the early works (CCW, CCN).

Although I consider some of Piaget's later empirical work in the context of my discussion of the theory of equilibration, I offer no systematic discussion of the empirical work by itself. I therefore include a few miscellaneous remarks here, before beginning the main part of my discussion.

As I already indicated, the later studies generally address more abstract issues than do the works I have considered in the preceding chapters, and the problems they deal with, as well as the data generated, are much more narrowly derived from the theory. With the exception of the research on number noted in chapter 4, Piaget did not return to the topics covered in this book, at least not directly. A later discussion of causality (Piaget, 1971/1974), tangentially related to the section on causality in chapter 5, is discussed in section 3 of this chapter. Piaget did return to the question of the relation between action and thought, also treated in chapter 5, in his works *The grasp of consciousness* (Piaget, 1974/1976) and *Success and understanding* (Piaget, 1974/1978).

These works, however, deal with older children and the issue they focus on is quite different from those treated in *Origins*. They ask how children become reflectively aware of the mechanics of the actions they perform (e.g., crawling, producing backspin on a pingpong ball, building houses of cards). The allusions that are made to infancy or to the origins of thought depend entirely on the account in *Origins,* as does the treatment of the mechanism of developmental change (a grosser version of reciprocal assimilation; see section 4, this chapter). Hence, these works would not affect the conclusions reached in chapter 5.

In a separate empirical investigation (Sugarman, 1983), I reached the conclusion that Piaget's treatment of child logic (e.g., Inhelder & Piaget, 1959/1964; Piaget et al. 1968/1977), a main emphasis of his work not treated here, is derivative in much the same way I have argued for *Number* and *Morality*. One of the characteristics of Piaget's empirical program, throughout his career, is that his accounts always remain at the same level of analysis, although the conceptual terms of the analysis shift. The level of analysis is a problem, as I will attempt to show in the following discussions.

1. Structuralism

Piaget was committed to some form of structuralism from the start of his career (e.g., Chapman, in press; Gruber & Vonèche, 1982). However, structuralism became an increasingly official theme around which he organized his studies and theoretical syntheses (e.g., Piaget 1968/1971a). The main idea behind Piaget's structuralism, like that of the Gestaltists, is that the actual operation of such psychological processes as perception and thinking cannot be reduced to the elements they might be seen to be composed of (sensations in the case of perception, individual ideas in the case of thinking), but involves a larger organization. Perceptual illusions are an example of this principle. A divided space looks larger than an undivided one; a lead bar feels heavier when lifted by itself than when lifted while mounted on top of an empty box. Piaget believed that he was extending the same idea to children's thinking by showing, for example, that babies cannot connect just any action with any effect, but that the connections they can appreciate, or produce, depend on the level of intelligent organization ("sensorimotor intelligence") they have achieved (Piaget, 1936/1952, 1937/1954).

Piaget added that perception and thought were regulated not simply by an organization (a "structure") that was pregiven in the subject, in the environment, or "instantaneously" in the immediate interaction between the two. In any given *act* of thinking or perceiving, the subject played an active role in bringing the organization in question to bear on the objects or events encountered. There were processes of search, selection, adjustment, and compensation, in short, what Piaget called "self-regulation" (elsewhere "equilibration"; see Piaget, 1964/1967, 1975/1985). In addition, Piaget believed that these structures, or organizations, *developed.* They changed with age, and these changes were brought about specifically by the same processes of self-regulation and so on that operated in individual acts. They were not the result exclusively of maturation, the impress of environmental factors, or any simple combination of the two. In other words, structures are "constructed" (see Piaget, 1968/1971a).

Piaget distinguished various properties of structures, for example, that they are, at bottom, systems of "transformation" (Piaget, 1968/1971a). Intelligence, for instance, involves going beyond the actual perceived state of things to imagining or bringing about other possible states of those things. We imagine the depth and reverse side of objects, even when these features are not visible. The "structures" of intelligence are those systems of laws that govern these transformations.

Another central property of structures is that they are "closed." The transformations carried out under a structure never lead beyond the structure. In mathematics, for example, the addition of any two whole numbers yields another whole number. In human thinking, the conjoining of any two action patterns at any given stage of sensorimotor intelligence, for example, can yield a new pattern only at the level of organization of action characteristic of that stage. This remains the case even when the two action patterns, carried out separately, would exhibit this same level of organization. When hearing and looking first come together, for example, there is still only hearing for its own sake and looking for its own sake, not looking at the thing that is heard (see chapter 5).

Finally, like structuralists in other fields, Piaget had as a goal the identification of increasingly more basic structures to which all other structures reduce (see in particular Piaget, 1968/1971a, 1967/1971b). Thus, throughout his writings, he nearly always described what were already abstract accounts of children's behavior at the next higher level of abstraction. An example from his early work would be his attempt to trace child animism and realism to egocentrism (Piaget, 1960a). An example from his middle period would be his attempt to analyze children's understanding of numerous logical and physical concepts in terms of the "structures" of, for example, preoperational versus concrete operational intelligence (e.g., Inhelder & Piaget, 1959/1964). In his later works (e.g., Piaget, 1974/1980b, 1975/1985), Piaget analyzed children's understanding of the same or similar concepts with reference to the nature of the "regulations" allegedly resulting in these structures. His presentations suggest that this chronological sequence of hypothetical underlying "structures" is itself to be understood as the progressive recovery of ever deeper principles with which to explain children's behavior.

One can hardly dispute the advantages of Piaget's structural approach over the traditions, for example, of atomism and associationism, which he considered to be opposed to his approach (Piaget, 1968/1971a). Some of these advantages can be seen in the preceding chapters, in the way Piaget systematized masses of seemingly disparate data. As can also be seen, however, the advantages come at a terrific price, namely a serious deformation of the phenomena under study. A particularly telling example is Piaget's (1960a) attempt to construe child animism and realism as complementary aspects of the same, allegedly deeper property of thought: children's confusion of inner and outer reality. Quite apart from the question of whether children actually are confused in the way that Piaget says, the tight association of animism and realism led to some implausible consequences, not the least of which was the dissolution of the phenomena in question (see chapter 1). In his discussion of morality (chapter 3), the attempt to impose a tight unity on what, on analysis, are profoundly distinct ideas (e.g., the autonomous conception of duty, the valuing of reciprocity, the ideas of moral sentiment and moral motivation) obfuscated both the complex relation among these ideas and the truly central questions that a developmental psychology of morality ought to address.

As for the historical progression of integrative "structures" to which Piaget related his findings (egocentrism, operational structures, regulations), although different aspects of children's behavior and thought came to be emphasized, the same basic classifications always resulted. The same, very broad range of phenomena was always subsumed under any given structural description, and the same empirical states of development were always delineated. This immediately suggests that the more recent descriptions are not deeper than the old ones; they are merely different (see section 4, this chapter). Similarly, it seems reasonable to infer that, if Piaget had returned to the topics discussed in this book, he would not have drawn the essential distinctions we found lacking in his early treatments.

To put some of the same points a different way, a good structural account presupposes that valid groupings of phenomena have been acheived and appropriate distinctions drawn. For a psychological account the validity and appropriateness in question are psychological validity and appropriateness. One must divide and classify experience in a way that makes sense from the point of view of the human actor and, in the case of developmental psychology, from the point of view of children at the different stages of their development. Piaget, as we have seen, does not achieve the right groupings.

And yet his earlier works come closest to the ideal. They do so, I think, because the sweep is so large: because Piaget *attempts* to subsume animism and realism under one rubric or to group children's ad hoc answers to interview questions and their spontaneous magical practices under the same thought process. One gets a sense of the range of phenomena and concepts that could be relevant to the topics in question and hence a sense of the scope and complexity of the theory that would be needed to cover the topic adequately. Piaget was right, in a way, to push his unifying rubrics as far as he did. But he was right insofar as the failure of these rubrics to account for the data begins to expose the profound differences and complex relations among the phenomena and the concepts he tried to unite. By restricting the range of relevant phenomena to a much greater extent, his later works do not allow this complexity even to come into view.

2. Biology and knowledge

In his attempt to develop his biological account of intelligence in later writings (e.g., Piaget, 1967/1971b, 1974/1980b), Piaget encounters problems similar to those evident in his structuralism. Although the precise nature of the account changes in the course of his writings (e.g., Piaget, 1936/1952, 1964/1967, 1967/1971b, 1974/1980c), the basic idea remains the same. Intelligence is to be viewed as an instance of organic adaptation and its development as analogous to that of organic growth.

Piaget's view of intelligence as an adaptation was novel and in many ways highly productive. This productivity is evident in *Origins* (Piaget, 1936/1952), which traces in elegant detail the increasingly sophisticated means by which babies come to interact with their environment. The conception of intelligence as an adaptation, however, must be cast in a language that is general enough to cover both intelligence and organic life. Hence, Piaget speaks of such properties as memory and logic, for example, as expressions of an "autoregulatory mechanism" (Piaget, 1967/1971b, p. 13) and the intelligence of babies in terms of "assimilation" and "accommodation" (Piaget, 1936/1952). The result, as I argued in chapter 5, is that crucial psychological parameters of intelligence, in the end the mind itself, end up being taken for granted.

Another major problem with Piaget's biologically oriented theorizing, also discussed earlier, is the analogy between intellectual and organic development. In his early and his later works Piaget conceives of intellectual development as involving a "continuous construction" (Piaget 1964/1967, p. 4) entirely comparable to that involved, for example, in the differentiation of protoplasm in embryogenesis. In earlier chapters I argued that this concept presented two major difficulties. The first was that the particular behaviors or thought patterns between which Piaget was attempting to erect this kind of connection were not clearly related in the way Piaget attempted to show. For instance, it seemed plausible that there would not be a direct line of development from children's odd and ill-formed theories about the "animate" nature of physical objects to their later articulate understanding of the distinction between the animate and inert worlds. The second, and deeper, problem was that likening the actual process of idea change in development to a process as strictly continuous as organic growth does not really make sense under any circumstances. In what sense could the (e.g., biological) ideas of a 9-year-old actually be the direct "transforms" of the ideas of a 4-year-old? In what sense do *ideas* emerge, literally, one from the other in development? The development of mental life may not fall into neat sequences of transforming or otherwise continuous or ameliorating structures in the same way that structures persist and develop in other spheres. One of the defining characteristics of this development may be that it does not do this.

The work on biology and knowledge poses a final problem in that it postulates a continuous evolution or "filiation" (Piaget, 1967/1971b, 1974/1978) not only between successive stages of intellectual development, but between organic and intellectual development. In chapter 5 I argued that Piaget's attempt to demonstrate a direct filiation of one substage of sensorimotor intelligence into the next, minutely different one failed completely. Critical emergent properties (e.g., looking at the "thing" that is heard, having long-term goals, "wanting" to apply schemata) were being introduced, outside the theory. If my analysis is correct, it follows that the attempt to establish the still more remote connection between organic processes and intelligence must also fail. The connection to biology will not, therefore, help to explain intelligence or its development.

Piaget did not base his argument in favor of these continuities simply on the descriptive analogies that might be drawn between the higher and lower stages of intelligence or between intelligence and organic functioning. He believed he could identify the underlying "transformative mechanism" (Piaget, 1974/1978, p. v) that would actually account for the transition. The particulars of the account change over the course of Piaget's works, from the vague differentiation model of the early works (e.g., Piaget, 1960a, 1932/1965a) to the interplay of the adaptational processes of assimilation and accommodation in the infancy works (Piaget, 1936/ 1952, 1937/1954) to the regulatory processes connected with equilibration in the later works (Piaget, 1971/1974, 1974/1976, 1974/1978, 1974/1980b, 1975/1985).

When I say that the continuity argument fails in *Origins,* what I mean is that this account of transition, or transformative mechanism, fails. Given that Piaget developed his account of transition further after writing *Origins,* the question arises of whether any of the later developments would eliminate the problems of the earlier account and make it succeed. The answer is no. Much as there are, again, some productive insights in some of the later elaborations, all of them are essentially variations on the original theme. What is more, virtually all of the later accounts, including the most comprehensive one (Piaget, 1974/1985), appeal in the last analysis to the account in *Origins*. If that account does not succeed, it is unlikely that any extension of it at the grosser levels represented by the more recent work could. I will attempt to document this claim in section 4 of this chapter. First, however, I will comment briefly on the fate of the idea of differentiation in Piaget's later work, given that this was a dominant theme in his earlier developmental theorizing.

3. Development as differentiation

Piaget remained firm in his view that "the problem of going from cognitive structures initially undifferentiated . . . to structures both differentiated and coordinated in a coherent way dominates . . . the whole mental development" (Piaget, 1971–1974, p. 121). In one of his later works (Piaget, 1971–1974) he treated the question of how children develop causal understanding, on the one hand, and "logico-mathematical operations," on the other hand, from this vantage point. He tries to show first that these two forms of thought are deeply connected in their final adult state and yet at the same time are distinct. The development of either one, in his view, consists in significant part in their differentiation.

Causal understanding, according to this account, involves the attribution of a process to phenomena in the world. It is the attribution that some Event A causes another Event B. Logico-mathematical operations (briefly, any kind of ordering or arranging activity in action or thought), on the other hand, are a process a subject engages in while attempting to come to an understanding of the world. They are not a process "attributed" to something else.

Piaget infers that these two forms of intelligence must be interdependent. Causal attribution necessarily involves "operations," because it involves making an inference that goes beyond what is merely observed, and inferences involve the "operations" of the subject. (The "inference" involved in causal attribution is the notion that one movement caused another, as contrasted with the mere observation that the two movements occurred coincidentally in time.) Operations, in turn, are intimately tied to causal understanding, because, according to Piaget's account, they are internalized (causal) actions.

Causal constructions and logicomathematical operations also differ, however. If operations are internalized causal actions, then, as it turns out, most causal actions are "irreversible." They take place in one direction only. Event A comes before Event B and causes B, and that is the end of it. By Piaget's definition, however, operations are "reversible." They involve envisioning the inverse of an event that has taken place (say, envisioning the shortening of the row of objects that have been spread out in a number conservation experiment) and that would return things to their original state (the return of the objects to their original arrangement; see chapter 4).

Thus, a subject who makes appropriate causal attributions and who gives evidence of engaging in fully formed logicomathematical operations engages in two "differentiated" functions: making causal attributions and engaging in logicomathematical operations. But, Piaget reasons, both causal attribution and logicomathematical operations originate in the child's actions. They have a common source. For instance, the very act of ordering and arranging a group of objects has both a causal aspect (moving the objects) and a logical aspect (the production of the order itself). Hence, causal attribution and logicomathematical operations, or their predecessors, must be indistinct, or undifferentiated, initially. Piaget cites as evidence of this alleged nondifferentiation, for instance, young children's failure to "reverse" events they have witnessed when they are trying to draw logicomathematical inferences (as in conservation tasks). Therefore, the argument concludes, the *development* of causal understanding and of logicomathematical operations must consist of the differentiation of causal and operational constructions.

There is a simpler alternative. To engage in logicomathematical operations, for instance, children have to be able to reverse real or imagined sequences of events. They do not readily make these reversals, because this is not something that, in the course of acting in the world, they would normally do. It takes an extra, specific kind of reflective act to do it, which, as Piaget documents, develops only slowly and with difficulty.

It is superfluous and unwarranted to add that "causality," as a whole, and "operations," as a whole, begin undifferentiated and then differentiate. The pattern of Piaget's argument here is exactly the same as that in *Child's conception of the world* and *Number* and has the same pitfalls.

Piaget does, however, add a new ingredient to the treatment of causality. He explicitly develops the notion, which is largely implicit in *Child's conception of the world* and *Number,* that the state of "undifferentiation" includes numerous contradictions, of which children may or may not be aware. These contradictions are the driving force of the differentiation. The operation of these contradictions is described in most detail in the theory of equilibration.

4. Equilibration

The basic idea of equilibration, elaborated primarily in Piaget's books on contradiction (Piaget, 1974/1980b) and equilibration (1975/1985) (however, see also Piaget, 1974/1976, 1974/1978), is as follows. Development takes place through the subject's own active "construction." The tendency toward new construction could be prompted only by a nonbalance ("disequilibrium") of some sort; otherwise the subject would have no reason to go beyond his or her current state, given that any particular "state" is itself an equilibrium. Any given state that the child is in, however, is "pregnant" with possibilities for disequilibrium or, as Piaget also calls it, disturbance. Disequilibrium is the first step toward an awareness of contradiction, and the discovery of contradiction is the specific catalyst of change.

Consider, for instance, the child who estimates the relative lengths of two lines by looking at their end points rather than at their full extension. Imagine that the child has been presented with a drawing of two lines that are in fact of equal length but that are imperfectly aligned, so that one protrudes beyond the other (see Figure 1). The child, seeing the unaligned end points (say, on the right), judges that the top line, extending further, is longer than the bottom line. This "state" is "pregnant" with possibilities for disturbance given that, if the child were to look at the opposite

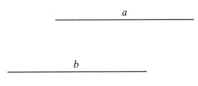

Figure 1. Two parallel lines of the same length.

end of the display, he or she should in principle conclude that the other line now appears longer.

The possibility for *disturbance* becomes real insofar as the child actually looks at the opposite end of the array and concludes this. The child arrives at one conclusion (*a* is longer than *b*) and then arrives at a different conclusion (*b* is longer than *a*), not expecting to do so. There is the further possibility for the recognition of a *contradiction,* insofar as the child does indeed conceive of both conclusions (*a* is longer than *b,* and *b* is longer than *a*), compares them, recognizes that he or she is asserting simultaneously both a proposition and its negation (*p* and *not-p:* "*a* is longer than *b,*" and "not: *a* is longer than *b*"), and knows that a proposition and its negation cannot both be true. Once a contradiction is recognized, the child will naturally attempt a reconciliation, because all organisms operate on a principle of noncontradiction, at whatever levels they may be said to function. (If humans operate at the level of thought, they strive to avoid contradiction in their thought; organisms operating at a sensorimotor level attempt, for example, to avoid a conflict of goals.)

The attempted reconciliation might take the form simply of the denial of one of the conflicting outcomes (e.g., that *b* is longer than *a*) or even a failure to perceive the relevant facts at all (that *b* extends beyond *a* on the left hand side of the figure). A more sophisticated form of reconciliation would be the search for a solution that takes account of both outcomes: One of the lines moved; the subject made an error of judgment the first time around. Weak though we as observers might find these inferences to be, they do represent a conceptual enrichment, by contrast with the first kind of attempted reconciliation through simple denial of the empirical outcomes. Finally, Piaget distinguishes a third kind of reconciliation, in which possible variations (e.g., one line protruding at one end, and the other line at the other end) are anticipated because they can be inferred as possible consequences of a general rule. These variations are organized into systems of inverses, such that various deductions follow: If *a* extends farther than *b* at one end of the array but not as far at the other end, then *a* and *b* may be the same length. If *a* extends farther than *b* at one end, and *a* and *b* are supposed to be the same length, then *b* must extend farther than *a* at the other end, and so on.

The most novel feature of this account, as compared with the accounts discussed in the preceding chapters, is the explicit separation of "disturbance" and "contradiction." Also new is the emphasis on the importance of (logical) negation in the detection of contradiction and hence in the generation of conceptual change generally. A less thoroughly analyzed version of conflict was given a central role in development in *Number,* a role similar to that of disturbance and contradiction combined in the new account. The different mechanisms of reconciliation (also called "compensations") have direct parallels in *Origins,* specifically in the account of reciprocal assimilation, as Piaget's account of sensorimotor intelligence in the new work makes clear. The accounts in *Number* and *Origins* had severe drawbacks. The same would apply, by extension, to the parallel accounts in the new formulation. Bearing these overlaps in mind, I now briefly describe the shortcomings I see in the new account. There are three, corresponding to each of the major aspects of the account I outlined: disturbances, contradictions/negations, and reconciliation.

Piaget's account of disturbances is mainly a comparison of disturbances with contradictions. One is subjectively aware of a contradiction only if one conceives two alternative judgments (*a* is longer than *b*, *b* is longer than *a*) as logical negations of one another ("*b* is longer than *a*" implies "not: *a* is longer than *b*"). With a disturbance, a subject experiences only a succession of *different* judgments, not logically incompatible ones. One has the experience of a violated expectancy, on the order of "I thought *x* was supposed to happen, but *y* took place instead."

The problem encountered in the disturbance thesis concerns the idea of disturbances itself, not the relation between disturbances and contradictions. How, we must ask, does the experience of a violated expectancy arise in the first place? There could be a sense of a violated expectancy only if the child had some reason to "expect" that his or her original judgment were the real or only judgment to be reached. In the case of the two lines, what could this reason be? It would seem to involve, at least in part, the notion that the same line judged on two different occasions should be judged to be the same (relative) length. Alternatively, the relation between the two lines should stay the same. (If *a* was initially longer than *b,* it should still be longer the next time the matter is considered.) Otherwise, why should the child worry whether his or her judgment were changing? (Weaker reasons, e.g., the assumption that the experimenter expects a single answer will ultimately reduce to this form. The child would still have to determine precisely under what circumstances the judgment should be held constant.)

The difficulty here is either that this notion of the "conservation" of the judgment is what Piaget is trying to explain or that it is a new and critical notion that should figure centrally in the account. In the latter case, it is never described or analyzed. Problems of exactly this form appear repeatedly in *Number* and the infancy books. Hence, Piaget's separation of disturbance and contradiction is largely a verbal solution to the problem that the original accounts raise.

With contradictions as well, it is difficult to conceive of the circumstances under which a child would come to the realization in question (which is now that "*a* is longer than *b*" and "*b* is longer than *a*" are not only different, but incompatible) without already having some appreciation of the point of view toward which he or she is allegedly moving. Piaget adds, however, that what is crucial is coming to see "*b* is longer than *a*" exactly as the *negation* of "*a* is longer than *b.*" Only then can a contradiction be said to exist. So far, however, this is just an argument of logical entailment, not one of psychological priority. To see "*b* is longer than *a*" as a contradiction of "*a* is longer than *b*" *is* in part to see it as the negation of "*a* is longer than *b.*"

Piaget does, however, allude to a kind of psychological priority that logical negations might have by themselves. Before having reached the point of noticing contradictions, children may realize that, if *a* is longer than *b,* there are various states of affairs that this judgment excludes, for example, that *b* is longer than *a.* Piaget aptly points out that this disposition to consider what is excluded is derived. When we gaze at something, we look at what is there. We do not, without an additional act of reflection, think about what we are not seeing. When we approach some goal in acting, we do not, without a conscious intellectual effort, conceive that we are necessarily moving that much farther away from our starting point. When we arrive at a judgment about something, we do not, again without an additional conscious effort, imagine what the judgments are that we have excluded (Piaget, 1980a, pp. xvii, 295–6).

Piaget's emphasis on this kind of "negative thinking" is a significant observation about human thought, one made by Dewey (1910), among others (see Baron, 1985, for a recent statement). It is not, however, what Piaget's whole project is really about. He is not examining some spontaneous tendency of children to generate a conception of what is excluded by the "affirmative" ascriptions they make (for an example of this kind of investigation see my reanalysis of children's ideas about "rules" in section 1.5 of the critique of morality, chapter 3; also Sugarman, in press *a*). He is giving children specially structured problems in which flagrant contradictions will arise if they do not recognize that they are asserting mutually incompatible views. Alternatively, he is concerned with a highly derivative sense of "negation" (Piaget, 1974/1980b, e.g., p. 153–5, 296; see also Inhelder & Piaget, 1959/1964, ch. 5), a sense that is linked, by definition, to late-emerging logical capacities. As before, this end point of development cannot be what pushes development toward that point.

Piaget's apparent way of grappling with this problem is to establish a category of "virtual" or "latent" contradictions or negations (Piaget, 1974/1980b, pp. 155–8). These are (what we know to be) contradictory judgments at which children arrive, judgments they do not perceive to be contradictions at the time but do recognize in this way later. Also in this category are contradictions that are never consciously confronted but that are eliminated as the result of some later development (e.g., the development of a concept of measurement that would simply prevent children from asserting that lines *a* and *b* in Figure 1 are of unequal length). Piaget then argues retrospectively that the initial (unrecognized) contradictions must have had some reality as contradictions or negations and that they form the basis of the full-blown negations that children later construct.

All we can say here, however, is that eventually children notice a contradiction (construct a negation, etc.). We cannot infer that the contradiction had any existence for them earlier or that their later recognition of a contradiction (or other elimination of it) derives in any direct way from the earlier "virtual" contradiction, as its necessary by-product.

Piaget's final retreat appears to be the notion that the contradiction (or negation), although not consciously noticed in the early stages, exerts an "influence" on children's thinking (e.g., Piaget, 1974/1980b, p. 156). This can be seen in their tendency to deny or overlook potentially troublesome facts. Piaget (1974/1980b) describes an experiment bearing on this claim, in which children were given a set of red, blue, and yellow cubes. They were shown that the red cubes had bells in them and were told that some of the blue or yellow cubes might or might not contain bells. They were then asked to select only the red cubes from behind a screen (i.e., without looking) and put them into a tube. In fact some of the blue and yellow cubes did contain bells. Hence a subject using the presence of a bell as a criterion for whether the cube was red would end up putting more than red cubes in the tube. Afterward the children were given the group of cubes again and were asked to put the red ones in the tube, while watching. This exercise would result in a shorter row than that produced in the screened selection.

The older children hesitated on the screened test, saying that they could not be sure that the cubes they were selecting were red. Although they knew the red cubes contained bells, they said, some of the yellow and blue cubes might also have them. Confronted with the short row of red cubes at the end of the experiment, these children immediately inferred that they must have put some yellow or blue cubes into the tube on the screened test. The younger children, on the other hand, put all of the cubes with bells into the tube on the screened test and appeared to regard the presence of some bells without cubes as evidence that only the red cubes had bells. Confronted with the shorter row of red cubes on the unscreened posttest, these children attempted to explain away the discrepancy. They said, for instance, that the row produced during the screened test did not really take up more room or that someone must have removed some of the red cubes.

The "influence" that Piaget is talking about is the impact of having obtained the shorter row on the younger children's description of the actual length of the two rows. They distort this description. Therefore, they have registered the troubling fact of the unequal rows, and it is only a matter of time before they will be led to confront this fact and resolve the contradiction.

Here again, however, we seem to have evidence only that, when they are younger, children deal with a potentially troubling fact in one way and, later, in another way. We do not have grounds to infer that the "pressure" somehow builds from the inadequacy of the earlier solution until some threshold is passed and a new perspective adopted (see in particular Piaget's 1980b discussion, p. 158 and elsewhere). It is difficult, among other problems, to give this decidedly physical metaphor clear psychological content.

As to what would push the children to this threshold, Piaget cites "greater decentration and objectivity" (p. 157). But now the argument has come full circle. It was presumably the development of such cognitive advances as greater decentration and objectivity that the construction of negations was supposed to bring about. In this as in other work, Piaget concedes this circularity and maintains that it is intentional. The developments he is describing form a "functional circle" (see, e.g., OI), each cultivating and supporting the other, eventually creating a spiral of development. The trouble is, as I argued with regard to *Origins* and *Number*, that Piaget cannot get the spiral started. The arguments are simply tautologous.

This is exactly the difficulty with Piaget's account of the reconciliations that purportedly follow the detection of a contradiction. Reconciliations are important because they are what moves the system forward to higher stages of development. I will discuss Piaget's application of his three-tiered scheme of reconciliations (simple denial, subsumption under a general scheme, and organization into a system of affirmations and negations) to the stages of sensorimotor intelligence elaborated in *Origins*. Piaget takes on, once again, the particular problem of the coordination of actions in different modalities, for instance, vision and hearing.

According to the account in *Origins*, babies' intelligence is such that initially activity in these different modalities is separate. Babies look and they listen, but they do not put together what they see and hear. Even if they look at the bell that sounds, they are not, in their view, looking at the thing that sounds. They are just looking at something and listening to something.

According to the new account, they come to coordinate these

activities, that is, to look at the thing that sounds, insofar as the environment normally presents sights when there are sounds, and babies come to experience a gap when, for example, they hear something but do not see anything. Through various adjustments (described under the process of reciprocal assimilation) babies come to integrate the two actions, so that, in effect, a sound will prompt a visual search in the direction of the sound, presumably for its source.

The coordination of actions at this very primitive level makes babies susceptible to another sort of disturbance; the attempted grasp of an object that fails and results instead in the swinging or displacement of the object. This effect, initially perturbing (as a failure) to babies, also interests them. They then endeavor to reproduce the effect through a series of adjustments ("regulations and corrections"; see Piaget, 1975/1985, p. 74), until a new action pattern (hitting to swing or hitting to displace) is consolidated. At an entirely practical level, these two new coordinations involve Piaget's second kind of reconciliation: the attempt to incorporate a "disturbance" into a novel scheme.

There is something more, however, in these advances than the mere integration of actions. The child is coming to view the objects of these actions in a new way. Whereas previously the "object" seen had no particular relation to the "object" heard, now, according to Piaget's description, the object that is seen is the same as the object that is heard. Piaget's new equilibration account does not even deal with this problem. *Origins* does, and fails.

The result is not only, and not even primarily, that Piaget fails to give a convincing account of the process by which this development occurs, but that we gradually realize we have lost track of the thing that was supposed to be developing: the child's mind. There is a further problem. Suppose that stripped of its excesses, and amended where necessary, the equilibration account could be made cogent. We could envision a process unfolding in time in which perturbing "facts" are registered in a peripheral way; are gradually understood as logically incompatible with the child's current way of understanding something; and are eventually surmounted by a process in which they are progressively incorporated into a scheme that eliminates the contradiction. This account might describe the directed and highly reflective problem solving in which adults sometimes engage. It is less clear that it describes the process of natural, long-term development.

The absence of an account of mind and the absence of an account of development are the two problems that arise in Piaget's earlier works. The earlier works lead closer to the sources of these problems and provide more material to go on in constructing alternatives.

5. Contemporary research

Despite appearances to the contrary, Piaget's ideas and overall approach continue to dominate much of developmental psychology. Hence, these two problems continue to persist in some form.

The contemporary work pertinent to this discussion can be conceived of as progressing along three lines. It develops certain Piagetian themes, it criticizes particular details of Piaget's execution, or it claims, falsely, to have overcome the Piagetian project altogether while actually remaining bound to some of the same problematic assumptions that Piaget made and the methods he used.

It would be superfluous for me to comment on the work that directly elaborates Piaget's themes. As for the critics, what they question, in large part, is the way in which Piaget operationalized his concepts (for reviews see, e.g., Bryant, 1982; Brainerd, 1978; Donaldson, 1979; Gelman & Baillargeon, 1983). Alternatively, Piaget is considered to have underspecified the information-processing mechanisms, "performance," and other causal factors underlying the phenomena he described (e.g., Halford, 1982; Sternberg, 1984). Along similar lines, certain more abstract and philosophical critiques have focused on the lack of an adequate explanatory or "learning" theory in the account (e.g., Fodor, 1975; Haroutunian, 1983).

These programs presuppose that Piaget told an approximately correct developmental story (see, however, Halford, 1982; Harris, 1983; Russell, 1981). The concepts in terms of which he attempted to tell it are the real dimensions along which conceptual development proceeds, and the stages he delineated in connection with these concepts are the significant benchmarks of developmental change.

It is precisely this presupposition I question. It is not clear whether the concepts with which Piaget evaluated child thought in fact have much to do with child thought or whether the stages he delineated form actual sequences of growth from children's point of view. Insofar as these programs inherently accept these concepts and stages as given, they raise the same questions.

As for the work that might be seen to offer a more genuine alternative to Piaget, essential ingredients of his conception are still present. Perhaps one of the most diametrically opposed views is the idea that children's conceptual development involves in significant part the progressive "accessing" of principles that they already implicitly understand. The evidence usually cited for this view is that children's behavior in a specially devised task (say, a modified number conservation task) is consistent with a principle (conservation of number) that they will apply only later in a different task (e.g., Piaget's number conservation task) (see e.g., Bullock et al., 1982; Carey, 1983; Donaldson, 1979; Flavell, Flavell & Green, 1985; Fodor, 1975; Greeno, Riley & Gelman, 1984; Rozin, 1976). This view might be seen to be opposed to Piaget's general conception insofar as it posits that the basic concepts of thought remain invariant across development and are merely extended in their application. Piaget conceived that the basic concepts change.

Both views, however, share the underlying conception that children's thought and action are the direct and unproblematic predecessors of one form of adult thought or another, and development is the continuous transformation of these predecessors into the corresponding adult forms. I argued that Piaget had insufficient evidence for the continuities that he conceived and that the attempt to pick out these continuities led him to distort and impoverish his description of both children's thought and the process of development.

As revealing of children's early competencies as the contemporary work may be, it runs the same risk. The fact that we as external observers identify the same principle in children's earlier and later behavior does not automatically mean either that children's understanding on the two separate occasions is appropriately characterized as involving the same principle or that the developmental pathway leading from the first instance to the second involves the simple extension of the very same resource. Children might, for example, reinvent the conservation principle the second time it appears. Moreover, when it reappears it might be a different principle, from a child's point of view. No two tasks, however similar from our perspective of watching from the outside, are necessarily analyzed into the same set of conceptual components by children. That their analysis of the earlier and later tasks might differ in this way would seem all the more plausible if the tasks are solved at different ages. Other conceptual advances might have intervened so that what is formally the same principle from our point of view is embedded in a quite different conceptual structure in children's thought (see Carey, 1985, and Piaget, 1975/1985 for accounts along these lines, and Sugarman, in press *b*, for further discussion of all of these points).

Somewhat closer to Piaget's specific theses, the idea that adult notions develop through the differentiation of childhood conceptions is still applied today (e.g., Brent, 1984; Keil, 1979; Smith, Carey & Wiser, 1985). Although these new accounts differ, both from one another and from Piaget's differentiation concept, all of them invoke a substantive continuity of some kind between the earlier and later behaviors in question that goes beyond mere formal description (however, see Smith et al., 1985, for some qualifications). Although I do not wish here to discuss the cogency of any particular claim that has been made, I would question again the ultimate applicability of the idea of differentiation to the process involved in the natural development of ideas, or what it really means.

The further notion of development as an instance of directed problem solving is quite prevalent. Children's conceptual growth has been characterized variously as involving stepwise changes in "self-modifying systems" (Klahr, 1984; see Case, 1985, for a similar kind of account), as a series of novice-to-expert shifts (e.g., Chi, Glaser, & Rees, 1982), and as comparable to theory change in the history of science (Carey, 1985). I do not question the possibility that these accounts are applicable at some level of description or that they apply in isolated cases of idea change. I only allude again to the presupposition they entail. It is that when they are in the process of developing increasingly mature ideas in the areas in question, children are engaged in a disciplined, more or less intentional and conscious process of discovery or apprenticeship. That development proceeds in this way in general, or in any specific case, is not at all clear.

That development appears to be a series of focused, continuous changes of one state into other, more complex or more elaborated states may be, rather, a deformation caused by the way developmental psychologists look at the process. The actual process by which our adult conceptions come about might be significantly more convoluted, with many more obscure backtrackings and complicated and unpredictable interactions among different components of experience.

The account of development, however, is only half of the agenda of developmental psychology. The other half is the description of the child's own mental reality. I have just finished arguing that it may be wrong to think about development as a process in which certain relatively simple, abstract forms of childhood thought are transformed in a continuous line of development into corresponding adult forms. If one takes this point, one will not be quite so sure of discovering the essential constitutive features of the child's mental reality by looking back in a straightforward empirical way for these abstract predecessors.

To some extent, where there are specific forms of knowledge or thought whose direct predecessors we want to identify, this approach makes sense and should be productive. Piaget presented an alternative. He encouraged us to seek the child in the child and to use this inquiry as a basis for understanding how adult mentality comes about and what it consists of. He did not follow through. His successors could, and might thereby deepen our understanding of mental life in both child and adult.

References

Baron, J. (1985). *Rationality and intelligence.* Cambridge: Cambridge University Press.

Brainerd, C. J. (1978). *Piaget's theory of intelligence.* Englewood Cliffs, NJ: Prentice-Hall.

Brent, S. B. (1984). *Psychological and social structures.* Hillsdale, NJ: Erlbaum.

Bryant, P. E. (1974). *Perception and understanding in young children.* New York: Basic.

Bryant, P. E. (1982). Piaget's questions. *British Journal of Psychology, 73,* 157–61.

Bullock, M. (1985). Animism in childhood thinking: A new look at an old question. *Developmental Psychology, 21,* 217–25.

Bullock, M., Gelman, R., & Baillargeon, R. (1982). The development of causal reasoning. In W. J. Friedman (Ed.), *The developmental psychology of time* (pp. 209–54). New York: Academic Press.

Carey, S. (1983). Cognitive development: The descriptive problem. In M. Gazzaniga (Ed.), *Handbook for cognitive neurology* (pp. 37–66). Hillsdale, NJ: Erlbaum.

Carey, S. (1985). *Conceptual change in childhood.* Cambridge, MA: MIT/Bradford.

Case, R. (1985). *Intellectual development from birth to adulthood.* New York: Academic Press.

Cassirer, E. (1955). *The philosophy of symbolic forms: Vol. 2. Mythical thought.* New Haven, CT: Yale University Press.

Chapman, M. (in press). *Piaget and the problem of universals.* Cambridge: Cambridge University Press.

Chi, M., Glaser, R., & Rees, E. (1982). Expertise in problem solving. In R. Sternberg (Ed.), *Advances in the psychology of human intelligence* Vol. 1, pp. 7–75. Hillsdale, NJ: Erlbaum.

Dewey, J. (1910). *How we think.* Lexington, MA: Heath.

Donaldson, M. (1979). *Children's minds.* New York: Norton.

Flavell, J. H. (1963). *The developmental psychology of Jean Piaget.* New York: Van Nostrand.

Flavell, J. H. (1985). *Cognitive development* 2nd ed. Englewood Cliffs, NJ: Prentice-Hall.

Flavell, J. H., Flavell, E. R., & Green, F. L. (1985). Development of the appearance in reality distinction. *Cognitive Psychology, 15,* 95–120.

Fodor, J. A. (1975). *The language of thought.* Cambridge, MA: MIT Press.

Freud, S. (1952a). *Totem and taboo* (standard ed., Vol. 13). London: Hogarth Press. (Original German, 1913)

Freud, S. (1952b). *The "Uncanny"* (standard ed., Vol. 17). London: Hogarth Press. (Original German, 1919)

Furth, H. G. (1981). *Piaget and knowledge: Theoretical foundations* (2nd ed.). Chicago: University of Chicago Press.

Gelman, R. (1972). The nature and development of early number concepts. In H. W. Reese (Ed.), *Advances in child development and behavior* (Vol. 7, pp. 116–67). New York: Academic Press.

Gelman, R., & Baillargeon, R. (1983). A review of some Piagetian concepts. In P. Mussen (Ser. Ed.), *Handbook of child psychology* (4th ed.): *Vol. 3. Cognitive development* (J. H. Flavell & E. M. Markman, Eds., pp. 167–230). New York: Wiley.

Ginsburg, H., & Opper, S. (1979). *Piaget's theory of intellectual development: An introduction* (2nd ed.). Englewood Cliffs, NJ: Prentice-Hall.

Gréco, P. (1962). Quantité et quotité. In P. Gréco & A. Morf (Eds.), *Structures numériques élémentaires: Vol. 13. Études d'épistemologie génétique.* Paris: Presses Universitaires de France.

Greeno, J. G., Riley, M. S., & Gelman, R. (1984). Conceptual competence in children's counting. *Cognitive Psychology, 16,* 94–143.

Gruber, H. E., & Vonèche, J. J. (1982). *The essential Piaget: An interpretive reference and guide.* New York: Routledge & Kegan Paul.

Halford, G. S. (1982). *The development of thought.* Hillsdale, NJ: Erlbaum.

Haroutunian, S. (1983). *Equilibrium in the balance.* New York: Springer-Verlag.

Harris, P. L. (1983). Infant cognition. In P. Mussen (Ser. Ed.), *Handbook of child psychology* (4th ed.): *Vol. 2. Infancy and developmental psychobiology* (M. Haith & J. Campos, Vol. Eds.) (pp. 689–782). New York: Wiley.

Inhelder, B., & Piaget, J. (1958). *The growth of logical thinking from childhood to adolescence: An essay on the construction of formal operational structures.* New York: Basic. (Original French, 1955)

Inhelder, B., & Piaget, J. (1963). De l'itération des actions à la recurrence élémentaire. In P. Gréco, B. Inhelder, B. Matalon, & J. Piaget, (Eds.), *La formation des raisonnements recurrentiels: Vol. 17. Études d'épistemologie génétique* (pp. 47–120). Paris: Presses Universitaires de France.

Inhelder, B., & Piaget, J. (1964). *The early growth of logic in the child.* New York: Routledge & Kegan Paul. (Original French, 1959)

Keil, F. C. (1979). *Semantic and conceptual development: An ontological perspective.* Cambridge, MA: Harvard University Press.

Klahr, D. (1984). Transition processes in quantitative development. In R. Sternberg (Ed.), *Mechanisms of cognitive development* (pp. 101–40). New York: Freeman.

Piaget, J. (1952). *The origins of intelligence in children.* New York: International Universities Press. (Original French, 1936)

Piaget, J. (1954). *The construction of reality in the child.* New York: Basic. (Original French, 1937)

Piaget, J. (1955). *The language and thought of the child.* New York: Meridian. (Original French, 1923)

Piaget, J. (1960a). *The child's conception of the world.* Totowa, NJ: Littlefield, Adams. (Original French, 1926)

Piaget, J. (1960b). *The child's conception of physical causality.* Totowa, NJ: Littlefield, Adams. (Original French, 1927)

Piaget, J. (1962). *Play, dreams, and imitation in childhood.* New York: Norton. (Original French, 1945)

Piaget, J. (1965a). *The moral judgment of the child.* New York: Free Press. (Original French, 1932)

Piaget, J. (1965b). *The child's conception of number.* New York: Norton. (Original French, 1941)

Piaget, J. (1967). *Six psychological studies.* New York: Random House. (Original French, 1964).

Piaget, J. (1968). *Judgment and reasoning in the child.* Totowa, NJ: Littlefield, Adams. (Original French, 1924)

Piaget, J. (1971a). *Structuralism.* New York: Harper & Row. (Original French, 1968)

Piaget, J. (1971b). *Biology and knowledge.* Chicago: University of Chicago Press. (Original French, 1967)

Piaget, J. (1974). *Understanding causality.* New York: Norton. (Original French, 1971)

Piaget, J. (1976). *The grasp of consciousness.* Cambridge, MA: Harvard University Press. (Original French, 1974)

Piaget, J. (1978). *Success and understanding.* Cambridge, MA: Harvard University Press. (Original French, 1974)

Piaget, J. (1979). Correspondences and transformations. In F. B. Murray (Ed.), *The impact of Piagetian theory: On education, philoso-*

phy, psychiatry, and psychology (pp. 17–27). Baltimore, MD: University Park Press.

Piaget, J. (1980a). *Recherches sur les correspondances: Vol. 37. Études d'épistemologie génétique* Paris: Presses Universitaires de France.

Piaget, J. (1980b). *Experiments in contradiction.* Chicago: University of Chicago Press. (Original French, 1974)

Piaget, J. (1980c). *Adaptation and intelligence: Organic selection and phenocopy.* Chicago: University of Chicago Press. (Original French, 1974)

Piaget, J. (1985). *The equilibration of cognitive structures: The central problem of intellectual development.* Chicago: University of Chicago Press. (Original French, 1975)

Piaget, J., Grize, J., Szeminska, A., & Vinh-Bang. (1977). *Epistemology and psychology of functions.* Boston: Reidel. (Original French, 1968)

Piaget, J., & Inhelder, B. (1956). *The child's conception of space.* New York: Norton. (Original French, 1948)

Piaget, J., & Inhelder, B. (1969). *The psychology of the child.* New York: Basic. (Original French, 1966)

Robert, M., Cellérier, G., & Sinclair, H. (1972). Une observation de la genèse du nombre. *Archives de Psychologie, 41,* 289–301.

Rozin, P. (1976). The evolution of intelligence and access to the cognitive unconscious. In J. M. Sprague & A. D. Epstein (Eds.), *Progress in psychobiology and physiological psychology* (pp. 245–80). New York: Academic Press.

Russell, J. (1981). Piaget's theory of sensorimotor development: Outline, assumptions, and problems. In G. Butterworth (Ed.), *Infancy and epistemology: An evaluation of Piaget's theory* (pp. 3–29). Brighton, UK: Harvester Press.

Saussure, F. de (1966). *Course in general linguistics.* New York: McGraw-Hill.

Smith, C., Carey, S.., & Wiser, H. (1985). On differentiation: A case study of the concepts of size, weight, and density. *Cognition, 21,* 177–237.

Starkey, P., & Cooper, R. G. (1980). Perception of numbers by human infants. *Science, 210,* 1033–5.

Sternberg, R. (Ed.) (1984). *Mechanisms of cognitive development.* New York: Freeman.

Sugarman, S. (1983). *Children's early thought: Developments in classification.* Cambridge: Cambridge University Press.

Sugarman, S. (in press *a*). Young children's spontaneous inspection of negative instances in a search task. *Journal of Experimental Child Psychology.*

Sugarman, S. (in press *b*). The priority of description in developmental psychology. *International Journal of Behavioral Development*.

Sully, J. (1914). *Studies of childhood*. New York: Appleton.

Turiel, E. (1983). *The development of social knowledge: Morality and convention*. Cambridge: Cambridge University Press.

Vygotsky, L. S. (1962). *Thought and Language*. Cambridge, MA: MIT Press.

Watson, J. S. (1977). Depression and the perception of control in early childhood. In J. G. Schulterbrandt and A. Raskin (Ed.), *Depression in childhood: Diagnosis, treatment, and conceptual models* (pp. 123–33). New York: Raven Press.

Winch, P. (1958). *The idea of a social science and its relation to philosophy*. New York: Humanities Press.

Index

accommodation, *see under* intelligence, origins of, in infancy
action and thought, *see* thought and action
adaptation, 173–7, 229–30
animism, 6–8, 12, 13–15, 16, 18–20, 28
  development away from, 39–49
  egocentrism in, 23–30, 33–9, 227
  and indissociation of ideas, 14–15, 17–23
  spontaneous, 30, 33–9
  and structuralism, 227–8
anomie, 93, 99–100
appearance-reality distinction
  in childhood, 29–30
  in infancy, 146, 151, 161
apriorism, 18, 147, 178, 226
assimilation, *see under* intelligence, origins of, in infancy
associationism, 178, 227
atomism, 17, 227
authority, children's relation to, 102; *see also* morality, heteronomous conception of
autoeroticism, 28
autoregulation, *see* self-regulation

Baillargeon, R., 172, 241
Baron, J., 237
biology and knowledge, 224, 229–31
Biran, Maine de, 178
Brainerd, C., 4, 241
Brent, S., 243
Bryant, P., 135, 241
Bullock, M., 172, 242
Buytendijk, F., 178

Cantor, G., 121–2
capacity argument, 54–5, 95–9, 110–12, 203–4
Carey, S., 172, 242, 243
Case, R., 243
Cassirer, E., 27n3
causal efficacy (infancy), 161–2, 164–70, 199, 201–4; *see also* magicophenomenalistic causality (infancy)
causality
  children's concept of, 31–2, 114–16, 145–6, 198, 224, 231–3; *see also* animism; magic in childhood; physical-determinism, children's concept of
  infants' conception of, *see* reality, infants' conception of
Cellérier, G., 115
Chapman, M., 225
Chi, M., 243
child psychology, 1
circular reactions, *see under* intelligence, origins of, in infancy
Claparède, E., 1
clinical interview, technique of, 7–8, 59, 61, 69
commensurability (in theories), 22–3, 49
communication
  and "absolutist" egocentrism thesis, 52–5
  capacity argument in, 54–5
  collective monologue, 51, 62
  egocentrism in, 5, 50–5, 111–12
  explanation and justification in, 51
  intentionality in, 52–3
  logical discourse in, 51, 53